An American in Hyderabad
Life in India in the 1970s

by
David Courtney

Sur Sangeet Services

Sur Sangeet Services
Houston Texas, USA

isbn(10) 1-893644-05-7
isbn(13) 978-1-893644-05-2

An American in Hyderabad:

Life in India in the 1970s

by David Courtney

Table of Contents

Preface

It is a warm, almost hot morning here in the South Indian city of Secunderabad. I am sitting on an upper story veranda of my brother-in-law's house.

Secunderabad, along with its sister city Hyderabad, are known for their high-tech industries. Throughout the municipality, there are computer firms, call-centres, and innumerable degree and non-degree courses available for every aspect of the IT (Information Technology) industry with which Hyderabad has become synonymous.

The movers and shakers of this industry are young. Most of them were not even born when I first came to this city more than three decades ago. It was a very different place then. There was not nearly the degree of pollution or crowding that one finds today. Computers were almost unheard of. Certainly the concept of people actually owning their own computer was unthinkable, and outsourcing and call centres did not exist.

My own memories of Secunderabad reflect a more relaxed atmosphere. I remember warm afternoons in the cantonment area. Those were lazy days spent sipping "Rosy Pelican" beer, eating *bhajis bhajis* and *pakodas*, and whiling away the hours with good friends talking about politics, films, and other unimportant topics.

This book is written with two types of readers in mind. One class of readers are Indians and Indian expatriates. The other class of readers are Westerners with a serious interest in Indian culture. Obviously these are two very different groups of people. There are times when I am writing for an Indian audience, often with the goal of invoking a deep feeling of nostalgia. Unfortunately this will leave the Western readers cold. There are other times when I discuss at great lengths something which is very common in India yet foreign to Western readers. Indian readers will wonder why I am spending so much time on some trivial thing. It is something which may be trivial to an Indian reader, but of considerable interest to a Western reader. Unfortunately this is unavoidable and I request your indulgence whenever you encounter a section that is not written for you.

This book emphasises topics over the narrative, therefore there are many irregularities in chronology. In many cases events that were spread over a period of time were compressed into a single narration. Related events are sometimes aggregated into the appropriate chapter when they may have actually occurred at different times. The greatest liberties in chronology were taken with the Kundula Nagbani incident which occurred in 1981 and the Mohammad Hanif Shah incident which occurred in 2008. These events are clearly out of the 1970s timeframe, but I feel that these were stories that needed to be told.

The book also covers a fair amount of geography. One should not conclude from the title that all events occurred in Hyderabad. Hyderabad should be considered the epicentre of the book from which events may have occurred at some distance. I usually indicate where things happened.

When you buy a book, you expect to find a cohesive and readable narrative. But life does not unfold in this manner. Life is a jumble of random events, which collectively, move us from the womb to the tomb. It is impossible to precisely follow these erratic tacks of life and produce a book that is readable. A book that is unreadable is unpublishable. The simple act of writing forces me to cherry-pick information from years of random events and arrange it in a form that makes sense.

I must also explain something about the characters Ram and Lalitha. They are composites. In this book they function as mentors, examples, and narrators.

At times they represent my mentors. Over the years that I lived in India, I met hundreds of people, had many friends, and they all instructed me in the ways of Indian life. But I cannot introduce hundreds of characters, as this would make the book impossible to follow. The creation of Ram and Lalitha helps keep the number of characters to a minimum.

Ram and Lalitha sometimes represent typical Indians in typical situations. Remember, the central subject of this book is India in the 1970s. It is neither myself, Ram, Lalitha, nor any person mentioned in this work.

The liberties taken in chronology and the composite characters are distortions that I own up to. Any other *errata* that you encounter are purely the result of my flawed memory, for which I offer my apology.

I must thank many people for making this book possible. I would first and foremost like to thank Michael Gouch whose offhand suggestion made me start to write this in the first place. Then there are the good people who did a lot of work to read the manuscript and offer their suggestions. I would like to thank Linda Bird, Gaynor Blight, Rochelle Brackman, Morgan Bradford, Dan Clark, Lakshmi Gopal, Kalyani Giri, Neha Gupta, Giridhar Kalamangalam, Mary Koenig, Yashashree Kulkarni, Justin Lasiewicz, Raj Mankad, Prathiba Natesan, Rashida Parmer, and Bert Samples. In this last regard, I would especially like to thank Samhita Sunya. I must also thank the countless people in India who took me into their homes, into their lives, and gave me these experiences. Finally I must thank my wife Chandrakantha, for her patience and indulgence through all of these years.

Chapter 1
No Time, No Space, No Connection

"How long is this killing going to continue?" I thought to myself. It was a night in 1978. I had grown tired of reading by the light of a kerosene lamp. It was difficult sitting in the hot room, but there was no relief in sight. It had been a week since the electricity went out, so the ceiling fan sat motionless. Its blades reminded me of some stuffed bird of prey, permanently set with outstretched wings by some taxidermist - lifeless, and pointless.

It was not just the electricity that was gone, for the water too went out about the same time. The same was true for garbage collection and every other municipal service.

Somewhere on the opposite side of the planet, my old friends were leading normal lives. They were watching TV, eating frozen dinners, visiting each other, and simply engaging in normal day to day lives. But I was sitting in this old house in Hyderabad, India. I tried to do some productive work, but the heat, the lack of electricity, and the tension in the air made this impossible.

I got up from my seat and made my way across the courtyard. I could hear the servant in the kitchen cleaning up after the night's meal. Food was not really a problem. Although there was a twenty-hour-a-day curfew, the four hours that it was lifted allowed us to obtain food and water for our needs. But the cost was considerably higher.

I walked up the dark stairs aided by a small torchlight (flashlight). Carefully I made my way onto the broad, flat roof and started to move closer to the street. I knew the roof well, so I was very mindful of water-pipes and its other obstacles. I moved closer to the edge of the roof so I could see what as going on in the street.

1

The street below was almost unrecognisable. The normal hustle and bustle that I had come to expect was gone. During that time of the evening, the streets should have been teaming with people. Some people would be heading home after shopping, others would be going to a late night showing of a film. There should have been auto drivers and customers attempting to fix a price for their services. Instead the street was deserted and strewn with rocks. Its emptiness was occasionally intruded upon by monstrous military trucks carrying heavy loads of soldiers. Each soldier was dressed in military green, and carrying a gun. Sometimes it was a submachine gun, but more often it was an old dull Enfield, antiquated but still lethal. Although there was no electricity in the city, the night sky glowed a bright orange. It glowed from the reflection of numerous fires.

It wasn't clear exactly where the fires were. The light could have come from shops in the bazaar not far from our house. Perhaps a shop-owner had the misfortune of belonging to a religion different from those of a roaming gang of miscreants. Perhaps the light emanated from a local police station that had been set on fire. I couldn't know for sure. In that situation it was difficult for me to maintain a sense of distance.

My entire sense of space contracted. There were no newspapers, no electronic media, no connection with the outside world, so getting any type of perspective was impossible. The only information were rumours that came from immediate neighbours. We gleaned this information during the few hours a day that the curfew was lifted. My entire universe collapsed to the size of myself and the four other people in this house. It was a peculiar existence with no time, no space, nor connection to the outside world.

Chapter 2
How Did I Get Here?

I sat there on the roof of the house, admiring the surrealistic beauty of the orange sky. It danced and pulsated like some demonic phantasmagoria. It seemed that even in death and destruction there was beauty. As I sat there, I reflected on the chain of events which brought me here.

To begin with, I was born in St. Joseph's Hospital in Houston, Texas, in 1953. The year I was born, David was one of the most popular male names in the US. To be precise, it was ranked at number five, right after Michael, Robert, James, and John.

I have a sister named Cathleen Courtney. She is two years younger than myself.

My mother was Jo Anne Courtney. Her name reflected a curious Southern propensity towards double names. In this part of the country, there were many Mary Elizabeths, Mary Sues, Bobby Joes, and John Wesleys. She was of European and Cherokee extraction, a very common mix in Texas. Most of her family settled in Texas in the 1830s and 1840s. She was raised in a strict Baptist household, but as a young woman she rebelled against what she felt were arbitrary rules and irrational worldviews imposed by this upbringing. Thereafter, she was liberal in religious matters.

My father was Cecil Joseph Courtney. Although the name Courtney is generally associated with the British Isles, he was actually from an old New Orleans French family. He was born into the Catholic Church as most Louisianans are, but from the age of six, he was raised by an aunt in Arkansas. She was Methodist, so he too became a Methodist.

Cecil J. Courtney and myself (circa 1955)

From a religious point of view, my childhood was liberal. Neither of my parents were strong churchgoers, and it was always understood that when I matured I would make my own decision in these matters.

Travel was much more important than religion to my family. My mother had the wanderlust, which she indulged any way that she could. She frequently dragged the whole family around the country to go camping. By her 40s and 50s, the family's economic situation had improved to the extent that she was traveling around Europe and the Far East.

Under ideal circumstances politics do not play a part in one's upbringing, but the 1950s and 1960s were far from ideal times. We were in the midst of the Cold War and America was awash with a "John-Wayne-cowboy" mentality. There were "good guys" and "bad guys". Americans were the good guys, and the "Ruskie Commies" were the bad guys. It was a basic article of faith, and no one dared to question it. My family may have been liberal with regards to religion, but on social and political issues they were considerably more conservative. I remember my father, and to a somewhat lesser extent my mother, as strong Goldwater supporters in the 1960 presidential election. My family remained Republican throughout my childhood years.

But of all the political issues, it was race relations that had the most impact on my early upbringing. I remember segregated public restrooms and water fountains. Communities were almost entirely racially segregated. But racially segregated social institutions were being dismantled, yet it was unclear what was going to replace them. This created a tense environment that touched every aspect of life. This is all well known, yet there was a twist in my own upbringing that gave me a considerably more complex view on the subject.

In a sense, I had two different upbringings. During the school year, I lived in Houston with my parents. This was a typical White suburban community which aspired in every way to mimic the lifestyle of *Leave it to Beaver*. Life in Houston consisted of the usual round of going to school (all White, of course), and learning the basics of reading, writing, and arithmetic. There were weekly rounds of "Duck and Cover" atomic bomb emergency survival drills. We were all indoctrinated as to why the US was the greatest country in the world, and that the "Godless Communism" of the Soviets was something to be feared. We watched a lot of TV, common favourites were *Jack Parr*, *Ed Sullivan*, *I Love Lucy*, and *Gunsmoke*.

However, the typical suburban environment of my school year stood in sharp contrast to my life during the summer. I spent most of this time in the small town of Altair, Texas, where my mother was raised. If you look on the maps, you probably won't find it. (You can find what is left of it on Google Earth at 29°34'20N 96°27'34W). It was always unincorporated, and I doubt that its present population exceeds 40 people. Yet in the 1950s and 1960s, it had several hundred people living either directly in town or in small outlying farms.

Altair was almost entirely African-American. There were no more than a dozen "White folks" in the entire town. There was a strong attempt to maintain segregation, but given the demographics, it was more a frame of mind than a functioning system. Apparently the town was at one time a large plantation. After the Civil War, the slaves were freed, but there was no place to go, so everyone just stayed on. The old plantation system morphed into a system of land owners and share croppers. But socially and culturally, nothing really changed.

It was in this predominately African-American community that I spent the summers of my youth. My close friends and loved ones were largely African-American. Given this upbringing, it was no surprise that both my mother and myself never quite agreed with my father's segregationist leanings or racial stereotyping. Our own experiences told us that there was a universality of human experience that linked Black and White communities, and that concepts of racial essentialism were false. This rejection of racial prejudice became an important part of my worldviews.

The summers spent in Altair were very happy ones. There were endless opportunities for amusement. We could play in the barns which were always full of hay, so we climbed and burrowed in them to our hearts' delight. There was an odd array of old tools, many of which were specialised for long-abandoned manual agricultural practices. The attic too provided numerous opportunities for exploration. It was a veritable museum of magazines from the 1920s, button hooks, radios from the 1930s, manual sewing machines, and an assortment of other things.

In those days firearms were an essential part of our upbringing. No one thought twice about turning twelve-year-old children loose in the pasture with .22 caliber rifles or 410 gauge shotguns - all without adult supervision. We would spend hours plinking away at tin cans. (I must say that we got VERY good). Today people may give a six-year old toy guns, but in those days the elders treated things very differently. We were constantly told: "Hold it this way... don't point it that way.... squeeze the trigger, don't pull it." By the time we were adolescents, we had gone from toy rifles, to BB guns, to pellet rifles, and finally to .22 calibre carbines. We already had six years of training before we turned twelve.

Hunting and fishing were important skills in this culture, and I engaged in both to some degree. But they became less interesting to me as I grew older. Today, I cannot see them as being leisure activities, but rather work. It is something that is done to put food on the table. I find it much easier to simply go to the grocery store and buy the meat that I want.

Coming of age in this environment would probably have proceeded as it had for the last hundred years, except for one thing. This was the mid 1960s, and the United States was in the midst of a cultural revolution. The iniquities of segregation were being addressed by the integration movement. The criminality of the military industrial complex, coupled with the short-sighted political vision of Cold War politicians produced the Vietnam War. Its disastrous consequences forced everyone to question decades-old political norms. Once people started to question orthodoxy, there was no stopping, for the questions kept coming. The end of the 1960s saw people addressing sexual politics as well. This gave rise to the feminist and gay rights movements. It was in this turbulent social environment that I came of age. Looking back, I can see how unstable everything was. But at the time I had nothing to compare it to, so everything seemed normal to me.

Although these were turbulent times, I did not have to face the tough personal decisions that people just a few years older than myself did. Those slightly older had to do a lot of soul searching to decide whether Vietnam was justifiable, and whether they should join the military. By the time I had to register for the draft, the answer was crystal clear: Vietnam was bad, it was wrong, and it was a disaster. Those same people had to think hard over what sort of alcohol or recreational drugs they should indulge in. By the time I came along, there was no question that "weed" and LSD were *de rigueur*, and alcohol was *passe*. It was the same for virtually every personal decision, from clothing to sex. Since the difficult issues had already been addressed by those a few years older, our path was easy and clear. It was not a counter-culture, but THE culture.

One strong aspect of this new culture was a strong sense of internationalism. The *Tibetan Book of the Dead* was virtually required reading. Jack Kerouac's semi-autobiographical escapades in Mexico in his *On the Road* were not merely narratives, but studied as though they were the gospel. Che Guevara's journeys throughout the world were not merely idle curiosity, but a metaphoric guide to our own political and spiritual growth.

The position of India in this new internationalism cannot be underestimated. Within the popular culture, the explosion began when the Beatles started studying with the Maharishi Mahesh Yogi. Concurrent with this was George Harrison's study of the sitar under Ravi Shankar. Members of

ISKCON (a.k.a., *Hare Krishnas*) could be seen proselytising on the street corners of most Western cities. The sitar was freely mixed with electric guitars in popular music. The youth regularly sat around in their flats smoking "good old mother nature's best" and listening to Ravi Shankar. Public lectures given by Indian holy men were always well attended. Today these things are considered a cliche of the 1960s; but they were true.

Was I right in the middle of all of this? Well, not entirely. There were many things about the music that I liked, and I was beginning to get vague glimpses of a country whose worldviews attracted me. But as I looked around, much of this struck me as being a bit fatuous. It was clear that my peers' embrace of India as part of this 1960s internationalism was very superficial. For myself, the seminal event was my embrace of a musical group known as the "Incredible String Band". Their strong use of the sitar and exotic, otherworldly themes resonated within my adolescent mind. Eventually this too seemed shallow, so I immersed myself in the music of Ravi Shankar, Ali Akbar Khan, and Bismillah Khan.

By 1971, I had a formidable collection of recordings of Indian music. Through a series of events, this led to a short stint as a host and programmer for the local Pacifica networks (KPFT Houston) radio show *Evening Ragas*.

KPFT Button

8

This period of my life was marked by close personal friendships with a number of Indian students at Rice University. Although I was still in high school and many of these students were graduate students, I attached myself to them, moved in their circles, and enjoyed their friendship. It was in their company that I started to learn about the Indian way of doing things. One key person in all of this was Jayant Kirtane. When I first met him he was a graduate student in computer science at Rice University. More significantly for myself, he was a knowledgeable connoisseur of North Indian classical music with an impressive collection of recordings. I spent many hours with him listening to these recordings and learning about the music. It was from him that I inherited the radio program.

In 1971, I started to make the transition from a listening knowledge of music to a practical one. I had a close friend by the name of Kamaljit Singh Kalsi. He had a dilettante interest in a number of Indian instruments. One of these instruments was the tabla. I acquired a pair due to the kind services of another friend by the name of Yashpal Singh Sodhi, and I started to learn whatever I could.

Things started to change when I went to Texas A&M University in 1972. It was an excellent university, but conservative even by Texas standards. By the time I was eighteen, I had left any trace of conservatism a long way behind. Consequently, I felt the environment to be stuffy, rigid, and parochial. The only comfort I had in Texas A&M was the association with the Indian students and faculty there. In particular there was a professor of meteorology there by the name of P. Das. He introduced me to the beauty of a style of Bengali music known as *Rabindra Sangeet.*

It was in my second year of college that things just became too much. I looked around and realised that if I stayed there, I would wind up in some corporate environment as an engineer. I would have my one-and-half wives, my two-and-half children, my house in the suburbs, and a dog. This conventional lifestyle was approaching me as though it were a train, and I was a small animal on the tracks. If I were to avoid being crushed by this hideosity of conventionality, the only course of action was to get off the tracks.

So that is exactly what I did.

I made the change. I left the university, and I did a short stint with a seismograph crew in West Texas, and then I moved to the Ali Akbar College of Music in California.

It was in January of 1974 that I enrolled as a tabla student at the Ali Akbar College of Music. Ali Akbar Khan and Zakir Hussain were in India that particular session, so my instructors were Vince Delgado (tabla), Peter Van Gelder (formerly with Grace Slick and the "Great Society"), and a couple of other instructors. By the next semester, Ali Akbar Khan and Zakir Hussain returned. I started to learn a barrel shaped drum known as *pakhawaj*, under Zakir Hussain, and Ali Akbar Khan was my teacher for general music theory and vocal.

I spent nearly two years at the Ali Akbar College of Music. These were formative years, and I learned many things about music, at the same time I was learning about life. But after awhile, I knew that I had to move on.

One might wonder why I left. Ali Akbar Khan and Zakir Hussain were regarded as some of the greatest Indian musicians to have ever lived, and to study with them was something that every music student dreamed of. The answer was the environment. Although the instruction was world class, learning Indian music in California was in many ways like learning the Blues in Scandinavia. I saw students who had been there for a number of years and were technically very good, but unfortunately, there was an indefinable something that was missing. Being cut off from the culture that generated the music also cut the students off from this "something" that was necessary to make the music work. Therefore, I resolved that I would move to India to further my studies.

I left the Ali Akbar College of Music in December of 1975. I returned to Houston with the intention of working to earn some money. I would set my affairs in order, and then move to India.

The intention of moving to India to study music was all very well, but how I was going to do it? Where would I get money? How much would everything cost? Where would I live? These were only a few considerations. The question of money was addressed by my getting a job for a few months at the Houston Public Library. The rate of exchange was so skewed that a few American dollars converted into a lot of Indian money. Other logistical concerns were partially addressed by my continued correspondence with Jayant Kirtane. He had recently moved back to India and managed to get a deal for putting a computer together. I would have to procure a few things for him in this regard.

But things didn't work out this way. My resident's visa took several months, when I thought that it would only take only a few weeks. This was in the middle of the "Emergency," and it is amazing that I got a resident's visa at all. In that period of time, Jayant's computer deal dissolved, and he moved to Pennsylvania to pursue graduate studies. Nevertheless, about nine months after I left the Ali Akbar College of Music, I had my visa in hand.

In September 1976, I boarded a jet plane and made my way to India.

Chapter 3
First Glimpses of India

"What the hell am I doing?" I thought to myself. The doors of the jet plane opened and I was immediately assaulted by the musky Bombay air. Its strangeness was unsettling. The first thing that crossed my mind was that I was making a big mistake, for I had heard stories of people who died attempting to do what I was doing. I pondered simply going back to my seat and returning to the US.

It was an early morning in September of 1976. Although it was about 2:00 a.m., it was already very hot and humid. Coming from Texas, I thought that I was used to heat, but this was extraordinary. The most unusual thing was the musky quality of the air. It was a curious combination of smoke from open fires, untreated sewage, cooking food, urine, diesel exhaust, and virtually everything else imaginable.

"Thank you for travelling Air India," said the air hostess. "Have a nice trip." Her stale wish was not particularly convincing, but then I couldn't expect it to be after saying the same thing, day after day. Her accent screamed of a convent school education. She was dressed in a thin blue printed Kashmir silk *sari*, that was identical to that of the other air hostess. She wore it with the *pallu* folded tightly over the left shoulder in a manner that seemed particular to Air India hostesses. This had the practical benefit of keeping the left hand unimpeded; but it also made a very strong and daring fashion statement by leaving large portions of midriff bare.

If I had not been so overwhelmed, I would have been concentrating on how beautiful she was. But all air hostesses were beautiful. Every "modren" girl aspired to be either a film actress, a model, or an air hostess, but only the most beautiful, educated, and well connected were able to land these jobs.

13

I walked down the steps that were wheeled up to the door of the plane. This led to a shuttle bus that waited on the tarmac.

This bus was my first exposure to the rough, hand-forged quality of Indian manufactured goods. Its skin, both inside and out, was wavy and crinkled. Its attachment to the chassis was tenuous, and the entire vehicle roared and rattled with a sound that was reminiscent of a giant, poorly-maintained farm machine. Indian industry in the 1970s was definitely not up to world standards. The raw quality of the bus was, in part, a reflection of the many sheets of metal that were shaped by hand. It also attested to the fact that nothing was ever thrown away, but repaired countless times with all parts pressed back into service.

We were herded into Immigration. Herded is the most appropriate term for the process, for this hall was more reminiscent of a stockyard than an immigration centre. This effect was further amplified by the crowd's resistance to queuing up for anything. It was just a mass of people shoving and pushing in an attempt to get through the various stages of processing. These stages involved the usual health certificates, passports, disembarkation cards, and paperwork imposed by the "Emergency." (The "Emergency" was the time when Indira Gandhi, the prime minister, ignored the constitution, and set herself up as absolute ruler of the country). There was also Customs which had to be cleared. The entire Immigration process seemed to have no order, and it went on for hours.

Continuing the Journey

I awkwardly made my way out of the Immigration/Customs facility, and found a seat near the entrance to the airport terminal. The quiet lounge was a welcome relief from the chaotic stockyards through which I had just passed. I felt like a drowning man who was suddenly able to come up for air.

Now I could actually see India for the first time. It was early morning, and the sun was beginning to shine. I still had several hours before my flight, so I carefully absorbed all that I saw.

The terminal in Bombay was functional and utilitarian, but it had a drab quality. It would have been more typical of the Soviet Union. This was no accident, because every Indian administration since Independence proudly declared their goal of modelling the Indian economy after the Soviet Union's.

Several hours later, the queue for the Hyderabad flight opened up. After an uneventful security check, I, along with the rest of the Hyderabad-bound passengers, were trundled off to the plane.

Fortunately, I had a window seat that afforded me my first aerial view of the country. This revealed a curious criss-cross of lanes. From the air, I could see *bastis* which were crudely-thatched wall-to-wall shelters. I could also see many *pakkah* houses made of cement. From the plane, I was a voyeur as I watched the scenes of life unfold below me.

The plane ride from Bombay to Hyderabad gave me time to reflect upon my situation as I headed towards my new home.

Map of India

Reflections

"Is this my new home?" I thought to myself. Yes, this was going to be my new home. I came to India to find a guru and study music, but was I up to the task? How would I adjust? I knew that there were going to be great difficulties, for I had heard stories of other people trying to do what I was attempting. Some gave up and returned to the US, disillusioned and bitter. I had even heard stories of others who came here and contracted some strange disease and died. Questions and doubts moved about my mind like flies trapped in a bottle.

But I had no time to continue thinking about such matters. The plane was coming in for a landing and there were many mundane things I would have to attend to.

Chapter 4
The Twin Cities

The scene in front of the Hyderabad airport was one of complete confusion. A dozen taxi drivers, rikshaw drivers, and others hovered about me. They were bombarding me with questions in languages I didn't understand. I tried to leave the terminal, but there was an army of people blocking the way. Many were friends and relatives of people arriving on flights. They looked at me quizzically as they waited. Somehow, I negotiated a taxi and a coolie, and the three of us, along with my bags, pushed our way through the mass of people and headed for the vehicle. I got into the back of an old black Ambassador car, and we drove off. As we left the airport, I saw a sign in the parking lot that said, "Welcome to the Twin Cities."

I reflected on some reading that I had done earlier. Previously they were merely abstract words in a book, but now they assumed a special significance. As you move around the world, you will encounter a number of places where two municipalities grow up in close proximity to each other. Many of which bill themselves as "Twin Cities." The Hyderabad/Secunderabad municipality is one example.

Hyderabad developed as the administrative centre for the southern part of the Mogul empire. After the collapse of the empire, the rulers of Hyderabad became autonomous. These rulers grew in wealth after the failed uprising of 1857, in part as a reward by the British for Hyderabad's non-participation in this uprising. By the time of Independence in 1947, the ruler of Hyderabad, known as the *Nizam*, was reputed to be the wealthiest man in the world.

Secunderabad, on the other hand, was originally a small British holding used to garrison troops. Although it was in the middle of Hyderabad state, it was technically British soil. Hyderabad and Secunderabad may have been close geographically, but before independence they were culturally very different. Secunderabad had a very strong British feel to it while Hyderabad was infused with a strong, Islamic/Mogul ethos.

Old tomb stands as quiet testimony to Hyderabad's Mogul past.

The conditions in Hyderabad and Secunderabad changed in the 1950s. During this time, India was reorganised along linguistic lines. In the process, the earlier feudal boundaries were eliminated. This restructuring was quite appropriately referred to as the "Reorganisation." The Marathi-speaking district of Marathwada and the Kannada-speaking district of Karnataka were separated. This left the surrounding districts of Telangana. The people of Telangana spoke a dialect that was a mix of Telugu and Urdu. Telangana was fused with Andhra and Rayalaseema, which were Telugu-speaking areas of the former Madras presidency. This fusion created the Telugu-speaking state known as Andhra Pradesh.

View of Hyderabad from atop Naubat Pahad

The formation of Andhra Pradesh had a tremendous influence over the culture of both Hyderabad and Secunderabad. The Andhra culture became dominant and overwhelmed the British quality of Secunderabad. The Mogul quality of Hyderabad was also weakened under a tidal wave of Andhras. This did not completely eliminate the cultural differences between the two cities, but it did reduce them. If you didn't know where the boundaries were, you wouldn't feel them by moving around.

At least that was what I remembered from my reading, as the taxi rushed me to my new life.

Journey By Ground

The taxi wove its way through the streets of Secunderabad, slowly heading toward Hyderabad. Everything was so different from the US that it was absolutely overwhelming. I could now see the *pakkah* houses and *jhopdis* that I had seen from air.

Roadside commerce in India was extensive. The most common were stalls that were occupied by the *paanwallas*. They dispensed cigarettes, a variety of tobacco products, and most famously, *paan*. There were mechanics of every ilk, many whose only job was to fix punctures in tyres and fill them with air. Other people would simply lay out a cloth upon which they sold a variety of day-to-day items. Another form of roadside commerce was the *bandi*. This was nothing more than a simple, shallow wooden cart, upon which flowers, snack foods, or any number of other items might be sold.

Typical street scene

Shopping on the roadside

I also came in contact with totally new forms of transportation. Perhaps the most striking were the "autos." These were three-wheeled gas-powered vehicles, slightly reminiscent of a golf cart. Although some were for private commercial use, the majority were rented in the same manner that one would rent a taxi. Another unusual mode of transportation was the cycle rikshaw. These were large tricycles that could be engaged the same way that you might engage a taxi. For this the passenger would sit in the back, while a *rikshawalla* would pedal in front. Equally intriguing was the bullock cart. As the name implies, the bullock cart was a cart that was pulled not by a horse, but by a bull.

Cycle rikshaw

Bullock cart

I was in awe of all the animals that I saw in the streets. Dogs and cats were no surprise, but I was taken aback by the large number of goats, cattle, and water buffalo.

The taxi continued across *tank-bund*. This was an earthen dam that created a large lake in the centre of the Hyderabad /Secunderabad municipality. This man-made lake was known as the Hussain Sagar. It was a famous landmark and the only easily recognisable separation between Secunderabad and Hyderabad. The taxi moved toward Basheerbagh, and then on to its final destination - All India Radio.

Cattle were a common sight even in the centre of the city.

Chapter 5
Seetha Devi

We pulled into the compound of All India Radio. There was heightened security due to the Emergency, and my presence created a flurry of activity on the part of the guards. Just as the taxi driver was trying to straighten things out, my contact suddenly walked along. Her name was Vinjamuri Seetha Devi, and she was the aunt of a close friend of mine in the US. She was with a friend of hers named Sunandani Eypes. Sunandani Eypes was a producer in the English section, while Vinjamuri Seetha Devi was a producer of Telugu folk music. Both were women in their early fifties. Although I didn't know it at the time, they would play a crucial role in my marriage a few years later.

"You must be David," Seetha Devi said with a smile. "Rathna-*Papa* told me all about you. Let me take leave, and then we'll go."

Seetha Devi took me to her small flat located only about half a mile away.

"Here, let me make some *chai* for you. *Aayo papam*, you must be tired," she said.

We talked a bit as she made me some tea. After that, she said I could rest while she went out to attend to some work.

Although I was thoroughly exhausted, I could not sleep. I was overwhelmed with a tidal wave of unfamiliarity.

For reasons of economy and practicality the room was painted in a two-tone fashion. The lower portion was painted in enamel, while the upper portion was covered with whitewash. This was something that I had not encountered in the US. Whitewash was little more than chalk that was painted on. It was economical, but you could not use it all the way to the ground, or it

25

would wash away every time the floors were washed. Therefore, a permanent enamel was used on the lower portions. The enamel was far more durable, but since it was expensive, few would paint the entire wall with it. The dividing line between the enamel and the wash was invariably rough and sloppy. In those days, everything was rough and sloppy. The labourers who painted the houses had no interest in doing a neat job of it, and strangely enough the house owners were equally unconcerned.

There were concrete lattices mounted in the walls right up near the ceiling. This aspect of Seetha Devi's flat struck me as being very curious. These lattices were about 1 x 1.5 feet in size. A typical wall might have them spaced at about 10-foot intervals. These allowed air to circulate and kept the rooms relatively cool.

But the presence of these lattices meant that rooms could not be isolated. As I lay there, the flat filled with a fantasia of aromas that defined India, but this time the predominant scent was one of Indian food. Outside noise added to the ambience as the sound of every passing vehicle reverberated through the concrete room. Not only sounds and smells had easy access to the houses, but every manner of small creature would come and go at will. I lay there trying to sleep, but I was distracted by sparrows flying around. They would enter by way of a lattice, and fly to the top of a large Godrej *almirah*, where they were building a nest.

The *almirah* was a ubiquitous component of most rooms. Closets were rare in Indian houses, and cupboards were usually confined to the kitchen. Thus the need for a place to store things was fulfilled by the *almirah*. This was a very large, free-standing metal box that was locked with a large key. It was in these that one kept clothing, jewellery, and other valuables. In the West, we do not generally equate clothing with valuables, but in India a women's formal dress *sari* might represent a month's salary. Considering the disparity in income between middle or upper class Indians and their servants, to have *saris* laying about presented too great a temptation for theft. The cost of clothing might explain the need for a locked *almirah*, but there was another reason for keeping one's clothing packed away - dust. Dust was all-pervasive in Hyderabad. You could wash the floors in the morning and by the afternoon there would be a thin layer on everything.

Even though I had only been in India for less than a day, there was one theme that was clear. There was an openness about Indian life that was a striking contrast to life in the US. Most activities were conducted on the street. Commerce, socialising, eating, weddings, funerals, it didn't matter what it was, it could be seen in the street. Coupled with the open style of architecture, it meant that even when one was inside, the street still encroached upon one's life.

However, I would later find out that there existed an opposite to this openness. There was a private part of Indian lives that was kept hidden, almost as though it was locked inside a Godrej *almirah*. Indians spent their lives in a world that oscillated between the two extremes of the "fishbowl" and the secretive lifestyle.

My attention wandered around the room as I perused many of the new things that I saw, then my attention shifted to the doors. In the West, most doors were hinged only on one side. For reasons that were unclear to me, Indian dwellings tended to have double doors, even when the portal was small. There were usually no doorknobs, but instead an array of metal handles and bolts.

The threshold was also interesting. In the West, the threshold was a small strip, seldom higher than half an inch, made of rubber and located on the floor where the door closes. Its function was to seal the door, thus keeping cool air in during the summer, and hot air in during the winter. But the Indian threshold was very large. It was a strip of wood that was two to three inches high. A small opening at the base allowed water to flow outside whenever the floors were washed. The threshold of Vinjamuri Seetha Devi's flat was typical of most in southern India. It was painted bright yellow and decorated with white and red stripes. This was a striking contrast to the turquoise green that was the predominant colour of the rest of the door jamb.

Living spaces are not only a reflection of the material culture of a people, for there are always individual touches that reflect the personalities of their occupants. In the case of Vinjamuri Seetha Devi's flat, its individuality was apparent by virtue of several items. One was a black and white picture. This showed Indira Gandhi flanked on both sides by Vinjamuri Seetha Devi and her sister Anasuya Devi. The other item that gave a distinctive character to the flat was a folk musical instrument known as an *ektar*. Together the *ektar* and the picture with Indira Gandhi, defined her flat.

Seetha Devi's flat may have been modest by Indian standards, but it was palatial compared to what was outside. Next to her outside wall was a *jhopdi*. A *jhopdi* was a crude thatched structure. It was often constructed of scavenged materials. Typically, it was a simple framework of bamboo that supported crudely woven mats. These mats formed the walls and roofs. Occasionally the occupants might "find" some corrugated sheets of metal. These too, would be incorporated into the structure. Even cardboard boxes could be pressed into service during the dry months.

Jhopdis

The juxtaposition of crude *jhopdis* and *pakkah* houses was the norm for any middle or upper-class neighbourhood. The well-heeled residents of the locality needed servants, and these servants needed places to stay. Although many of these servants might have lived in the *bastis* (slums), and come in for work, some found it easier to just construct a crude *jhopdi* in these posh localities and stay there.

Vinjamuri Seetha Devi: The Woman

In 1976, while in her mid 50s, Vinjamuri Seetha Devi was a producer of folk music at All India Radio. In her younger days, she and her sister Anasuya were known as the "Vinjamuri Sisters." They were some of the first musicians in India to take folk music from the villages to the urban stage. This afforded them a considerable amount of fame among the older generation of Telugu-speaking people.

Vinjamuri Sisters (1978)

Seetha Devi was a remarkable person. She was warm and matronly. She was becoming a bit portly, but this was not unusual for a woman of her age. She moved with a slow, nearly-imperceptible limp.

Her life was different from many Telugu women of her generation. She was one of the first people to get an advanced degree in folk music. The modern, upper-class women might have had degrees in medicine or some academic subject, but to do so in folk music was unheard of. Equally unusual was the fact that she never married. Although unmarried, she was so attached to her sister's children that they referred to her as *Amma-pinni*, which translated to "Mother-Aunt."

Vinjamuri Seetha Devi

She had the habit of wrapping her *sari* with a preference towards roomy pleats about her waist. This had the effect of leaving the section of *sari* that hangs over the shoulder (*pallu*), a comically short length.

She represented the new Hyderabad, one which had a strong reflection of Coastal Andhra. She spoke very little Urdu, but she was very comfortable in Tamil, Telugu, and English.

I didn't realise it at the time, but Seetha Devi's life was destined to be inextricably linked to my own. It was a connection that would extend through many decades.

Chapter 6
The Auto Ride

At some point in Seetha Devi's flat I fell asleep. I have no recollection of it because it was that dreamless, timeless state that envelopes one in extreme exhaustion.

After a while Seetha Devi came back with a friend. She was a dance teacher. Seetha and her friend talked on various topics. But chief among them was myself, and how to best handle my training. Since almost all the discussion was in Telugu, I did not understand what was happening. I just went with the flow. After dark, we packed into an auto and headed to Secunderabad to go to the Government College of Music and Dance.

This was my first time to ride in an Indian auto. It presented me with a very intimate connection with Indian traffic. There was a chaotic quality about it, with cars and trucks coming directly at you, only to veer to the right at the last instant. This veering to the right was a reflection of the fact that Indians drove on the left hand side of the road. This was a holdover from the days that India was ruled by Great Britain. Actually, it was not really correct to say that they drove on the left hand side of the road. It would be more correct to say Indian driving statistically favoured the left side - but just barely so.

We made it to the Government College of Music and Dance. Unfortunately, I was a foreigner, and this was a government college, so it was not possible for me to study there. But I was assured that this was not a problem because there were numerous other possibilities.

Autos in Hyderabad

View from inside auto.

At this point my memory is unclear. I was overwhelmed by fatigue. Somehow we made it through the hustle and bustle of the traffic back to the flat. Seetha Devi prepared a meal, and I fell into a deep sleep.

I often look upon this auto ride as being a metaphor of my first month in India. There was a random quality to its turns, stops, and starts, but in the long run, it was possible to make a progress in the right direction. But what was the "right" direction? I didn't know, but it was one hell of a ride.

Chapter 7
Finding a Guru

It was a golden morning, and the sun bathed Hyderabad in its warm radiance. The arid Hyderabad air usually gave the sun's rays an oppressive quality, but this early in the day it felt wonderful. The air was full of the gentle musky aroma which typifies the country.

This was my second day in India, and I was sitting in Seetha Devi's flat along with her sister Anasuya Devi. It was important to find a teacher to begin my training. However, in India things never happened quickly. Invariably important decisions were group decisions involving elders and much discussion.

But the city was oblivious to our discussion. This was evidenced by a symphony of sounds permeating the flat.

There was a rhythmic "*tak, tak, tak*" emanating from an adjacent plot of land. These were the sounds of workers breaking roughly cut stones into smaller, equally rough ashlars. The quality of their work left much to be desired. It was definitely a reflection of the Hyderabadi "*chalta hai*" (literally "it goes") attitude. For this, one put enough effort into something to make it functional, and no more. The refinement of the stone in pursuit of a "perfect ashlar" could not have been further from their minds.

There was the sound of a vegetable seller announcing her goods. She walked down the street with a wicker *gampa* (basket) balanced on her head. The *gampa* was filled with potatoes, okra (ladies' fingers), and *surakai*. These were all of dubious freshness, but this bothered neither the hawker nor her customers. She was convenient, and she was always ready to negotiate the price downward.

35

There was a "*ching, ching, ching*" of bells that were crudely attached to the axle of a modified rikshaw carrying children. The back seat was removed, and a large cage was put in its place. About eight small children whose ages ran between five and seven sat in this cage. They crouched there, huddled in their crisply-starched green and white school uniforms. They reminded me of chickens being sent to market, and like chickens they seemed unperturbed by their caged transport.

Not all of the sounds came from outside, for there was a "*clink...clink...*" pizzicato coming from the kitchen. This was the sound of dishes being cleaned. The servant-girl came, and was busily crouched over her pile of dishes and cooking vessels. She washed them with ash and tamarind, and for a scrubber she used coconut husks. It seemed crude, but it worked as well as commercial soaps and brushes, but was considerably more eco-friendly. Her simple, coarse cotton *sari* was lifted up to her shins exposing an equally-coarse, white cotton petticoat. The *pallu* was pulled tightly across her back, and tucked into the petticoat at her stomach. Her hair ran down her back in a single tight braid. She occasionally conversed in a rough, rustic Telugu with Seetha Devi. She quickly yet skilfully restored the brass vessels to a clean golden lustre. These vessels were made of brass but were coated on the inside with tin. They had to be coated in this fashion, or they could not have been used for cooking. The copper would have reacted with food to produce a poison that would make people sick.

This concerto of morning sounds only provided the background score for the work that was going on. We were making a decision as to whom we should approach for my instruction. Anasuya Devi had just arrived from Madras that morning, and they were both discussing this in great depth.

Anasuya Devi

Anasuya Devi was, and still is, an extremely interesting person. She was a well-known vocalist with an amazing ability on the harmonium. She had a mercurial bend of mind, and was as ambitious and strong-willed as she was intelligent. Her marriage to her husband Giri was permanently on a rocky course. The reasons for this lack of marital harmony were varied, but included the fact that she was not the passive, yielding personality that was typically desired in an Indian woman in those days.

I placed my fate as to who my guru should be in both of their hands. Many names were tossed about, but none of them had any ring of familiarity. That was to be expected. After some time they reached a consensus.

Anasuya Devi

"*Babu*," said Anasuya Devi. "We think we should approach Shaik Dawood Khan. He is the best tabla player in this part of India."

"He is a staff artist in AIR," continued Seetha Devi. "I don't know if he will accept you as his student, but we can go ask. There just seems to be one problem."

What's the trouble?" I asked.

"He doesn't know any English," replied Seetha Devi.

After more discussions, they concluded that his inability to speak English was merely an inconvenience, it was more than compensated by his skill as a performer and teacher. So we decided to contact him.

All India Radio

We went back to All India Radio, later that morning. This time I was able to get a better picture of the radio station. All India Radio, more popularly known as AIR, had facilities that were typical of the time.

Like so many public buildings in India, it was at one time a great mansion, but at some point it came to house the studios and offices for AIR. The walls of the offices were made of cement. They were painted with the ubiquitous two-tone enamel / whitewash scheme. The offices were once living quarters that opened onto a large porch. However, this porch did not open directly into the garden, but was closed off with a large wooden grill or *jali* consisting of a lattice of wooden slats. This arrangement was typical of old Muslim households in the area. The purpose of the *jali* was to let air circulate, and allow women a view of the outside, but keep people outside from seeing in. This allowed women a degree of freedom to move about while still maintaining their privacy.

The equipment at AIR was crude, even by 1970s standards. The recorders were full track 1/4-inch tape machines. This was the first time in my life that I had ever seen such machines, I had only heard of such equipment existing in the early 1950s in the US. The mixers were large and cumbersome and also reflected a 1940s and 1950s technology. I often wondered why they even bothered with mixers. Most of the recordings usually involved nothing more than the placement of one large ancient microphone in the centre of the room. The studio walls were covered in a *desi* (locally made) version of an acoustic tile.

There was an extremely rigid and well-defined social structure at All India Radio. This approach was inherited from the British, but it acquired a unique Indian colour. At the top of this social structure was the SD or Station Director. No one was his equal and no one socialised with him. It was necessary to have his blessings for every undertaking. Below the SD was the next rung of administration, which consisted mainly of producers. Lower down were vocalists and engineers. Although the engineers and vocalists were on a comparable level in the social hierarchy, each looked upon themselves as being superior and did not socialise with the other. Instrumental accompanists were lower still. And at the lowest rung of the AIR hierarchy were the maids, cleaners, *chaprasis* (peons), gardeners, *chowkidars* (guards), and other common servants. Yet even within these major groups there were sub-groups and cliques.

Shaik Dawood Khan's clique was permanently ensconced outside the studios in an area where the bicycles were kept. There was a large box of some indiscernible function under a massive and ancient tree. Since only a very small portion of the day was devoted to rehearsals and recordings, most of their time was spent whiling away the hours, gossiping, smoking *beedis* (a small, rough, *desi* version of a cigarette), drinking *chai*, and eating *paan*. This group consisted of instrumental accompanists, largely Muslim with an occasional Hindu or Christian. They were all what one would describe as *mulki Hyderabadis*.

The term "*mulki*" was an extremely pregnant term. It conveyed volumes of information, not just about the person involved, but also about the state of affairs in Hyderabad in general. It was an Urdu term that meant the same thing as the Hindi term *desi* and implied a "countryman" or perhaps even "native son." However, in the Hyderabadi context of the day, it had a special significance. Before 1947, Hyderabad was an autonomous kingdom. In the space of about 10 years, Hyderabad was absorbed into independent India. Its king, the *Nizam*, was deposed, and its borders violated by the loss of the districts of Karnataka and Marathwada. Furthermore its culture was confused by its sudden merger with large portions of the erstwhile Madras Presidency. It would be an understatement to say that not everyone was happy with these changes. When a person was referred to as *mulki*, you were saying that a person represented "old" Hyderabad, replete with all its cultural, and at times political implications.

Anasuya Devi, Seetha Devi, and myself approached Dawood in his cluster of *mulkis* to discuss the possibility of my study under him. It was not customary for traditional ustads to easily accept students in those days, yet, he readily agreed to teach me. Perhaps it was the novelty of my being an American that impressed him. Maybe the fact that I came all the way from the US proved that I was serious about my study. Possibly it was Seetha and Anasuya Devi's recommendation that persuaded him. Perhaps it was just a display of Dawood's magnanimous personality that guided his decision. For whatever reason, he agreed.

Seetha and Anasuya quickly consulted their *panchangam* (a traditional Hindu calendar) to find an auspicious day. They decided that I should meet him the next day for my *ganda-bandhan* ceremony.

My Ganda Bandhan

September 21, 1976 was the day that I officially began my training under Shaik Dawood Khan. This was marked by a *ganda-bandhan* ceremony. In this ceremony, I officially took Dawood as my ustad or guru (teacher), and he officially acknowledged me as being his *chela* or *shagird* (student). I am so sure of the date, because this also happened to be my 23rd Birthday. For my initiation, I brought some cloth, some fruit, some sweets, and a monetary offering of 201 rupees (roughly US $40 in those days). This ceremony was attended by members of Dawood's family, fellow students, and other Muslim musicians of the area. There was a short prayer, after which I gave my offering to Dawood. He then tied a red thread around my wrist. I touched his feet in a pranaam, and at that point I was officially his student.

My goal of finding a guru was accomplished. But this signalled the start of something and not an end. Was this "something" good, bad, practical, or what? At this point I couldn't know.

Chapter 8
Shaik Dawood Khan

Shaik Dawood Khan was my guru. In India, this relationship was considered to be one of the most important in one's life. It was considered to be just under one's parents in terms of importance, and was sometimes felt to be as important as one's spouse.

Shaik Dawood Khan was born on December 16, 1916 in Sholapur. He was born into a modest, middle-class family. His father was a draftsman in the Public Works Department of Bijapur.

His early years were the foundation upon which he built his career. He began his formal training in music when he was eight years old. He received his instruction in the basics of vocal music and tabla under Ameer Qawal. By the age of twelve he started to focus on tabla. It was at this time that he became a student of Ustad Khasim *Sahib*. Shaik Dawood made such progress on the tabla that by the age of twenty, he was regularly invited to accompany artists on the Hyderabad radio station. This was in the pre-AIR period, when it was a private radio station. He was in such demand as an accompanist that in 1937, Dawood moved to Hyderabad where he accepted a permanent job with the radio. (Recording technologies were in their infancy, therefore all music that was broadcast from the radio was live.)

Within months of Dawood's arrival at the radio station, it was taken over by the *Nizam* (the ruler of Hyderabad). This proved to be advantageous to the young Dawood, because it brought him in contact with various nobility who took charge of its administration. In particular, it was the Nawab Ali Yavar Jung and the Nawab Zaheer Yar Jung Bahadur (Minister of Religious and Cultural affairs), who took a liking to the young Shaik Dawood and helped advance his career. During the time that he was attached to the radio station, Shaik Dawood accompanied most of the great musicians of that period. These included Ravi Shankar, Ali Akbar Khan, Bade Ghulam Ali Khan, D.V. Paluskar, Allaudin Khan, and a host of others.

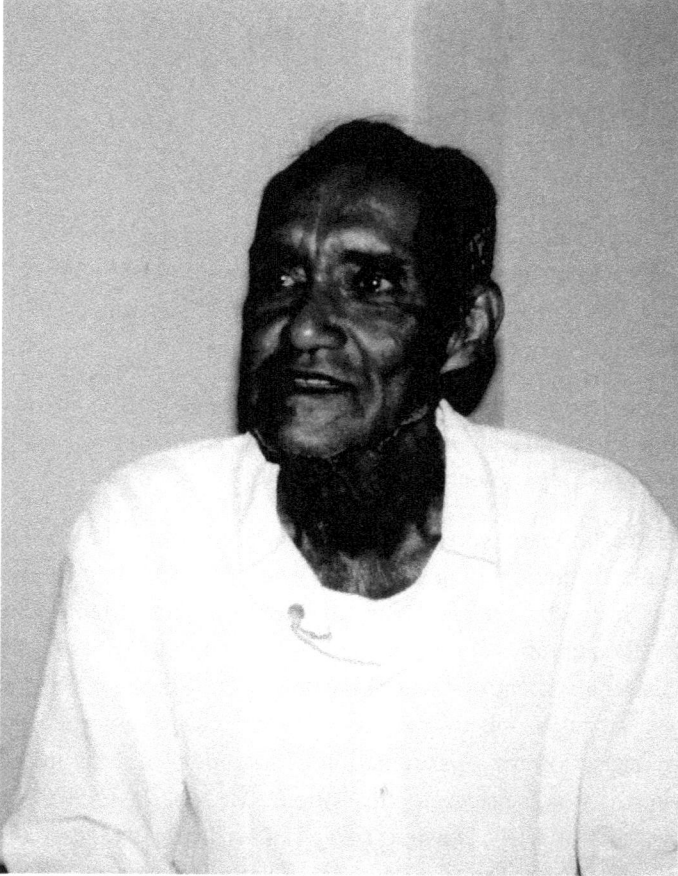

Shaik Dawood Khan (circa 1985)

During this period, Dawood did something very unusual. Although he was a well established professional, he continued to apprentice himself to other great musicians. He apprenticed himself to the great Alladia Khan and then to his two sons, Ustad Mohammed Khan and Ustad Chote Khan. It was under Mohammed Khan that Dawood *Sahib* learned *pakhawaj* (a barrel-shaped drum that is considered to be the ancestor to the tabla). Finally at the age of 45 and at the peak of his career, he became a student of the great Mehboob Khan Mirajkar.

Shaik Dawood Khan on tabla in early radio broadcast

Dawood was a very good and kind teacher. We affectionately referred to him as *Baba*, which literally meant "father." His reputation as an excellent teacher was in part due to his openness and willingness to impart information and compositions to his students. It was also due to his great knowledge of the tabla.

Shaik Dawood's Generation as a Cultural Bridge

Dawood *Sahib* and his generation bridged the old feudal approach to tabla and the modern, urban approach. In the 18th and 19th centuries, there were three places that served as centres for high culture in India. These were the temples (*mandir*), the royal courts, and the *kothas*.

Historically, Hindu temples served as centres of culture. In the south, they played an extremely important role in the maintenance and propagation of the *Carnatic* Indian system of music. However, due to the dearth of Hindu kingdoms in Northern India, they played a very limited role in the development of the North Indian style of music.

Shaik Dawood Khan with tabla

The royal courts were much more important for the development of the arts in the North. The contributions of nobility such as the Wazid Ali Shah were legendary. But as far as tabla was concerned, the royal courts seemed to have contributed only slightly to its development. The tabla, with its delicate sound, was ill-suited to the large *darbars* (large royal halls) in which state functions were held. There was a tendency to use the much louder *pakhawaj* for courtly purposes.

The culture that generated and supported the tabla was the *kotha* culture. The *kothas* were the mansions of the *tawaifs*. Although the term *tawaif* is today equated with a prostitute, in many ways it was similar to the geisha tradition of Japan. The *kothas* were the meeting places for artists, poets, aristocrats, musicians, and dancers; but they were closed environments. The only way to gain access to the gatherings and performances (*mehafil*) was by great personal wealth, political connections, nobility of birth, or some outstanding musical or artistic ability. Yet even after gaining access to the *kothas*, there was no degree of egalitarianism. This environment, like that of Indian society as a whole, was strictly stratified. There was a rigidly-enforced system of etiquette that determined who did what, who could come, who could not, who were paid, and who were required to pay. At the top of the *kotha*'s social structure there was a *bai* (madam) who had the reputation of being highly educated, wealthy, and having impeccable etiquette; but also mercenary and prone to political machinations in the affairs of the kingdom. Below her were a cadre of lesser *tawaifs*, musicians, apprentice *tawaifs*, and servants.

The position of the tabla player in this environment was mixed. They were definitely "hired help," but the years of practice required to master the instrument set them apart from the common servants. Tabla players were often illiterate. This was typical of other musical accompanists as well. Although exact numbers may never be known, virtually no books, poetry, or other literary works come from tabla players in this period.

Today the tabla player lives in a very different world. The *kothas* and the *bais* have largely disappeared, so they have ceased to be a source of patronage. The tabla players of today are often well-educated, a major contrast from those of past generations. Furthermore, the prevailing attitude is one of relative openness about the art. The professional aspect of tabla is also considerably more complicated than it was in ages past. Relying upon public support for one's livelihood is more challenging than living off the patronage of a king or *bai*. Additionally, there is the necessity of having a degree of technical literacy so that one may deal with the challenges of recording, sound reinforcement, media distribution, and the other realities of the modern world.

This drastic change in the culture of tabla did not happen overnight. There had to be a generation of performers capable of bridging the gap between the *kotha* culture and the mp3 culture. This was where Shaik Dawood Khan fit the bill perfectly. He was able to free himself from the fetters of the old feudal mindset. He was comfortable with being recorded, performing on the radio, and being on the television. He freely imparted his knowledge to all of his students. These were remarkable breaks from the past. But he also retained many of the positive aspects of previous generations. He was acknowledged to be one of the most knowledgeable people in India with regards to traditional compositions and techniques.

Yet Dawood was not completely unfettered by problems that afflicted previous generations. To begin with, his formal education was somewhat limited. To his credit, he was literate in Hindi, Urdu, and Marathi. However, his lack of ability in English and limited familiarity with the post-independence "modren" culture made it difficult for him to move in high society.

Today the image of the tabla player is epitomised by Zakir Hussain. This is one who is innovative, intelligent, educated, and has no difficulty moving in the higher echelons of international society. But Zakir and others could not have accomplished this without the tireless struggle of many Dawood Khans across the country. These artists, often unnoticed and unappreciated, lifted the artform from the ashes of a decaying feudal society, suffered the ostracism of the anti-*nautch* movement, endured the cultural upheavals of the Independence struggle, and finally brought it to the point where it is today.

Chapter 9
Settling In - The Kirtane Household

My lessons under Shaik Dawood commenced nicely, and I was just beginning to get a feel for the country. But I still had a few things that needed to be taken care of. One of which was finding a permanent place to live.

Accommodation for the first week was not a problem. Seetha Devi's flat was minuscule, so it was obvious that I could not stay there. But she made arrangements for me to spend a few days with a kind Maharashtrian family by the name of Chitale. They were conveniently located next to her flat. But I could not stay with the Chitale's indefinitely, so I moved into the house of Dr. Gouribai Kirtane. For the next two years, the Kirtanes would be my surrogate family.

Dr. Gouribai Kirtane

Dr. Kirtane, more commonly known as Gouribai, was a delightful woman in her late 50s. She was a small, thin woman, and of very fair complexion. She studied medicine in England in her younger days. Before marriage, she was a Kirloskar, this was a very prominent Maharashtrian industrialist family.

She had three sons. Jayant was the oldest and was my friend back in the US. It was through his friendship that I made the connection with her. There was Sanjay who was a physician in the US. He was the most well-known of the Kirtanes, this degree of fame came from his earlier days as a cricketer. Finally, there was Dhananjay, who was the youngest. He was the only son still living at home.

However, the household was not limited to just us. There was a servant by the name of Kamal, and a dog named Peter. Furthermore, over the next two years that I lived in the house, other people came and went.

Dr. G. Kirtane

Dr. Kirtane's lifestyle was spartan. She always wore a clean, ironed *sari* of a modest and conservative style. She had absolutely no interest in fashion, consumerism, or ostentation. Any purchase was made strictly according to utilitarian considerations. Aside from work, her main interests were religion, philosophy, history, and reading general non-fiction.

Professionally, Dr. Kirtane was what was known as a "lady doctor." This was a specialisation that was unheard of in the West. It was a combination of Ob/Gyn, paediatrics, and family practice. It stemmed from the fact that an Indian woman would not go to a male doctor.

I moved into Dr. Kirtane's house as a "paying guest." Basically, I lived in her house in exchange for money. It was somewhat akin to the old "boarding house," with the major difference being that I lived as a member of the family.

There was always the question as to what motivated Dr. Kirtane to accept paying guests. I am sure that money was not a reason. I feel that the home environment was the important factor. She was raised in her very large house when it was teeming with activity. There were several generations of Kirloskars, all living together in a bustling, vibrant, extended family. But, when I was there, her husband and parents were dead, two of her three sons were out of the country, and it was clear that there were not going to be any daughters-in-law or grandchildren living there in the immediate future. Living in that same house with just one servant and a dog must have been a depressing change from the dynamic household of her youth. Another motivating factor was Dr. Kirtane's magnanimous personality. By accepting paying guests she was helping people she deemed to be worthy.

In my case, I think there was an additional motivation. When she studied medicine in England, she enjoyed the hospitality of many people there. Accepting the kindness of people in a foreign country is an experience that is not easily forgotten. I think that she felt a debt that might only partially be repaid by extending hospitality to a foreigner such as myself.

Furthermore, if you were a close friend of someone, you were considered to be a friend of the entire family. Curiously enough, this friendship exists even if two individuals have never actually met. I, along with the other paying guests, were all friends of the family.

The Kirtane House

The house was the most interesting place that I have ever seen. It was extremely large and spacious, but its style was somewhat dated even by the standards of the day. It was located in Troop Bazaar, at the intersection of Bank Street and Reddy Hostel Road. (The house no longer exists, but the location can be found on Google Earth at 17°23'15.25N 78°28'39.14E).

View from veranda of the Kirtane house

The house was built around 1915 and reflected the kind of mansion that was common among wealthy Indians at that time. There was an internal courtyard, which was surrounded on three sides by living quarters, and on one side by a wall. All of the outer walls were painted in a peculiar off-yellow colour. Many of the doors and shutters were turquoise green, but a few were stained and varnished brown. Every window had the ubiquitous iron bars that were there to deter burglary. It had a flat cement roof, which allowed one to go up for a nice view of the locality.

The compound had a wall that was roughly ten feet (3 metres) in height. The top edge of this wall was lined with bits of broken bottles, pointing upwards, and affixed with cement. This was an extremely common way to deter would-be thieves.

The accommodations at the Kirtane household were spacious by any standards. The building was originally designed to support a household of about ten to fifteen people. But in the two years that I was there, the occupancy seldom exceeded four people.

Because the building was under-utilised, large portions of it were closed off. At one time, an unused back section was broken into by a thief. He stole vessels and anything that he found, and then took them to the market and sold them. Normally a thief would make a hasty escape to avoid capture after burgling a place, but he felt so secure that he just moved in. He was never discovered by members of the Kirtane house. It was only after he was captured by the police and questioned for a different set of burglaries, that his dwelling place was discovered. Needless to say, the Kirtanes were surprised and perplexed when the police called one day and informed them that a thief had been living in their house without their knowledge.

Although the house was very roomy, in the past it was even more spacious. The jagged glass-covered wall partitioned the household off from a much larger area of land which had once been a large front garden. This partition resulted from a property dispute arising after the death of Gouribai's (Dr. Kirtane) father. Another sign of a reduction in usable area was to be found in the back. There was a Muslim graveyard known as a *khabarstan*, or at least it appeared to be a *khabarstan*. There seemed to be some doubt as to whether any of the graves were actually occupied. This land too was involved in a dispute over its ownership.

Ownership of land should have been a simple affair, but in India, it was a particularly thorny matter. This was probably the most common source of civil litigation in the country. There were two major reasons that land disputes clogged the courts. The first was greed, as there are always going to be people who will attempt to acquire property by any means. The other reason was that land ownership in India was often unclear. Land ownership laws followed the old feudal system, the British system, and that of post-Independence India. In the last hundred years, all three systems existed, often overlapping with each other. When one mixed avarice with a dysfunctional system of civil law, the results could be particularly bad. The Kirloskar family, which included Gouribai, was in the midst of a land dispute that lasted for decades.

The Kirloskar family was very famous. There were two professional wings of this family. One wing of Kirloskars were industrialists and another were doctors. In the West, we do not think of families as being involved in professions, but in India this was the norm.

There were many reasons why professions tended to cluster in families. Some of these were nepotism, professional politics, and general lack of independence on the part of the youth.

Professional politics was a major reason. If you were involved in any profession, you would attempt to keep other people out, this would enhance your own material security. This tactic was used by the American Medical Association and other labour unions in the US for ages, so there was nothing surprising about this. But the degree to which this was carried out in India was extraordinary.

Nepotism was another reason. It was probably the most important exception to the exclusionary tactic. In India, nepotism was not considered to be a character flaw, but a deeply-rooted way of life.

Furthermore, most Indian youth were not very independent, this lack of independence provided yet another reason for which professions clustered in families.

Kamal

Next to Dr. Kirtane, the senior-most member of the household was Kamal. She was a servant. Servants were not normally considered to be part of Indian households. Still, she had lived there for decades, and become an important component of the household dynamics. Kamal was a Maharashtrian woman who was about forty. She came from a small town in Maharashtra. One might think that this last statement is redundant, but it is not. The majority of Maharashtrians in Hyderabad settled there so many generations ago that they had no attachment to the state of Maharashtra. Kamal had been married, but had some marital problems. In those days, divorce was not an option in her community, so she felt that the only thing she could do was to run away. After leaving her husband, she came to Dr. Kirtane in a destitute condition, whereupon Dr. Kirtane took her into the household as a servant.

People are a mixture of good and bad, and Kamal was no exception. As servants go, she was hardly a model worker. She was overweight, slothful, moody to the point of being surly, and a terrible cook. Nevertheless, she did not steal things. In India, this last trait was extremely rare in servants and would trump any other personal deficiency. She also didn't seem to be capable of duplicity in any way, another rare trait. Her education was deficient, which was no personal weakness but merely an unfortunate consequence of her social condition at birth. In spite of her lack of education, she had a good command over three languages. She was fluent in her mother tongue Marathi, albeit a rough rural dialect. She was comfortable with the Hyderabadi dialect of Urdu, and she also seemed to be comfortable with Telugu. She had no fluency in English, so this forced me to develop a rudimentary ability to speak in Marathi, a skill that has long since disappeared.

Although I am digressing a bit, I should say a few words about language in India. India has about eighteen languages and roughly eight-hundred dialects. (People argue over the exact numbers, but you get the idea). Being multilingual was the norm, especially for those who live in the cities. I have seen many people who were poorly educated, but could still hold their own in five different languages.

Let me digress no further and return to the topic of Kamal. She may have had her deficiencies as a servant, but she was Dr. Kirtane's companion for most of her adult life. In spite of the vast chasm that existed between them in terms of education and social position, they lived together until Kamal was roughly seventy years of age.

Kamal

Kamal and the dog Peter

Dhananjay Kirtane

Some of my happiest memories are of Dhananjay Kirtane. He was Dr. Kirtane's youngest son. He was a year younger than me, and this closeness in age afforded an almost immediate bonding. I can't say how many times Dhananjay, his cousin Suhas, and I, would go about the city just having a great time doing the things that young people did.

Dhananjay Kirtane

This was the environment in which I lived from October 1976 until my marriage in November 1978. It was one of the happiest periods of my life, and certainly one that had significant influence on my personality.

Chapter 10
My Training

The red thread tied around my wrist was a constant reminder of my bondage. The only way this bond could be broken was by death, either mine or my guru's.

These thoughts echoed through my mind as I left the Kirtane compound and headed to the house of a senior student. It was my second week in India and this opportunity to move with other English speaking students would help me understand many things. I arrived and found several people there, and was immediately offered some *chai*.

"We are your guru-*bhais* - your 'brothers under the guru,'" I was instructed by one one senior student. "You treat us in the same way that you would treat your own brothers. You must learn your lessons, well and practice daily!"

I was filled with self-doubt and apprehension. Was I up to this obligation? Could I handle the practice? I knew no Urdu, so how would I even manage my lessons? I knew that I was involved in a form of apprenticeship, but there were still so many unanswered questions.

"Continuity is extremely important in our culture," a senior student said. "Of particular importance is a tradition which in Sanskrit is called *guru-shishya-parampara*, this term literally translates to 'unbroken chain of teacher and disciple.' You recently acknowledged *Baba* as your teacher. Dawood *Sahib* was previously taken by his teachers, who were taken by their teachers. After some years, you too may take students, and thus the chain will continue. According to tradition, this chain goes back to the earliest period of history. People say that it goes all the way back to the time of the Vedas."

"It is not only the student/teacher tradition, but the art too is tied to this continuum," he continued. "There is a body of material that is the basis of your training, and this is called *taleem*. Whenever you perform, even if it is improvised and thus existing 'in the moment,' it is still based upon your *taleem*, and therefore linked with antiquity."

I reflected upon the words my guru-*bhai* told me. In years to come, it formed the context in which everything I did, and everything I studied made sense.

Dawood's Residence

All of my training took place in Dawood's home. He lived in an area just off Lakadi-ka-Pul, known quite unglamorously as Chintal Basti. The term *basti* translated to "slum." Still, I never actually saw a *basti* in the area the entire time that I was there. Presumably, it had once been filled with *jhopdis*, but at some point these were replaced with *pakkah* houses, and only the name was retained. The lanes were narrow, even by Indian standards, and the congestion made it difficult to travel by car. However this latter condition was largely academic, since the major forms of transportation were seldom larger than a three-wheeled auto.

Dawood lived in a typical Hyderabadi Muslim's home. There was a room in the front that was roughly comparable to a parlour. Chairs could be offered should an elderly person be present, but usually people sat upon a large thin mattress that covered a dais which occupied most of the available floor. The general absence of chairs was partly custom and partly a requirement for playing music. Traditional Indian instruments are played while sitting on the ground.

Dawood's family observed a strict *purdah* system of sexual segregation. For this, there was a door that was curtained off, and this led to the back living quarters. The curtain demarcated the *zanana*, or the place where the women lived. When guests arrived in the parlour, a bangle-clad female hand thrust out from behind the *purdah* holding a small tray with water, *chai*, and an occasional snack of biscuits, or *khaara*. This was all that was ever seen of the women. Over the two decades that I studied there, I saw whole crops of young girls emerge, grow to the age of about twelve, and then disappear behind the *purdah* and *burkha*, never to be seen in public again. Nobody ever gave a second thought to it, this simply was just "the way things were."

Woman in *burkha*

Dawood's residence was always bustling with activity. A variety of musicians came and went. Most were my guru-*bhais*, but there were other artists as well.

Sayeed-ur-Rehman in particular stands out. He was noteworthy because he was one of the few *sarangi* players in the Hyderabad area. The *sarangi* is a very difficult instrument, and one that acquired a dubious reputation due to its association with the *tawaif*. I used to wonder what kind of person embraced an instrument that had such a deep social stigma. Was it lack of other professional opportunities, was it a streak of rebelliousness, was it an anachronistic personality? In Sayeed's case it may have been a mixture of all these things. I know that he suffered ostracism. I know that he was moving with *kathak* dancers, some with dubious reputations. These social forces made him at times defensive and impenetrable. But all in all, he was a likeable character. Together we moved about in the artistic circles of Hyderabad, and I learned many things about India and the life of Indian artists from him. Today the *sarangi* is making a comeback, and we all owe artists such as Sayeed a great debt for keeping the art alive during this difficult period.

Sayeed-ur-Rehman with *sarangi*

(l to r) Shaik Dawood Khan (siting), myself (tabla), and Sayeed-ur-Rehman (*sarangi*) (1977)

Shabbir Nisar was another person who was part of Dawood's home. He was Shaik Dawood's third son, and the only one who had taken to music. Shabbir was born in 1960. He started learning the tabla at a very young age. When I first began to learn under Dawood, he was only sixteen, but was playing tabla very well.

An additional noteworthy person that I met at Dawood's residence was Ram. He was my guru-*bhai*, and he was about a year older than I. He worked in a medical supply company in sales, and was passionate about the tabla. But his passions went beyond music, for he had a remarkable knowledge of India, its history, and its traditions. Yet his knowledge extended far beyond the academic, for he was also street-smart. He freely shared this knowledge with me and became my teacher in the ways of this country.

My Lessons

I rode my bicycle to my lessons about three times a week. It was a large, iron, single speed "Hero" bicycle of pre-World War II design. It was a clunker, but serviceable. I rode from the Kirtane house in Troop Bazaar to Chintal Basti, this was approximately two miles (three kilometres). In the US this is considered to be a negligible distance; but in India, with its traffic and winding roads this was a respectable trip.

My lessons were routine. Sometimes I was the only person present for my lessons, but often there were other students. First, I would show my progress in the previous material. Then Shaik Dawood would carefully write down my next lessons in a large ledger book. After this, I did my best to memorise them, but I always needed to take them home and practice.

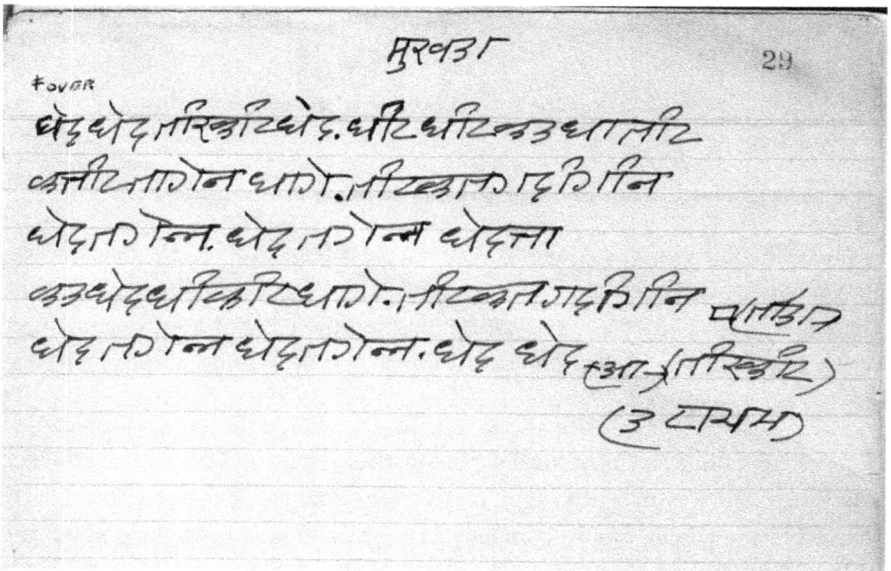

Lesson in Shaik Dawood's handwriting

There were no prescribed fees, but I gave *guru-dakshana* (an offering to the teacher) on occasion. Usually this was a box of sweets with some money inside. Sometimes it was cloth. Sometimes I made short trips to the US, and on such occasions, I always made it a point to bring back gifts for him. On one occasion, a few days before *Bakr-Eid*, I went to the market and bought a live goat. I gave it to him in anticipation of the upcoming festivities.

After each lesson, I made my way back the two miles to Troop Bazaar and the Kirtane household.

Three Weeks

I was sitting in my room in Troop Bazaar. I just finished a couple of hours of practice, so it was time to take a break. I climbed the winding stairs that took me to the roof of the Kirtane house. It was dark, and the steps were irregularly spaced, so I had to be careful. The stairs were completely dark, so I had to keep my hands on the walls to maintain a sense of orientation. The walls were rough cement, but the feel was inconsistent as I encountered portions that had been patched and repaired over the last few decades. I reached the top of the stairs where there was a pair of weather-worn doors, and upon opening it, I was dazzled by the blinding afternoon sunlight. Slowly my eyes adjusted to the light.

I was alone on the roof. This was level with the tops of trees that were in the *khabarstan* behind the house. A parrot and crow noisily flitted from branch to branch. I watched them engage in their small territorial dispute. I also saw some mechanics who had a work shed on Reddy Hostile Road. They went about their business of fixing vehicles, unaware of my presence. There was the sound of traffic in the street near the mechanics. But all of this merely brought my solitude into sharp relief. I felt like an island.

The solitude struck me. It seemed that from the moment I stepped off the plane, I was constantly surrounded by people. This was one of the few times that I had to be by myself. This gave me a chance to reflect upon my situation. Three weeks had passed since I arrived in India. Things were finally getting under control. I had my teacher and a place to live. I was beginning to have a circle of friends and acquaintances. But it was starting to get tiresome. The initial rush of enthusiasm and excitement was wearing off. It was going to be a lot of hard work, and I had a long journey ahead of me. It was not a physical journey, but a psychological one.

I thought of the US, and the people I left behind. Although it was only a short time, so much had happened, and so much had changed. It seemed like an eternity. For the first time, I was beginning to descend into that melancholy that is so tritely referred to as homesickness.

"David..." I heard Dr. Kirtane call from the courtyard below.

I immediately curtailed my reflections to attend to this distant summons. I knew what the purpose of this call was. It was teatime.

I passed through the weathered, wooden doors, and latched them behind me. It was almost complete darkness, but I made my way down several flights of stairs by memory. Tap... tap... tap..., I heard the sound of my Bata sandals as they connected with the stone steps. Without the distraction of sight, the sound of each footstep seemed to be amplified to unimaginable proportions. They seemed to echo endlessly in the concrete and stone stairwell. Finally I reached the bottom.

Chapter 11
Names

Teatime was an indispensable part of the daily routine at the Kirtane household. Indians acquired many habits from the British and this was one of the most conspicuous. Today a number physicians from the area were coming by. They had been meeting once a month for a long time. Ostensibly these meetings were professional, but I knew that these tea-parties were more social than professional.

A gentleman in his mid 50s entered the door and was introduced to me as Dr. Shauche.

"What is your good-name?" he asked me in a friendly manner. I wondered if I had a "bad-name." I didn't know it at the time, but I later found out that the peculiar Indian usage of "good name" was a literal translation of *sunaam*. But it seemed to lose something in translation.

I had my tea, and afterwards Dr. Kirtane, Dr. Shauche, and the half-dozen other physicians attended to their business. I retired to the sitting room to read a copy of *Illustrated Weekly of India* which had just arrived. But I was not really interested in the magazine. I started to reflect upon the different way that names were handled here.

In the West, a person could have four names. There was the family name (a.k.a. surname or last name), there was the given name (a.k.a. first name), there was the middle name (a.k.a. the Christian name or maiden name), and then there could be a nickname. Names in India had a similar breakdown, but there were some important differences.

The first thing that struck me was the order in which names appeared. As a general rule, South Indians had the family name first and the given name last. North Indians on the other hand, had the given name first, and the family name last. Did this cause confusion? Yes, it certainly did.

Villages, towns, and districts were commonly used as family names. Just as Western family names such as "Rosenberg" or "Townsend" reflected place names, so too did Indian family names such as "Sardhana" or "Tenali" reflect places.

Many names were derived from professions. Sometimes these translated exactly into their Western counterparts. For instance, the name "Mistri" directly translated to "Mason," "Mirza" translated to "Clark," "Shah" translated to "King," etc.

However, names that showed a familial relationship seem to be found only among Muslims and even then, they were rare. Therefore, you generally did not find names corresponding to Johnson (i.e., son of John) or Robinson (i.e., son of Robin).

Caste was also commonly used as a family name. For instance, the name Shastri or Sharma indicated that a person was a brahmin, while Thakur or Khatri indicated that a person was a *kshatriya* (warrior class). There could be confusion when the caste name was used in addition to a place name. For instance, the south Indian name Tenali Krishna Shastri, could for official purposes have either Tenali (a place) or Shastri (the caste) as the official family name on a passport.

Compound given names were often a source of confusion. Depending upon how a name was conjugated, it could completely change the gender. For instance the name Durga was a common girl's name, but the name Durga-Prasad became a boy's name. In a similar manner among the Sikhs, the name Devinder-Singh was a boy's name, while Devinder-Kaur was a girl's name. All Sikhs had either Kaur or Singh in their name, but it was common practice not to use this appendage. Therefore in practice, Sikh names like Devinder, Kulvinder, etc. became genderless.

There were other cases where a name could be either male or female. For instance Apurva (literally "unprecedented") could be either a boy's or a girl's name.

An entire book could be written just describing nicknames. Many times such names were meaningless. The Telugu nickname "*Ammulu*" for a girl, meant nothing, it was somewhat analogous to "Tootsie". Sometimes the meaning of a nickname was patently obvious, such as the Telugu nickname *Papa* (lit. "baby girl") or *Babu* (lit. "baby boy"). It was not unusual in

Hyderabad to find sixty-year-old men being referred to as *Babu* by their family. The most common nicknames were short derivatives of the given name. For instance the nickname Dhannu was a derivative of Dhananjay, Shai was a derivative of Shailaja, etc.

In India, the nickname often assumed a special importance due to the sometimes protracted delay in coming up with an official name. Unlike in the West where the name was usually chosen well before the child was born, in India, a name was often not chosen until just before the naming ceremony. This naming ceremony was usually performed when the child was still an infant; but I know of cases in which this was not done until the child was nearly five. Obviously the child was not going to be referred to as "It" for this long period, hence the popularity of generic nicknames such as *Babu*, *Papa*, *Chitibabu*, *Chinnababu*, etc.

Women's names were perhaps the most confusing. This reflected the fact that Indian women traditionally had no recognised identity separate from their husband's or father's. For instance when a girl was single, she took her father's family name, but after marriage she took her husband's family name. This is commonly done in the West and should not be a cause for confusion, but there was more. For instance, it was common in many South Indian communities for a woman to adopt her husband's first name as her last name. Therefore, the name "Girija Balaji" reflected her given name (Girija) and her husband's given name (Balaji). It is comparable to a woman in the West having the name "Julie John" with "Julie" being her given name and "John" not actually a family name, but her husband's given name. This was often done in addition to assuming the husband's family name!

This brings up the question of who actually has "given" a girl's name. In the West, it was given by the girl's parents, but in India, this was not always the case. In some communities people had the option of renaming their daughter-in-law. If a girl was renamed at marriage, did her given name at birth disappear entirely? No, not necessarily. When she went back to visit her parent's house, she typically went by her given name at birth, but when she returned to her in-laws' house, she assumed the name given her at the time of marriage. This reflected the curious trait of having people's names being somewhat relative. There could be one set of names used for official purposes, another name used by friends and co-workers, and yet another name used at home.

As a general rule, a person's given name was only used if you were addressing someone of equal or lower social position. For instance, if a man's given name was "Ram," you would only address him as such if he were a close friend, if he was much younger than you, or perhaps in some other socially inferior position to you. If the person was older or in any way deserving special consideration, you could use the name "Ram" only if it was appended with some term of respect, for instance "Ramji," "Ramsahib," or "Ramgaru." Now if that man were of a considerably higher social position, then using the name Ram under any condition was simply not done. For instance, most Indian women would not address their husbands by name. They would address them as "*Ji*" (in North India), *Undi*, or *Emundi* (in Andhra Pradesh), or some similar term of respect.

The appendage *Bai* deserves some discussion. *Bai* translates almost fully to the term *Madam*. Like the term Madam, it was at one time a fully respectable term that at some point came to be associated with prostitution. Still, this association was not universal. The Maharashtrian community did not make this association, and it was very commonly used as an affectionate term of respect. However, even within the Maharashtrian community, its usage was confined to being appended to names. Although it might be grammatically correct to address a woman directly as *Bai* as you might address a man as *Sahib* or *Ji*, this was not something that I would recommend.

Many times people were referred to only by their familial relationship. The most important was one's mother and father. For instance, respect was implicit in addressing your father as *Baba* and your mother as *Maa*. Still, it was not unusual to see terms of respect appended to these already respectful forms of address (e.g., *Maaji* for mother).

A very curious treatment of names occurred when a person became a renunciate. According to Hindu tradition, after one has fulfilled one's worldly duties, one had the option of taking *sanyas*. Traditionally, one would divest oneself of all material possessions, go into the wild, and live the rest of one's life in meditation and the pursuit of spiritual goals. A *sanyasi* was legally dead. His property passed to his heirs, the wife assumed the manner of a widow, and more significantly for the topic at hand, the person taking *sanyas* assumed a new name and identity. Their names (*yogi* such-and-such, this-and-that-*ananda*) reflected this new identity and did not necessarily give any indication of their previous worldly life.

All of this underscored a simple point: names in India were not just a question of defining a person, but of defining relationships as well. Thus the common Western concept of "first name, middle name, last name" was meaningless in India.

Chapter 12
What's the Sex of a Banana?

"Go get me some bananas," my Hindi teacher ordered.

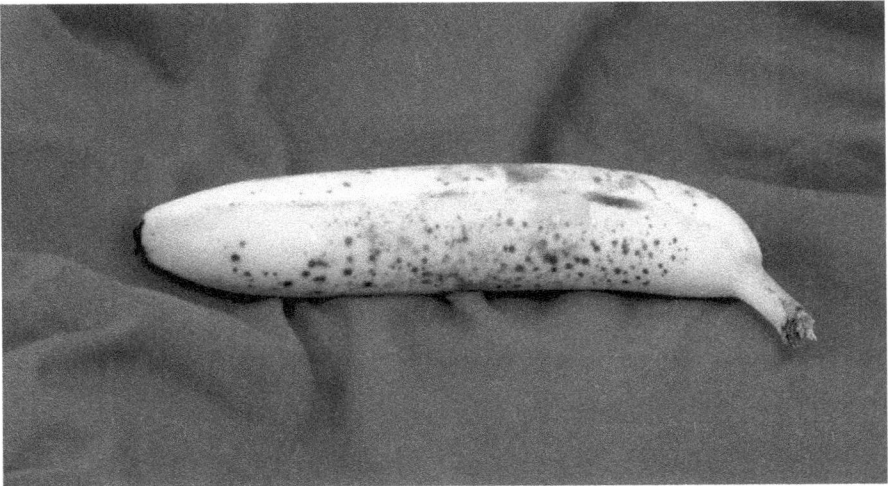

Is it male or female?

I knew what he was doing. In countries like Japan or Germany it was possible to just walk into a shop, point to what you want, lay down some money, and come away with change and your item without ever speaking a word. But this was impossible in India. My teacher knew that the only way that I could possibly come back with bananas was by going to a fruit-seller and engaging in *sauda bazi* (haggling). None of this would be in English.

I had only been in India for six weeks, so my Hindi skills were abysmal. But I had to do it.

I quickly looked up at a chart that was on his wall. This chart had the entire *devnagri* alphabet with small pictures of items that began with the letters. This chart was clearly oriented towards a first grader. Maybe I could find a first grader somewhere to help me? - no, probably not. I saw that the first consonant ("k") stood for "*kela*" and had a picture of a banana. It seems that most of the pictures were fruit. It started with pomegranate ("a"-*anaar*), mango ("aa" - *aam*), and went through the whole alphabet. If this chart was any reflection of Indian mentality, these people must have a very deep fruit fetish.

Ok, so I knew the word for banana, but what about the rest of the stuff that went around it? Damn - I had no idea as to the gender of kela (banana). Every noun in Hindi had a gender and I couldn't construct a sentence properly without knowing it.

Somehow with my horrible Hindi, supplemented with a lot of finger pointing and gestures, I managed the transaction and returned with the bananas.

Learning the language was one of the most difficult adjustments that I had to make. It was difficult because one cannot just translate a language. You have to be able to think in it. Fortunately there were some very useful tools that made the job somewhat easier.

One helpful tool was to look very closely at the errors that Indians made when speaking English. For instance Indians often referred to "empty sheets of paper" when referring to "blank sheets of paper". Or a person might say, "Meet me outside when I am empty." In the Hindi/Urdu mindset, "blank," "empty," "unoccupied," and "free," were all classified under the concept of *khali*. Although this was but a single example, when numerous mistakes were taken together, it gave me a very good picture of Indian lexical tendencies. It made me aware of the large number of distinct concepts in English that were covered by only a single term in Hindi/Urdu.

But there were also many concepts which were vague in English, but very precisely defined in Hindi. The most notable were familial relations. Where an English word like "Brother-in-law" can be applied equally for wife's-brother as well as sister's-husband, such ambiguity was missing in most Indian languages.

The most difficult aspect of Hindi and Urdu was its gendering of inanimate objects. Every item had a gender, and its proper recognition was essential to the correct construction of a sentence. In many cases the gender was obvious, especially with people. In many cases it wasn't too difficult, for instance a sledge hammer (*hathoda*) was masculine, while an ordinary hammer (*hathodi*) was feminine. Sometimes the pronunciation indicated the gender; but many times there was no indication at all. For some inexplicable reason a pen (*qalam*) was considered to be feminine, while a pencil (*pensil*) was masculine. After some time I actually began to associate gender qualities with some objects. Unfortunately, there are many things in this world, and I have only been able to internalise the association for a few. Therefore, I still make many grammatical mistakes in this regard.

As I was learning to associate gender with inanimate objects, I started to think a lot about the English language. The concept of gender for inanimate objects may be dormant, but it is still there under the surface. For instance, take the words "case" and "cassette", which one is masculine and which one is feminine? In a similar manner, think of "figure/figurine", "drop/droplet", or "eye/eyelet". If you present the words in pairs and ask any English speaker to assign a gender, you will be surprised at the consistency of the answers. I think that fundamental Indo-European concepts of gender are still sensed by English speakers, even if the grammar no longer reflect this.

The assigning of gender to inherently non-gendered items yielded certain insights. For instance "energy" (*shakti*) was feminine. This was not just a linguistic curiosity, but a very significant reflection of the position of femininity in traditional Hindu worldviews.

By the way, the gender of banana (*kela*) is masculine. But it's not because of what you are thinking, (my you have a dirty mind)!

Chapter 13
My Frame of Mind?

It was a week since my Hindi class and the business with the bananas. There was one important thing that I learned from these classes, I learned that I was ill suited to the banana trade.

I went with a friend to his village to attend a family celebration. Everyone was happy, talking, eating, and having fun. I was having fun too, but then I just had to slip away for a bit. I had just finished my seventh week in India, and I was exhausted. From morning to night it was a struggle. But this was my problem, not theirs. Everyone around me was kind and extended to me every consideration that was humanly possible. Still I was tired, so I wandered off in search of some solitude.

A village path at sunset

I strolled down a dusty path. Presumably it led to some agricultural fields. The walk was pleasant, and I started to relax. After some time, I found an inviting log by the path, and after a quick perusal to satisfy myself that there were neither ants, scorpions, nor cobras, I sat down.

The sun was setting, and I was overcome with a sense of introspection. What was my frame of mind? In the last seven weeks, I went through two stages. The first stage lasted roughly a month. In that stage I was completely overwhelmed. It was a very turbulent and bittersweet period. There were times when I was exuberant and excited about the possibilities that were at hand. And there were other periods of irrational fear, confusion, and disorientation.

But I was in the middle of my second stage of changing. In this stage I was able to settle down to the long task of acquiring the cultural skills necessary to live in India. The initial turbulence had subsided, and I could now "get down to business."

But psychologically, this stage was similar to having an arm or leg amputated. This may sound harsh, but in both cases there was a permanent loss of something integral to one's sense of self identity. Unlike an amputation which is sudden, my loss of self identity was much more drawn out.

Was I displeased over the psychological pressure I was under? Not really. I dissociated myself from being pleased or displeased. It was my reality. I was as immersed in it as I was in the air that I breathed. And like the air, I did not even bother to think about it.

Suddenly my contemplation was interrupted.

"David-*bhai*", I heard my friend calling from a distance.

The sun had set, and I really shouldn't have been in this isolated place after dark. I could hear the sound of music playing in the distance. My friend beckoned me, so I returned with him to the family celebration.

Evening in Village

Chapter 14
A Typical Day

"....*Allahu Akbar....Ash-had al-la ilaha illa llah...*"

I halfway emerged from my slumber. It was over a month since my visit to the village with my friend, so I had been in India for three months. In this time I learned the daily routine well.

"....*Ash-hadu anna Muhammadan rasulullah....*"

The chant from the nearby *masjid* slowly, almost mournfully, announced the start of a new day. Even though I was not fully awake, the early-morning *azaan* couldn't be ignored.

The *azaan* called the Islamic faithful to their morning prayers.

".....*Hayya 'ala-salahh......,*" continued the loud speaker from the *masjid*.

I knew that outside the Kirtane compound things were happening. Muslims were going to prayer. People were getting out of bed, bathing, and cooking. All over Hyderabad, people were starting another productive day.

I was not one of them. I rolled over, determined to squeeze in as much unproductive sleep as I possibly could, and I nodded off.

Other sounds attempted to interrupt my slumber. There was an early morning *suprabhatham*. This was the sound that came from the Hindu temples as the morning *poojas* were conducted. The *suprabhatham* is a Sanskrit hymn to awaken the deity. Unlike the Islamic *azaan* that was broadcast to the community because of tradition, there was no tradition in Hinduism that said that the morning *suprabhatham* should be similarly broadcast. I felt that this was just the temple's way to show that it was not only the *masjids* that had a presence in the locality.

Typical *masjid* with multiple minars

The city was determined that on this morning I should not sleep. I heard the singsong declarations of a hawker selling bread. This hawker had a large, broad basket (*gampa*) affixed to the rear carrier of his bicycle, in which he carried a variety of breads, buns, and baked goods. He slowly made his way up one lane and down the next, announcing his products and stopping at all of his regular customers' houses.

Poojari conducting a Hindu ritual

But the bread hawker was merely adding his own sounds to the rising cadence of large lorries barreling up and down the roads. These lorries (large diesel trucks) were laden with vegetables and other goods destined for market. These markets had to be supplied with fresh produce before the morning shoppers came. But it was a race for the lorry-drivers to make their rounds before the morning traffic made it impossible. The lorries were invariably in a questionable state of repair, and their engines roared with a fury that could be heard for great distances.

Phulwali selling flowers by the roadside. The flowers had to be supplied fresh daily.

I was resolute. I was going to sleep as much as I could.

Still, at about 7:00a.m., Dr. Kirtane summoned Dhananjay and myself up from our sleep. This absolutely could not be ignored!

As I woke up, I saw the room through the mosquito net. This mosquito net, known as *machardani*, afforded me only a fuzzy view. The room was medium-sized and was painted with an off-white coloured whitewash. The walls were cement. There were several windows with internal shutters, that when opened exposed a series of vertical iron bars. These bars deterred burglars and were a ubiquitous part of Indian houses. There was a large ceiling fan suspended from a U-shaped iron hook embedded in the ceiling.

"I look a mess, I need to make myself somewhat presentable," I thought to myself. Quickly I combed my hair and secured the *lungi* that worked itself loose during the night. The *lungi* is a sarong-like garb that men use as casual wear in southern India. When I was satisfied that I was reasonably presentable, I went down a short flight of stairs and across a small courtyard.

The first order of business was to brush my teeth. In many parts of the world, dental hygiene was a relatively recent affair, but not so in India. Brushing one's teeth was universal. Before the introduction of toothbrushes, this was done by chewing and rubbing the teeth and gums with sticks from the *neem* tree (*Azadirachta indica*). This practice was still used in many rural areas during the 1970s, and continues even today. This widespread habit was responsible for the relative low rate of dental problems, even though villagers did not have access to modern dentistry.

Next stop was the dining area.

"Good morning," I greeted Dhananjay and Dr. Kirtane as I entered the veranda. We all sat at a large DecoLam (Formica) covered table. The chairs were large, high-backed wooden ones, with a strong European feel about them. We went through the Hindu and the *Deccan Chronicle* newspapers while we waited for breakfast.

Press censorship was extreme due to the Emergency, so newspapers could not say what they wanted. But there were standard conventions that allowed the newspapers to get around this. For instance, if the newspapers reported that XYZ had been killed in a "police encounter," they often made a point to enclose it in quotation marks. This was their way of signalling that XYZ had been arrested, taken to an isolated place, and extrajudicially executed.

There were a number of topics of interest in the newspaper. These were usually local events and politics, but film advertisements and their showtimes were definitely high priority. Dr. Kirtane seldom read the papers at the breakfast table. She had already been up for hours, performed her morning *pooja* (prayers), and read the paper, long before the rest of us were roused from our sleep.

Our perusal of the newspapers was interrupted when Kamal came with breakfast. This varied a bit, but it was always centred around the morning cup of *chai*, toast, and butter. One thing that struck me about breakfast was the butter, which was white and looked very much like "Crisco." It tasted fine, but it had a slightly different flavour due to the fact that it came from water buffaloes instead of cows.

Water-buffalo were the most common source of milk and dairy products in the 1970s

Breakfast in Hyderabad varied tremendously according to community. Muslims tended toward a bread called sheermal which was often eaten with some heavy curry of *paaya* (goat knuckles) and a thick soup known as *shorba*. Most of the Hindus of the area ate *iddli* (a kind of fermented steamed rice cake), *dosa* (a thin lentil and rice pancake), and a lentil-based soup called sambar. Anglo-Indians commonly ate eggs and toast. The Kirtane propensity towards a more European-style breakfast may have reflected the time Dr. Kirtane spent in England; but it may have just been a remnant of the Indian upper-class British bourgeois culture that was common before Independence.

"*Ring....ring...*" sounded the telephone as it interrupted our conversation.

Dr. Kirtane slowly yet deliberately rose and answered the phone. This was a large, black bakelite affair similar to those seen in old American films from the 1940s and 1950s.

"*Kaun bol rehen hain?*" I heard Dr. Kirtane inquire. One always spent the first part of any phone conversation making sure that it was the right connection.

The Kirtane household had two means of connecting electronically with the outside world. We had a telephone when most households didn't, and there was also a large, vacuum-tube-driven short-wave radio receiver. This receiver could occasionally pick up stations as far as the Middle East, but normally it was tuned to All India Radio or Radio Sri Lanka.

"Brooooooooommmmm..." came another sound. It was the sound of an electric pump that the servant boy Yadeya had just turned on. The municipality supplied water twice a day: once in the morning and once in the evening. This water collected in a cistern that was located in the ground. It was the duty of the servant boy to operate the switch and pump the water up to a tank that was located on the roof. This tank then supplied water to the taps that were located around the house. This whole system was awkward, but it was functional, and it allowed us to have water in the taps 24 hours a day. This was a luxury that few people in Hyderabad enjoyed.

This interruption in the breakfast table conversation was my cue to attend to my "morning duties." This was a delicate way of referring to defecation and a bath.

The toilet was just a small room about the size of a closet. There was a large, oval-shaped hole in the floor. There was a faucet in the wall and a heavy, dented brass vessel known as a *lota* underneath it. The *lota* and faucet compensated for the lack of toilet paper. On the rear wall was a pipe running from the floor to a water tank located about five feet above the ground. This tank stored water for flushing. Flushing was effected by pulling a long chain that ran from a lever on the side of the tank. A flushing toilet too was a luxury. After this job was finished, it was time for the morning bath.

The bathroom was a separate room about ten feet square. The floors and sides were white marble. There was a raised block about a foot high, and roughly two feet square, where one could sit. This too was white marble. Curiously enough, the bathroom had several entrances. There were several fixtures, even one for a shower, though I don't think they had worked in years. The procedure for taking a bath was to take a brass bucket to a water heater that was located just outside the bathroom. This water heater was a large, cylindrical contraption several feet high. It had a central chamber in which you could put wood, coal, paper, or anything else that would burn. There was an opening and a series of pipes so that if you poured a bucket of cold water into the top, the pipe would yield an equivalent quantity of hot water. This contraption was typical of water heaters that were used in India in the early 20th century.

Once my "morning duties" were completed, I then attended to my daily matters. These varied from day to day. Often I went to my ustad's house, sometimes I went shopping, and sometimes my friend Sayeed came by with his *sarangi*, and we would practice.

One of my activities was learning the craft of tabla repair. For this I spent a lot of time with the *tablawallas* in Afzal Gunj. My presence was a novelty, because any type of job that involved skins was considered to be the lowest form of employment. I didn't worry too much about ostracism. Being a foreigner afforded me considerable latitude.

Dhananjay, Dr. Kirtane, and myself gathered again around two o'clock for lunch, after which the rest of the day's activities continued. However, we always looked forward to the evening activities. They often involved going out with friends or going to a film.

Settling Down for the Evening

After the day's activities, it was time to settle down. I put on my *lungi* and a loose fitting shirt, climbed under the mosquito net, and meticulously tucked the ends of the mosquito net under the mattress. Failure to secure these loose ends would let a few mosquitos in during the night. We generally went to sleep about 11:00, but possibly later if we decided to go to a "second show." A second show was the term used to describe the film showings that started about 9:00 p.m. and let out around midnight.

Just as the sounds of the city marked the start of the day, sounds of the night brought my day to a close.

"Chaand mera dil...... Chaandni ho tum...." I heard a song, distant and echoey as it wafted its way from the Sagar Talkies. The Kirtane house was next to this cinema hall, and every evening I heard the songs emanating from the theatre. They turned the volume up during the songs, and fight scenes, and then turned the volume back down during the dialogue.

After the second show, there was very little activity. There were the sounds of buses coming from outlying districts. Occasionally, some Hindu religious observance dictated all night *poojas*. In which case, chants were tinnily broadcast from ancient horn speakers affixed to the roof of the *mandir*. Sometimes it was a wedding that had the auspicious time (*muhurtham*) fall on some pre-dawn hour. But more often than not, the homeward march of the second show crowd marked the end of the day's activities, and Hyderabad became quiet.

One of the few sounds heard in the wee hours of the morning was the slow, rhythmic "*tak, tak, tak*" of the local *gurkha*. *Gurkas* were a community from Nepal. Years ago, they settled in Hyderabad, and many of them found work as freelance security guards. A gurkha staked out a locality and spent every night patrolling with a large stick. As he walked up and down, he would hit the ground to announce his presence. Hence the "*tak, tak, tak*", sound.

I lay there in bed thinking about my journey. I do not mean a physical journey, because I was settled into Hyderabad in the physical sense. I was instead thinking of the journey of the mind. I had seen things that I had never seen before. I had done things that I had never done before. I was ready to accept world views that I could not have even conceived of a few years earlier. I was becoming a different person. But for this new person to come to life, part of the old person had to die. But this introspection could not go on before I was overcome with sleep. Gently I descended into a warm nocturnal oblivion.

Chapter 15
Sleep

I laid there under the mosquito net asleep,

Sleeping...

Sleeping...

Resting in the lap of Morpheus.

Much of Hyderabad also slept.

The footpath-*walla* outside the Deccan Homeo Store slept.

Dreaming of his little *jhopdi* back in the village.

And of his wife and children asleep,

Sleeping...

Sleeping...

Resting in the lap of Morpheus.

My future wife, twenty two years old, slept on a cot.

Her deep brown eyes were closed,

She bathed in a dilute smoke of a "Tortoise" Mosquito Coil,

Sleeping...

Sleeping...

Resting in the lap of Morpheus

A prisoner slept in jail in Chanchalgudda.

A rich man slept in his mansion in Banjara Hills.

A dying man slept in the fever hospital in Nallakunta.

A stray dog, a film starlet, a politician, a sage, and a fool, all slept...

Sleeping...

Sleeping...

Resting in the lap of Morpheus.

A middle aged school teacher in Zamistanpur.

Her name was Lalitha.

I had not met her.

But when the forces of *runanubandh* became right

We would meet. But for now Lalitha slept,

Sleeping...

Sleeping...

Resting in the lap of Morpheus.

Chapter 16
Religion

"Watch where you're going beta!" Lalitha shouted at the young boy who almost ran into her. He ran down the lane with an old bicycle tyre. He propelled the tyre with the stick, attempting to roll it the entire length of Risala Gadda.

But Lalitha's protests were scarcely acknowledged by the lad. Lalitha couldn't get mad, for the boy was only about ten. This was the age of her students.

She was a school teacher in the government primary school in Zamistanpur. Although she was a teacher, she had not been to classes for the last week. Today, she was an enumerator taking information for the nation's census.

She made her way along the lane. It was a familiar one, with familiar people. There was an Irani hotel. It was not a hotel in the Western sense but a very small cafe which served only *chai*, *samosas*, and biscuits. It was too small to serve any real meals. This was run by a Muslim. She passed a small bakery that specialised in European style bread. It filled the street with the delightful, yeasty smell of baking bread. It too, was owned by a Muslim family. There was a small motorcycle repair shop, its proprietor was a Christian. There was a *kirana* store run by a Hindu, and a small tailor shop where she sometimes went to have blouses made, and its owner was also a Hindu.

Lalitha was going door-to-door getting information for the census. One of the questions that she always asked was in reference to the religion of the inhabitants.

India is a land of religious diversity. From her orientation as an enumerator, she knew that it was about 80% Hindu, 13% Muslim, 2% Christian, and about 2% Sikh. The remainder was a mixture of Buddhist, Jewish, Jain, and a few other religions.

But Lalitha lived near here, so she already knew the breakdown. She knew that Risala Gadda was roughly equal parts of Muslim, Christian, and Hindu. She didn't know why it had these proportions, but it seemed to work well. There were seldom any problems in this locality, even during times of communal unrest. Perhaps it was because there was so much familiarity that it was a quiet area.

Lalitha was a Hindu, but the Christians and Muslims were not abstract communal stereotypes to her, they were real people. There were several women of different communities that kept a watchful eye on both her children when they were younger. There was the time a few years ago when Lalithas's twelve year old son was smoking a cigarette at the *chaurasta*, and the Christian woman across the lane, came and told her. There was the Muslim taxi driver that drove his off-duty taxi and took them to the doctor when Lalitha's daughter was very sick. Even though many of them were not Hindu, they were her friends and neighbours, and she was very attached to them.

But Lalitha put her remembrances aside, for it was time to get to work. She came upon a compound. This was ringed by a wall made of bricks that had been fired to a deep rust red colour. Solidified mortar protruded from the cracks where they had oozed before setting. Although this was a less than ideal surface, remnants of a crudely painted political symbol and a caption which said "Vote Janata Party" could still be seen upon its outer surface.

A large tamarind tree dominated most of the free space of the compound. In this tree was a black crow, darker than a moonless light, but tinged with deep iridescent blue. At the corner of the compound was a bore well with a hand pump sticking up from its cement base.

Next to the hand pump was a small plastic bucket that was always filled with water. This small bucket was used to prime the pump to make it work. But the bucket had seen better days. It was originally red, but due to exposure to the elements it had faded to a sickly pink and puss-like yellow. Small broken protuberances indicated that at one time it had a handle. It was badly aged, but it was still serviceable so it occupied its position by the pump.

The ground was a sandy grassless Deccan soil, with but a few small plants tenuously making their presence felt.

A small chipmunk scurried away as Lalitha entered the compound. (For some reason, chipmunks were referred to as squirrels in the local English.) The chipmunk stopped about two metres from Lalitha, turned, gave an inscrutable look, then ran off.

Quickly Lalitha checked her papers to see that everything was in order, then entered the compound. She approached an old man who lay napping upon a teakwood cot. Its wooden frame was hewn by the simplest of tools. It was a deep dull brown, nearly black. At one time it sported a shiny French-polish and *laq* surface, but this was but an ancient memory. The cot did not even have cotton *nawaar*, but was intricately laced with jute cord.

Upon this cot was an old man. He dozed upon a thin mattress, but was quickly awaken by two small children who saw Lalitha enter.

"*Tata-Garu, Tata-Garu*," the children shouted as they ran to wake their grandfather. When the old man awoke, she could see that in spite of his apparent old age, he could hardly have been older than 60. Now the entire household turned out to see Lalitha.

Lalitha said that she was there to take the census, but this announcement was unnecessary. The fact that census takers were combing Risala Gadda was already known to all the inhabitants.

They offered her a seat, then proceeded to ask Lalitha questions. There were a few minutes of exchange that was completely irrelevant to census taking. Many of these questions were very personal by Western standards, but were a typical way in which most Indians created some type of social frame of reference. This frame of reference was necessary for any type of undertaking, even casual shopping. From this quick exchange it was found that the people of the compound knew some of the parents of her students. Furthermore, Lalitha's in-laws were from the same place as the family in the compound. Ok, now the work could proceed.

Lalitha got out her forms and proceeded to ask the census questions. Most of these questions were straight-forward. These concerned the names and number of people in the household, the relationships to each other, and similar things.

But there were also questions concerning their religion. She already knew the answer. She knew that they were Hindu. It was obvious from their home.

Every Indian home was full of small bits of art. Sometimes it was something substantial such as a framed picture, but more often it was something simpler such printed posters. Where Indian Christians may pepper their homes with pictures of crosses, Jesus, or the church at Velangani, or Muslims had pictures of the *Kabah* at Mecca, one could always tell a Hindu home by the pictures of Ganesh, Balaji, or other Hindu themes.

Lalitha particularly noticed a calendar on the wall. Upon this was a picture of a Hindu goddess, below which were printed in big letters "Sripathi Iron Works." It was a common form of advertising where calendars in various themes would have a company name printed into a spot left blank for this purpose. These calendars were then given to favoured customers. This particular calendar had a picture of Laxmi, the goddess of wealth.

Laxmi and the Charminar

I had never met Lalitha nor had I ever met the family that she was interviewing for the census. But by a curious quirk of fate, just as she noticed the calendar, I was passing the Laxmi temple in the Old City. This was a very small temple located at the base of a massive monument known as the Charminar.

I was with Dr. Kirtane, her daughter-in-law Yashodhara, Dhananjay, and my guru-*bhai* Ram. Yashodhara was in town for just a short time, so we were combining a bit of shopping with sightseeing. This Hindu temple in the very heart of Hyderabad's historic Muslim locality struck me as being interesting, so I asked a tour-guide about it.

"No one knows when or who built this," said the tour-guide. "But according to legend, the Goddess Laxmi became angry at Tana Shah and decided she would leave the kingdom. Tana Shah was a king in the 17th century. A guard who was stationed at the base of the Charminar saw Laxmi as she was leaving the kingdom, and realised how bad it would be for the goddess of wealth to depart in this manner. He pleaded with her not to leave, and said that he would go see the king to intercede on her behalf. So he made her promise not to leave until he returned.

The guard went to the king and explained the situation, but all were at a loss as to what to do. Then the guard asked the king to kill him. Since no other alternative could be found, the king complied and killed the guard. The guard never returned, so Laxmi, having promised that she would remain until his return, remained there at the guard's post. It is said she continues to remain there at the Charminar even today."

I thought that the story was very interesting. But the small Laxmi temple was completely dwarfed by the massive edifice of the *Charminar*. So we asked the tour-guide about the *Charminar*.

"The *Charminar* is a multi-storied *masjid* with four spires," said the guide. "The name '*Charminar*' means 'four-spires.' It is said that this building came about because Muhammad Quli Qutb Shah prayed at this very spot and asked God to rid his kingdom of a plague. According to legend, he promised to build a massive *masjid* if the plague was lifted. The pestilence subsided and true to his word, the king built the *masjid* in 1591."

The tour-guide then proceeded to give us a tour of the place.

Massive *Charminar* with small Laxmi temple at lower right hand corner (orange flags)

I started to think about the juxtaposition of this small Laxmi temple to the *Charminar*. Sometimes this was held to be symbolic of Hindus and Muslims living in peace. I would later find out that in far too many cases this was the epicentre of communal conflicts. Whenever times were tense, you could see a small army of policeman sitting opposite this small *mandir* just waiting for something to happen.

Islam

Most of the people in the Old City were Muslim. Many of my friends were Muslims, but their worldview was different from anything I encountered while growing up. It is difficult to reduce Islam into a single word, but if I had to, I would say that the word was "surrender." The idea was to completely surrender oneself to the will of God. This was not considered to be a mere abstraction, because every aspect of both civil and religious life was clearly spelled out. Therefore, the life of a good Muslim was one of strict adherence to these laws.

Roaming around the old city was fine, but when this shopping led us to Chuddi Bazaar, things came to a grinding halt. This was an area of the old city that specialised in bangles, most famously a kind of stone bangle. Although Dr. Kirtane and her daughter-in-law Yashodhara were completely absorbed by the details of every bangle they saw, for Dhananjay, Ram, and myself this was torture. At an opportune moment, we slipped away to a small Irani Hotel.

We sat for a while having *chai* and talking about various topics. Ram said that his family was having a *pooja* the next week and asked if I wanted to attend. I saw no reason to refuse so I accepted the invitation.

The Pooja

The day of the *pooja* came. Dr. Kirtane instructed me as to a few basic points of etiquette. As per her instructions, I took a complete bath before leaving the house and put on fresh clean clothes.

I arrived at Ram's house well after the time that he had given me, but still I was the first guest there. I knew that I should never arrive at the time that I was told, because invariably I would be the only guest there. The host and hostess would then feel embarrassed at having to dress and finish preparations with me around. But no matter how I tried to estimate things, I always tended to be early.

The *poojari* arrived, and started pulling out various paraphernalia. At the same time he was sending Ram's younger brother out on a veritable scavenger hunt for items. It wasn't very long before everyone assembled and the *pooja* started.

The *poojari* was chanting away in Sanskrit, and I had no idea what was going on. Then he started going down and asking everyone what their *gotram* (a Hindu way of categorising people) was. When he came upon me, I was naturally clueless. He made something up on the spot and continued.

This incident accidentally underscored something that was going on in my mind for some time. "Who am I?" Living in India these past four months was making me question many things, and I was no longer even sure of my own sense of self identity.

Chapter 17
Inter-Religious Competition

A week had passed since the *pooja*. I was just looking through some *Illustrated Weeklies* in the drawing room in the Kirtane house, and thinking about various topics. One of which was the interaction between religions.

Religions in India were not always contentious in their relations with each other. Once I was told a story of three religious leaders who had a friendly competition between themselves. According to this story, there was a Hindu *poojari*, a *mullah*, and a Christian preacher. They had known each other since childhood, so they were on very good terms in spite of their religious differences.

One day they were meeting and having some *chai*. The discussion turned to religion.

"What is this thing that you both have about converting people?" said the *poojari*. You "Don't see us Hindus running around trying to convert people."

"*Aare Bhai*," said the preacher. "You're just bitter because you know that you wouldn't be good at it."

"Right," said the *mullah*. "I don't think that you have the capacity to convert anyone."

"I certainly could convert someone," said the *poojari*. "Furthermore, I think that I could convert any living creature."

Now both the *mullah* and the preacher were amused by their close friend's outrageous boast. And they were not going to let it pass.

"Do you see that jungle over there?" said the *mullah*. "There's a bear living there. Go prove yourself by converting him to Hinduism."

"Ok I'll do it," replied the *poojari*.

Several days later the three good friends again met.

"*Bhai*," said the preacher to the *poojari*. "How did you do in converting the bear?"

The *poojari* was clearly mortified and said, "You know, I went there and for two days I tried everything. I sprinkled him with water from the holy river *Ganga*. I recited passages from the *Bhagawat Geeta*. I did everything that I could think of, but I failed."

His friends started to make fun of him, whereupon the *poojari* said. "You may laugh, but can you do it?"

Both the *mullah* and the preacher had not expected it to come back upon them in this manner, but they had been challenged and their honour was now at stake.

"I can do it," declared the preacher. "The Bible clearly says '... all things are possible to him that believeth'. My faith is strong and I will go and convert the bear."

A few days later the three again met. The *poojari* and the *mullah* enquired as to how the preacher did in his attempts at conversion. The preacher was dejected.

"I tried everything. I prayed, I read passages from the Bible to him, but nothing had any effect," the preacher said.

That just left the *mullah*. "You both failed because your religions are weak. I have the power of the one true faith, Islam!" Whereupon he too went into the jungle.

"A few days later the preacher and the *poojari* were summoned to the hospital. They were very distressed to find their old friend, the *mullah*, in a very bad state. He was covered from head to foot by bandages, and he was being given blood transfusions. They asked what happened.

The *mullah* feebly said, "I think that perhaps a circumcision was not the best way to proceed."

Chapter 18
Picture Time

The same time that I was amusing myself with stories I had heard of *mullahs*, *poojaris*, and preachers, a small drama was unfolding itself a few miles away in Secunderabad. An auto pulled up to the *Vishvavani* recording studios, which was part of the God Has Spoken Ministries. These studios specialised in gospel music in a variety of South Indian languages. A young man with a guitar exited the vehicle to do a recording. He had done this many times before, but this time things were different.

"We're taking pictures today," said the producer. "You'd better go back and wear some of your old ragged clothes."

"What are you talking about?" asked the guitarist. "I always wear these clothes."

"Poetker-*Dora* wants you to wear old clothes, so if you want to continue to get contracts, you'd better do it!" said the producer.

Begrudgingly the guitarist complied, and returned half-an-hour later.

"That's better. Now for the picture, don't use your guitar, use this one," said the producer as he handed the musician an old guitar.

"Why this one?" protested the guitarist. "This one is useless, it should be used as firewood!"

"How can you be such a *buddhu*? Haven't you figured it out yet?" said the producer. "Poetker-*Dora* is going back to Canada next month, and he'll use these pictures to beg for money, so he can continue to do 'God's work'."

"Why should I comply?" questioned the guitarist. "I won't see any of that money. That *maa-ka-lauda* Poetker will just use it to live in that luxurious house over there."

"Just do it!" commanded the producer.

And it was done.

Chapter 19
Caste and Community

Some weeks had passed since the drama at *Vishvavani* studios. Henry Poetker was in Canada, armed with his slides and pictures, and telling all his Mennonite brethren about the heathen natives in India and his noble efforts at bringing the Bible and civilisation to them. This would get him more money so he could return to India and peddle his pathological brand of Christianity, one that was completely bereft of love, compassion, forgiveness, or kindness. Thankfully I was blissfully unaware of his perfidy. It would be a couple of years before these matters came to my attention.

I was focused on a much more immediate problem. I was in Shaik Dawood's house trying to learn my lessons.

"*Dhin Dhin DhiTa DhiTa KiddaDha TiTa....*" Dawood patiently recited the *bols* (syllables) of the *paran* for the umpteenth time. I struggled to memorise them and get the technique right. I wasn't quite getting it, and I was starting to feel dense and foolish over what others were considering to be easy. Dawood then patiently wrote the composition in my notebook in a clear but somewhat idiosyncratic *devnagri* so that I could take it home and memorise it later. He then focused his attention on Shekhar and another student.

Shekhar was a very good student and a very good tabla player. He was about 23 years of age, slight build, thin moustache, and sported a somewhat longish hairstyle that was made popular by the film actor Amitabh Bachchan. He had a strong liking for the then stylish bellbottom pants.

Shekhar and the other student got a new composition and seemed to memorise it easily.

After the lesson, I suggested that we go for some tea and snacks. Both Shekhar and the other student readily agreed. I suggested that we go to the small cafe that one of Dawood's sons managed. Shekhar readily agreed, but the other student immediately became a little uneasy about this, and he made some polite excuse and left. I was a little surprised at this. Shekhar and I both got on our bicycles and rode the short distance to Dawood's son's cafe.

A short time later we arrived there and got our *chai*. While we were sipping away, I enquired as to the other student's hesitation.

"In his community they can't eat here because it's an Irani hotel, you know - run by Muslims!" Shekhar replied.

I immediately fixed my attention upon his use of the term "community." I frequently ran across this word, but I didn't really have a clear idea as to what he meant. So I enquired further.

"We are both Hindus, but there are many Hindu communities," Shekhar replied. "The way that Hindus define community is sometimes complicated."

"The cornerstone of the Hindu concept of community is the caste. Americans like yourself don't really understand what is caste. This isn't surprising because even here in India there are many misconceptions," Shekhar explained.

"The Sanskrit word for caste is jati. This word literally means a 'grouping' or a 'collection' of something." Shekhar continued, "India has a long academic tradition, and every aspect of the world was analysed and categorised to excruciating detail. One couldn't expect civil society to escape this intellectual scrutiny."

"How many castes are there?" I asked.

"There isn't really a clear answer on this," he continued. "Although the topic was addressed in a number of texts stretching over several millennia, it came to pass that all human society could be divided into four basic categories. At its base are the common labourers. It is their duty to produce the things that a society needs to function. These people were referred to as *shudra* in the old texts. But today, they are more likely to be referred to as *dalit*, backward caste, scheduled caste, or euphemistically as *harijan*, which means 'born of God'. The next level up are the business classes. It is their duty to sell and distribute things. Although the Sanskrit term *vaishya* was used in the past, the more common term is *baniya*. The next step up are the warrior classes. Their duty is to maintain the order and political structure of a civil society. Members of this class are generally referred to as *kshatriya*. At the top of society are the brahmins. High art, religious affairs, and academics are their functions."

"So there are four castes," I said.

"No, it's much more complicated than this," Shekhar replied. . "Although the ancient texts establish four broad classes of society, there were provisions for many sub-castes. When these are considered, the number of castes goes into dozens, possibly even hundreds. No one really knows."

"But the concept of caste was never meant to lock people into anything," continued Shekhar. "It was merely intended to be a description of civil society. A person's caste was supposed to be determined by their aptitudes, interests, and education, and not according to their birth. Nevertheless, we started equating profession with family, and this became fixed into the present caste system."

"That doesn't sound like a good idea to me," I said.

"It isn't," said Shekhar. "The caste system is broadly recognised as a social evil. It is criticised by social reformers and religious leaders alike. Yet it is so deeply ingrained in our society that it is almost impossible to dislodge."

"But Shekhar," I injected. "This tells me about the caste system, but what does this have to do with community?"

"Yes," said Shekhar, "This can be a little confusing, so I'll clarify this with a specific example. You know that a brahmin is a caste. But not every brahmin in India belongs to the same community. Language plays a very important part. For instance, we are in Andhra Pradesh, and Telugu is the official state language. Now, if we take the population of people who are both Telugu-speaking and of the brahmin caste, this comes very close to defining community. I say close, but in this case, close is not good enough. There are several major communities of Telugu brahmins, two common ones being the *Iyers* and the *Iyengars*. These communities, as well as the other communities, maintain their identities by a series of arcane religious, geographical, and social criteria."

"That explains a lot about Hindu communal attitudes but what about the non-Hindus," I asked.

"The non-Hindu communities may not use caste as a defining characteristic, but they still tend to define themselves as the intersection of their language and religion." replied Shekhar.

Bicycle Ride

A few weeks had passed since I had the discussion with Shekhar about caste and community. But it echoed in my mind as I rode my bicycle from Troop Bazaar to Afzal Gunj. I was at the large intersection near the Women's College, and there was a lot of traffic. I was in the big middle of it. Initially I found being in such crowded conditions to be stressful. But over the last four months I got used to it.

Not only had I gotten used to the crowds, I actually found it intellectually stimulating. I found myself looking at people and trying to guess their community. These were the days before the mass media homogenised much of the fashion, so you could still tell many communities by their dress and their jewellery, at least for the women. For instance, teenage Marwari girls used to have the strange habit of wearing blue jeans, a Western style shirt, but over that they wore a traditional *dupatta*. Parsi women of any age could be seen wearing sleeve-less blouses, while in other communities it was only the most daring younger girls that would do so. Teenage Andhra girls seemed to be very particular about wearing only half-*saris*. And among the elderly women, only Punjabis, Marwaris, and Muslims wore a style of earring called a *jhoomki*.

But fashions were not the only signs. For generations marriages tended to be made only within the community. Centuries of inbreeding meant that you could usually look at a person's face and tell what their community was.

But these reflections were curtailed as I moved away from the Women's College, and made my way closer to Afzal Gunj. I had other matters to attend to.

Chapter 20
The Tabla Dukaan

Noise - noise - noise, the street was filled with the most unbearable noise! There was honking, engine noises, and bells ringing. It was late one Friday morning during my fourth month in India. I was in Afzal Gunj. This was located near one of the few bridges which crossed the Moosi river, hence this locality was always congested with traffic.

I was in a small shop with several people making tablas. The sign over the door said Mehaboob Ali, but there was no Mehaboob Ali. Presumably the original proprietor of the shop was a man by that name, and that he had died some time ago. However, I had no idea whether he died a few months previously, or a hundred years ago. The shop was was no larger than a walk-in closet in the US, and this was small even by Hyderabadi standards. But crammed into this small room were four people who worked from 10:00 in the morning to 9:00 at night making tablas, dholaks, tashas, and other Indian drums.

I apprenticed myself to these craftsmen so that I could get a better understanding of tabla. I had only been in India for four months, so I was still struggling to get adjusted. No one in the tabla *dukaan* knew any English, and I was far from functional in Urdu. But through their association I was quickly learning the language, tabla making, and many other things.

A customer came to the door. He had dropped off a tabla for repair a few days previously, and he wanted to check on its status.

"*Abhi taiyar nahin Sahib, kal aiye,*" I heard one of the *tablawallas* say.

Tabla makers at Mehaboob Ali's

My Urdu was atrocious, but even I knew what this meant. It literally translated to "It is not ready Sir, please come back tomorrow." This was a ubiquitous mantra in India, one that reflected a laid-back approach to deadlines and getting work done. I knew that his tabla would not be ready tomorrow, he knew it, and the *tablawallas* knew it. But the customer also knew that he had to come in periodically and show his face, or his tabla would never be repaired.

The day passed, and customers came and went. But the mantra continued each time, "*Kal aiye... Kal aiye ... Kal Aiye...*"

Chapter 21
Sickness

"I'm sick again!" I thought to myself.

I had just finished eight months in India. Four months had passed since I sat in the tabla *dukaan* thinking about deadlines and work. It seemed that every two weeks I was getting sick. Public hygiene was very poor, and my body was struggling to get adjusted. I lay in bed with a high fever, but really no other symptoms. To others the weather was warm, but I felt cold. I drifted in and out of sleep, but my sleep was disturbed. Even while awake, my mind was still cloudy. Thoughts, ideas, dreams, and altered perceptions of reality ebbed, flowed, and mixed without any clear division. This phantasmagoria became my reality.

But the kaleidoscope of reality had a different colour. Thoughts barely thought, and ideas barely conceived, rushed to the surface like fish in a feeding frenzy. Who was I? Where was I? What I was doing? The orderly relationship between myself and the world was collapsing. Who were these people that I was surrounded by? What was my relationship to them? Was there some *runanubandh* which linked us across various births, or was it merely some Nietzschean chaos that only gave the illusion of connection and order? I had no answers. All that I knew was that with fever, disorientation, and a combination of powerful social and cultural pressures, all sense of self lay shattered like shards of broken glass upon the floor. And then I slipped back into a fevered, fitful sleep.

In a few days the fever broke. I was still weak, but my life was beginning to return to normal, or at least to what had become normal for me. But this latest bout of illness caused me to reflect upon the nature of health, sickness, and the state of medicine in India.

Most people immediately think of a dysentery, or the more common "Delhi Belly" class of abdominal troubles. I had my share of these problems. Yet for me, the most common ailments were tropical fevers.

I will never know exactly what these "tropical fevers" were. The system of diagnosing illnesses was not very precise, but it didn't have to be very precise. Generally there were only three classes of drugs used to treat a fever. These were APC (aspirin, phenacetin, and caffeine), sulfas/antibiotics, and quinine. The doctors would just guess as to which one to prescribe. If a particular drug worked, then everyone was happy. They were usually correct in their judgment.

But being sick for such a long time took a toll. This was my eighth month here, and I had lost a lot of weight. Although I could not know it at the time, it would only be in my second year that my body's immunities would catch up. After that, I wouldn't be ill any more often than the average Indian. But still it was stressful. I remembered stories of others who came to India to learn music, became sick, and died. There was no guarantee that I wouldn't become one of them.

Preparing for My Trip

I really didn't have too much time to worry about getting sick. Soon I would be making a short trip back to the US. Even though it was still a few weeks away, I had things to do. I needed to buy gifts for my old friends in the US. But that wasn't all. Since I was a resident of India, I had to get clearance certificates from the local police as well as the income tax offices. Dealing with government offices always took time.

Chapter 22
The Game of Customs

The trip to the US was pleasant. I gave a few performances, worked and earned a little money, and even performed on my first record. But on my return to India, I was very lucky to see a remarkable game. This was the game of "customs," which was on par with cricket, football, or any of the other great sports. However like baseball, which is now just a dim shadow of its once great past, the game of customs is no longer played as it was. I think that it will be agreed that this sport has never been played before or since with the same level of art, sophistication, and gusto.

There were two teams: "passengers," and "inspectors." Like most sports, the objective of the game was remarkably simple, yet the implementation was challenging. It was the passengers' objective to bring as much stuff into the country as possible, and it was the job of the inspectors to extract as many bribes as possible. It should be noted that keeping items out of the country was not an object of the game for the inspectors. Also, the collection of any tariffs was purely a secondary issue.

The game began like this. The government declared well ahead of time what items were dutiable. This was the list of items that every self-respecting Indian had to buy before returning home. It was totally irrelevant whether a person had any use for them. Simply the fact that something was on the list meant that it absolutely had to be purchased.

In the 1970s, the list of dutiable items was very large. It included cameras, film, *saris*, clothing, whiskey, and perfumes. All electronic items were on the list, among which cassette recorders were especially popular. Virtually any industrial device or raw material was also fair game.

The game of "customs" was played in the customs clearance hall. In Bombay, this was a massive hall with hundreds of participants divided into their respective teams. In the upper story, there was a massive glass wall, where people could observe the sport being played down below. Most of these spectators were relatives of the passengers. Friends and relatives of the inspectors seldom bothered to show up. (I suppose that support from fans is never uniform, but necessarily varies from team to team).

Games require participants to get into the proper frame of mind, and the sport of customs was no exception. In most sports, the proper frame of mind is attained by getting the adrenaline flowing, that is by getting "psyched up." For this game, the process of getting psyched up varied depending upon which team you were on. Getting "psyched up" was a very arduous process for the passengers. One would spend at least 10 hours cramped in an aeroplane seat. This would be followed by three hours of waiting in various queues to get into the arena. Furthermore, 4:00 a.m. was deemed by fans of the sport as the ideal time for playing. One would think that the long hours of preparation would give the passengers a tremendous psychological advantage. But the inspectors managed to hold their own. Their preparation often involved spending hours with friends, drinking imported whisky before showing up to work at midnight. The fact that the whiskey was imported was significant, but that is unnecessary to elaborate on here.

Every game must have a "moment of truth". This is the time when two professionals with well-honed skills came together for the crucial part of the match. After some insignificant and largely ceremonial interchange between the inspector and the passenger, the passenger led off with the first play. This was done by giving the inspector a customs declaration form. This was where the first use of tactics came to play. The usual gambit was for the passenger to submit forms with a small number of totally insignificant items on the list. This was considered to be a safe opening move. Submitting a customs form with all of one's dutiable items listed was simply not done!

Now it was the inspector's turn. He would ask the passengers to open up all of their bags. (This was the origin of the term "inspector". After all, an inspector must inspect.) The inspector then proceeded to go through every item in every suitcase. It was a cat-and-mouse game in which the mouse would always escape. In the game of customs it was a forgone conclusion that the passenger would be released, a bribe, variously known as baksheesh or inaam would be paid, and that everybody would move on.

We must discuss scoring. This indispensable part of the game was far more complicated than found in other sports such as cricket. The customs inspector proceeded to look at every item of clothing, every pen, and every rubber band. Every time a dutiable item was found by the inspector, he scored a point. Normally, when a team scores, the response is one of great jubilation for both the scoring team and the fans who turned out. Yet in the game of customs, every time the inspector scored a point, it would be met with a stoic look, possibly even a feigned look of disdain. In this regard the game had a lot in common with poker.

As the inspector went over every item, it was important to ask very personal questions. This would typically be things like "Why do you need five ballpoint pens, shouldn't two be sufficient?" One would think that in such an inspection, turning up items of women's underwear would draw particularly pointed inquiries concerning the sexual proclivities of a male passenger. However, even though such items commonly showed up in these searches, invariably they would be attributed as gifts for female members of the passenger's family. Sometimes these items turned into gifts for the female members of the inspector's family.

Once every item had been examined and tallied, one would think that the game was finished. Fortunately this was not the case. This just signalled the beginning of the "end-game", which fans of the sport universally acknowledged as the most exciting part.

The end-game proceeded in this fashion. The inspector presented a bill for duty which was to be paid. This essentially represented the points scored by the inspector in the previous round of play. But the inspector added a certain amount in excess of the actual points scored. This was of course all within the rules. The total figure would of course be exorbitant. Thereupon the process of negotiation would begin. Now this negotiation was derived from the art of haggling over the price of goods in the market, but it assumed a very particular significance in this game. The object of the end-game was to determine the ratio of bribes to duty. It was understood that in exchange for reducing or even eliminating the assessed duty, a certain amount of bribes would be paid. On occasion this amount was in the form of cash, but usually not. Typically the passenger would hand the inspector a bottle of perfume, imported whisky, cigarettes, or similar commodity while saying, "The duty on this is just too much. I'll not take it into the country. Here, you go ahead and dispose of these." This of course, was fully in the mind of the passenger when he purchased the items in Heathrow airport the day before.

There were four major gambits used in the endgame: sympathy, rank, friendship, and business. The passenger had to rely on his wits and his understanding of his opponent in order to know which one to use.

The "sympathy" gambit was very common. In this approach, you tried to convince the inspector that you were a poor man, you had three sisters who needed to get married, your mother was dying of cancer, and that these items were all that you had in the world. Now Indians have a very powerful empathy gene, which is either completely turned on or completely turned off in a most unpredictable manner. If this empathy is turned on, Indians are capable of generosity that is perhaps unmatched by any other people in the world. Therefore, if the passenger was able to turn on this empathy, then the duty-cum-bribe would be greatly reduced or even eliminated. Of course, this was dependent on the inspector not questioning why your poor cancer stricken mother should require Johnny Walker whisky, a carton of Dunhill cigarettes, and a bottle of French perfume.

The "status" or "rank" gambit was also a very common tactic. This approach was based upon the genetic propensity of Indians to rank everyone in relationship to themselves. If you could convince the inspector that your family connections were so much higher than his, then this rank afforded some privilege. Common tactics were "my uncle is the Minister of ...." or "my father works with..." These were threats implying that if the bribe-cum-duty was not reduced, then there would be retribution coming from certain quarters. On occasion this was very effective, but it had to be used with care. If these threats were not absolutely credible, the passenger ran the risk of losing the game.

There was also the "friendship" gambit. This required you to get the customs inspector to act as though you were both long lost buddies. It typically may have started as "I see that you are Marathi, you know I spent four years at IIT, Powai," or something to that extent. If the inspector was in a good mood and you were able to make a connection, then this was always good for a few points. This gambit was not always successful, but was considered to be a fairly safe move.

Finally, there was the "business as usual" move. In this approach you simply hinted that you want the matter resolved and that you wanted to cut through the games and get on to how much it would cost. You wouldn't want to lead off with this approach, but if you received hints that the inspector was open for this type of thing, you might respond to it.

You may wonder how foreigners such as myself handled this game. Our presence in the customs hall was analogous to that of stray dogs wandering onto the field. We were considered to be a disruption, and we were pushed on through as quickly as possible so that the players could get back to their sport.

Although it has been more than thirty years since I first encountered it, I consider myself very fortunate to have seen the game at its zenith. Perhaps never again will we see such skill and mastery. But alas, this sport has largely been consigned to history.

Chapter 23
All Things Foreign

"Do you have any cameras or tape recorders," asked a complete stranger outside the customs clearance hall.

I evaded the conversation with a polite "no". This was only the first in a long string of similar enquires that I would hear upon my return from the US.

I settled in my chair in the airport and waited for my Hyderabad flight. It was a year since the first time I came this way, now I knew the whole routine. As I waited there, I pondered the fascination that everyone had for all things from the West. Perhaps "fascination" was not the correct term, it was an absolute obsession.

Much of this obsession centred around consumer items. India modelled its economy after the Soviet Union. Although this may have made essential goods and services more accessible, consumer items were in short supply. Therefore, much of this obsession with foreign goods could be attributed to the "forbidden fruit syndrome." But it was something deeper than that. people imitated most Western attitudes. They had a fascination for Western drugs, tobacco, alcohol, clothing, films, and everything. The desire to imitate the West knew no rational boundaries.

But a wise person once said, "Be careful what you wish for, because you just might get it." I could not know this in the 1970s, but in the coming decades every international consumer good would be available. In the 21st century Indian trash TV would be just as bad as anything in the West. American junk food would cursed the diet and health of countless people. Would Indians be any happier for it? I will leave that question for others to answer.

But none of these things were known to me as I sat and awaited my Hyderabad flight.

Chapter 24
Meena Alexander

I returned to the Kirtane household to find a new addition. During my absence, we were joined by Meena Alexander. She was a teacher at the Central Institute. She was a friend of Dr. Kirtane's oldest son Jayant. She must have been about twenty-six at the time. She was originally of Malayali (Kerala) extraction, but born in Uttar Pradesh, and raised in the Sudan and in England. If I had to describe her, I would say that she was out to discover her Indian identity. This was reflected in numerous ways, one of which was the dropping of her birth name Mary to assume the name Meena. But the job of discovering her Indian-ness must have been a difficult task. Her independence, intelligence, and probing personality were at odds with the passive demeanour that was expected of Indian women.

This independence was demonstrated in numerous ways, one of which was her education. She had her doctorate at a time when many people still considered an intermediate education (comparable to high school) to be "all that a girl needed." Furthermore, she was one of the first female moped drivers in the twin cities. In those days, one would see females sitting side-saddle on the backs of scooters while male relatives drove them about, but here was a young women actually driving a moped alone - without any escort! This was certainly unusual, and in the eyes of many, it bordered on the scandalous. Frequently she would relate to me some incident of "Eve teasing" that occurred to her on that day. I have only fond memories of my association with Meena Alexander. I remember her with respect, admiration, and affection, in a brotherly sort of way.

Chapter 25
Respect, Etiquette, and Social Position

It was 1977 and the beginning of my second year in India. I was back in my usual routine, and everything was going along fine.

As I moved about the city attending to my daily matters, I saw posters for *Gharonda* everywhere. This was the latest Hindi hit film. These posters showed Amol Palekar, Zarina Wahab, and Dr. Shreeram Lagoo, in all of their day-glow glory. The film followed all the typical conventions, but with a minor twist on its theme. The basic theme was of a young couple in Bombay who wanted to get married, but were unable to do so because they could not find a place to live. In desperation, they conspired to have the girl (Zarina Wahab) marry their apparently dying boss (Dr. Shreeram Lagoo). The plan was that her inheritance would solve their problems.

But India was not ready for something like this. The premise cut at the very heart of traditional Indian values. Therefore, the director had the hapless boss miraculously cured after his marriage to his scheming and somewhat reluctant wife. This caused much melodrama, and finally resulted in Amol Palekar slipping away, while Zarina Wahab assumed all the responsibilities of a dutiful wife.

It wasn't necessary to go into a deep analysis of the film for any subtextual message, as it was right there on the surface. Like most Hindi films of the time, it was a morality play that told the audience that correct and respectable actions were the only options, and that any attempt to deviate from this would have serious consequences. But if one stepped outside for a bit, it raised interesting questions. What was respectable behaviour? For many Indians, this was axiomatic and subconsciously understood. But I had to examine every aspect of this in minute detail.

This film came at a crucial time in my integration into Indian society. I was in my second year and fairly adjusted to my new home. I lived within a very complex social framework, but I needed to know how it worked.

The best way to learn was to observe others. I saw how skilfully people handled their social obligations. But, I also observed that sometimes things went wrong. I saw the self-destructive measures that some people took to enhance their sense of prestige, and conversely, I saw problems when people abandoned their self-respect. Curiously enough, I also saw problems that came when people showed too much respect for other people.

Maryaada, Izzat, and Ghairat

"Respect" was covered by numerous terms, but *izzat*, *ghairat* and *maryaada* were the most common. Although the meanings of these words overlapped, there were slightly different connotations.

Maryaada was the respect that I showed to others, especially to those of a higher social standing. The Hindi term *maryaada* came from the Sanskrit word that meant "boundary," "limit," or "demarcation." As such, *maryaada*, was the boundary or the limit of my behaviour. However, the concept of a boundary also implied an interface with others.

Izzat and *ghairat* were also a common terms. The term *izzat* was an Urdu term that implied one's prestige in the eyes of the community. It could be translated as "reputation." *Ghairat* on the other hand, meant "self-respect." As such, it was more of an internal feeling. There were other terms, but these were the most important.

Please and Thank You

I had an old southern upbringing, and consequently, the terms "please" and "thank you" were drilled into me since childhood. One would think that these concepts would be the same in India. Curiously enough, this was not the case. I found that the term "please" was virtually unknown in north Indian languages. Dictionaries, and phrase-books all had words and expressions such as "*meharabani kar ke...*," but their use was very rare. If I attempted to use them, they were conspicuous due to their unusual level of formality. But if I addressed a person using the polite form of "you" (i.e., *aap*) and used all the structural elements that accompanied this form, then the concept of "please" was always understood.

Yet the same presumption could not be applied to "thank you." When I read beginning language books, I saw that the Urdu term for "thank you" was *shukriya*, and the Hindi term was *dhanyavaad*. This was technically correct, but Urdu speakers and Hindi speakers did not share the same worldviews. Etiquette was much more important to India's Urdu speaking population (i.e., India's Muslims), and the formal *shukriya* was thrown about quite freely. Yet among the Hindi speakers, the use of *dhanyavaad* was overly formal and rarely used.

Dealing with My Equals

I had to deal with my peers in such a way as to maintain my own self-respect and simultaneously be respectful of them. There were no linguistic concerns if we were speaking English, but I had to be careful when speaking Hindi or Urdu. It was important to use the correct forms. Yet linguistic factors alone could not solidify a friendship, as there were other points of etiquette to consider. Many of the considerations in maintaining friendships were universal. But there was one concern that was specific to the Indian condition, and that was that I always needed to be sensitive to communal sensibilities. Obviously, if we were with a Muslim, Sikh, or anyone, it would be bad form to make remarks or jokes that would offend someone.

Dealing with My Superiors

The core of *maryaada* was the way I dealt with my superiors. Indian tradition dictated that I give elders, learned people, and guests, the utmost in respect. This respect could be shown in many ways.

From a linguistic standpoint, I could show respect in very obvious ways. This could be reflected in my use of *aap* to the exclusion of *tum* or *tu*. But I could also use forms of address such as *maharaj* if the person was Hindu, or *janab* if the person was Muslim. Additionally, choosing words relating to some type of activity in the plural form made it even more polite.

But I could also display proper *maryaada* to my elders in body language. One way was to stand up when an elder entered the room. I could display respect by occupying less personal space. This was by sitting upright, hands either on my lap or to my side, and not stretching out and occupying more personal space than necessary. In extreme situations, I might even address an elderly or learned person with my hands folded as in prayer (pranaam). When addressing Muslims I sometimes placed my hand over my heart.

I could also show my respect toward elders by the nature of conversations. This involved nothing more than letting them determine the topics. When several or more elders were present, I usually let them do most of the talking. I would only occasionally inject some small point if it seemed appropriate.

One very strong form of respect was the pranaam. This took several forms depending upon the social gap, and the formality of the situation. But it usually involved touching another person's feet, or at least some point below the knee. The rational behind this was simple, a person's feet were considered to be some of the most unclean parts of the body. By touching the feet of another person in a deferential manner, you were saying that the social gap between you was so great, that even that person's feet were worthy of your veneration.

I also displayed my respect toward my superiors by giving gifts. This was the custom when meeting them after an extended absence. Typically, such gifts were sweets and clothing. Giving a *sari* was an especially common custom for showing respect to an elderly woman.

It may not be intuitive, but observing the proper *maryaada* towards elders and social superiors, was not always seen as giving, but of taking, in the sense of "taking their blessings."

Respectable Dealings with One's Inferiors

The rules of respect and etiquette were equally important for dealing with those younger than myself or otherwise socially inferior. This was not something that I had to concern myself with too much, because my youth and unmarried status put me low in terms of the traditional hierarchy. But I will describe an elder's position.

The etiquette that our elders and social superiors had to observe with us was nearly as rigid as the etiquette we had to observe with them. Respectful relationship with youth involved three things: bestowing blessings upon the young for their activities, behaving in such a way as to maintain self-respect, and imparting words of wisdom.

Giving one's blessing was a major activity. This was referred to in Hindi as *ashirvaad*. The way that this was done in India was very different from what I experienced in the West.

In the 1970s the Indian elders had (or at least believed they had,) complete veto powers over all of our activities. Decisions as to the course of studies in school, professions to pursue, and even who we would or would not marry, were all in their hands. But in practice, things were a bit more complicated.

There was often a tug-of-war between the elders and the young. Elders were constantly having to monitor their own activities in this regard. For instance, if a boy and girl had been seeing each other surreptitiously, and if it came to the parent's attention, then all concerned were in an awkward situation. If the youngsters wanted to marry, the elders were under great pressure as to what to do. The compatibility of the youngsters was actually only a very small part of the total equation. The propriety of the match among the extended family and larger community was often more of a consideration.

A key concern was their own prestige (*izzat*). If the parents refused to give their blessings, they ran the risk of the children eloping. This resulted in a major loss of dignity for the entire family in the eyes of the community. On the other hand, if the parents gave their blessings and performed the marriage, it was possible to lose their respect from this as well. This usually happened if there were age differences, caste differences, or something else out of the ordinary.

Giving blessings was not the only way in which the elders had to monitor themselves, they also needed to be respectable in the eyes of the community. They did this by their manner of speech (avoiding profanity), proper religious observances, proper maintenance of familial obligations, etc.

Another activity of elders was in the imparting of words of wisdom. It didn't matter who they were or what our relationship was. If they were much older they would tell us what we should and shouldn't do. The unsolicited advice bestowed upon the young by the elders was considered to be an obligation of advancing years. When I was young, I considered this to be a boon, because it provided me with an uninterrupted stream of consciousness that enabled me to peer into their minds. This greatly aided my assimilation into Indian society. But to Indians my age, this was received in a somewhat mixed fashion. Most young people didn't think much about it and ignored it as though it were some background noise. But thirty some odd years on, I observe my own children and the reaction of other Western born children of Indian expatriates. For them, this is often perceived as being "preachy."

But even in India, this uninterrupted, unsolicited advice on everything was not always graciously received. It was sometimes jokingly referred to by the Telugu term *akshintalu*. *Akshintalu* is the bestowing of blessings (*ashirvaad*) upon a newly wedded couple by throwing yellow coloured rice on them. This totally annoying yet well intentioned pelting of rice was humorously equated with the well intended, but at times annoying preaching of the elders to the young. Nevertheless, the demands of *maryaada* meant that whether the advice was desired, heeded, necessary, or not, we still listened to it. Or at least we all pretended to listen to it.

Dealings with the Opposite Sex

Dealing with the opposite sex was very delicate in those days. There were very strong rules as to what we could and could not do. As a general rule, socialising with the opposite sex was greatly frowned upon.

The first rule of respectful behaviour was that one did not touch a member of the opposite sex. This was in stark contrast to the touching that friends of the same sex engaged in. In India, it was very common to see members of the same sex walking down the street with their arms around each other. This was a normal sign of closeness, and did not signify any sexual attachment as it would in the West. However, in those days one didn't see the same behaviour between members of the opposite sex. Even married couples would not do this in public.

This prohibition against touching members of the opposite sex was relaxed during the festival of *Holi*. On this festival, it was not unusual to see a group of boys grab a girl and smear paint all over her face and arms. What's more, it was quite normal to see a gang of young girls grab a young boy and immerse him in a large cistern of paint and water.

But why were these rules relaxed during *Holi*? During this holiday it was generally viewed as innocent fun. To a great extent it was. But make no mistake about it, these activities were riddled with deep sexual overtones, even though such interactions rarely went beyond the spraying of paint. One might wonder why elders tolerated this behaviour on *Holi*, but not on other days. The answer was simple: on *Holi* no one would say anything.

Loss of Respect - "Log Kya Kahenge?"

When I first looked at this elaborate system of etiquette, the first thing I wondered was how it was enforced. I found that the most powerful enforcer was gossip (*bakwas*). A ubiquitous expression to describe this situation was "*Log kya kahenge?*" This translated to "What will people talk?" In India, to be the butt of critical gossip was considered to be one of the worst things that could befall an individual. It resulted in a loss of respect (*izzat*) and had very real repercussions.

The practical penalties of gossip (*bakwas*) and the loss of respect (*izzat*) were manifold. It could result in exclusion from community and family functions, and a narrowing of one's social circle. In the West, this might not seem like a problem, but in India this was a very serious matter. One's social connections were insurance for difficult times. Whenever one was in need of assistance in any form, one would fall back upon this circle. The narrowing or weakening of this circle resulted in a tangible loss of security. Perhaps the most significant penalty from the loss of respect was to be seen during marriages. If anyone in the entire family suffered a major loss of respect, it would adversely impact the ability of other family members to find a spouse.

The most vulnerable members of Indian society to a loss of respect were unmarried girls. For a girl to get married, it was very important that she conform to a very rigid set of dos-and-don'ts. The most important of all being that she be a virgin (*kanya*). For an unmarried girl, the term *izzat* and virginity were considered to be synonymous. It was because of these dire consequences that unmarried girls made very great efforts to monitor their activities in order to avoid any sign of impropriety.

Today things are slightly more relaxed in this regard. The reduced rate of arranged marriages in urban areas has slightly reduced the penalty imposed by gossip upon a girl's character. But only slightly.

Preoccupation with Prestige

I saw many problems that came from an excessive preoccupation with one's own sense of position and self-respect. This could come from a number of sources. The most immediate way in which one could artificially improve one's standing was with clothing. There was a common story told in India about the great poet Mirza Ghalib that illustrated this:

Ghalib's Clothes

Once, the *Nizam* of Hyderabad was having an assembly of great poets (*mushaira*), and Mirza Ghalib received an invitation. Ghalib accepted the invitation. Now Ghalib was a brilliant writer and poet, but was modest in his means as well as his character. He arrived at the gates of the palace wearing an old *shirvani* (similar to a"Nehru-jacket," but much longer like a coat). When Ghalib was met by the palace guards, they immediately denied him entrance due to the shabbiness of his dress. In a despondent state, Ghalib returned to his lodging and related the incident to his friend. The friend then gave Ghalib a very expensive and elegant outfit befitting a royal event. Ghalib returned to the *Nizam*'s palace, and this time he was admitted. The *mushaira* went very well and Ghalib received much acclaim. Afterwards, when everyone was settling down for dinner, Ghalib began to do the strangest thing. He started to take morsels of food and put them in his pockets, then in his pants, and finally on his hat. Now Ghalib had a reputation for being eccentric, but this was entirely too much for the guests. When Ghalib was asked about this unusual behaviour, he remarked that it was not himself who was welcomed into the palace, but his clothes. Therefore as the sumptuous meal was served, he felt that it was really more appropriate to give it to the clothing rather than eat it himself.

Now this story (or one of several variants that I have heard) was commonly told to children in order to teach them that it was the internal and not external characteristics that made a person. As far as I could tell, such stories fell upon deaf ears.

The degree to which a typical Indian would spend money on external trappings was at times ridiculous. Cooling-glasses (sunglasses) were not just to protect your eyes, because they had to be Ray-Ban in order to make a correct impression. A watch was not just to tell time, but had to be imported, if not a Rolex. One's clothing not only had to be of the finest material, but also in the latest style as well. Such ostentation was commonly summed up in the very common Urdu term *shaan*. The term *shaan* is not easily translatable, but perhaps "show" or "majesty" might come closest. Although the term *shaan* might be considered to have a neutral feel, it was usually considered to be synonymous with *naqali-shaan*. This literally translated to "false-majesty" or "ostentation."

When it came to ostentation, community functions such as weddings were common vehicles. Attendees would show up with everything they had. It was not just the bride that displayed great opulence, as every woman there could be seen with obscenely expensive *saris* and jewellery. When a woman went out for a function like this, her *sari* and jewellery might represent a year's salary for her husband.

Ostentation was problematic both for individuals and for their families. It diverted precious family resources from important areas (e.g., food, medical care, education) and put them into unproductive areas (more gold than useful, a bigger house than necessary, a fancier vehicle than appropriate). It was also harmful when bad times came. One's false sense of *izzat* could keep one from obtaining needed assistance from family or other members of the community.

Excessive attention to self-respect was not the only problem, I also saw problems when too much respect was afforded another person.

Chamchagiri

Showing respect to other people is normally held to be a sign of civility, but it can go too far. This is known as *chamchagiri*. This word is extremely expressive, very common, and almost untranslatable.

The root word was *chamcha*. In theory, *chamcha* should be considered to be synonymous with *chamach*, which means "spoon." Yet in common parlance, a *chamcha* was a fawning lackey, or one who was always at another person's beck and call. It seems that in the wealthy households of old, it was normal to find a servant hovering around the master at dinner time, ready to spoon helpings of food onto the master's plate. This was known as *chamchagiri*. Today anyone who is a hovering sycophant is referred to as a *chamcha*.

Chamchagiri was harmful to both parties. If it was perceived that the respect one person showed went beyond normal *maryaada*, then both lost a certain amount of prestige. It was probably more dangerous for the receiver of the *chamchagiri*. There are many situations where a true friend will tell you that your decision is probably wrong and will produce dire consequences. But when a person was surrounded by *chamchas* who constantly told them that they were smart and right, then such people began to believe that they could do anything. The absence of well intentioned, critical advice was the downfall of many people.

Chamchagiri was a perennial problem for certain professions. Politicians often insulated themselves from reality by surrounding themselves with *chamchas*. It was only their periodic losses at the polls (or assassinations) that jolted them to reality, often too late. There was a lot of *chamchagiri* in the arts as well. Although this was a problem for many musicians and poets, it seemed to be more of a problem for TV and film personalities.

The Journey Continues

Yes, the journey - the journey of the mind. Things were getting complicated. Living in this country, was psychologically akin to riding a kayak over rapids. Instead of just being able to chart a straight course from one point to another, I was forced to zigzag. I was constantly having to worry about showing the proper respect to the right people. At the same time I was often receiving what I felt was unwarranted respect from other people. I was having to worry about who was connected to who, and who could do what. I want to practice, learn, and take care of small business matters in a smooth fashion, yet it proved impossible. Was I up to the task? It was difficult but I was beginning to get a handle on things.

But I wasn't going to worry abut such things. I was tired - my mind was going blank. I was tired of thinking about heavy subjects. I needed some diversion. My mind started to wander to images of Zarin Wahab - she was gorgeous. My 24 year old mind started to succumb to the allure of the advertisements. Yes, I was going to go and see the film *Gharonda*.

Chapter 26
Hygiene

I was well into my second year living in India when I was sitting in the Kalpana theatre. The interval (intermission) just started. The film was *Gharonda*. The air conditioners just turned on, and the hawkers started coming down the aisles selling popcorn, potato chips, *murukkulu*, and cool drinks. The seats were dingy and the walls even more so, but no one seemed to care. Everyone was just out to enjoy a matinee show.

Even though the lights were on, a slide projector sprayed the screen with advertisements. "Rin" detergent bars with their deep blue colour, seemed to leap out at the viewers. Liril soap promised to exhilarate you. Nirma Washing Powder would save your prestige as a mother and daughter-in-law by making your clothes the cleanest that was humanly possible. As for Dettol, what can I say about that? From the advertisements, I figured that it would kill every germ within a ten-kilometer radius of your house. It seemed that cleaning and personal hygiene products were all that people thought about.

The film progressed with all of its predictability and finally finished. It was a matinee showing so it was just late afternoon when I exited the theatre. This was rush time, so I had some difficulty getting a bus for the trip back home.

A monstrously oversized, but pitifully underpowered local bus pulled up to the bus stop. It was painted a peculiar green colour. I climbed into the overcrowded bus with great difficulty, then it pulled away from the bus stop with a deafening roar.

When I rode the bus, people would sometimes offer their seats. This always made me feel a bit uncomfortable. I knew they were doing it because I was a foreigner, but this brought up questions. Was the fact that I was a *pardeshi* evidence that I should be treated like a *mehman* (guest)? If this was the case, then I was willing to accept these small considerations. But the reasons could also stem from the fact that I was a *gora* (white person)? This was not acceptable to me, and made me very uncomfortable. It was sometimes possible to ascertain the reasons if they made some small comment among themselves in Hindi. (By then I was functional in the language.) But usually there was no indication. I suspect that in most cases the motivation may not have been clear to them as well.

I stood there holding on to the bar, attentive the genders and ages of the passengers. As per custom, I gave preference to the females and the elderly, but when I felt that it was appropriate, I grabbed a seat.

As the bus moved slowly through the traffic, I was able to reflect upon the public hygiene situation. This was atrocious. I looked out the window and saw men and boys of all ages relieving themselves against the walls. I also saw piles of garbage amass and go uncollected for long periods of time. In most places there was open sewage. Not surprisingly this created major public health problems.

It seemed that many of the reasons for this poor state developed centuries ago when India was a smaller agricultural country. In the old days, going out into the fields to defecate was reasonable. But in the 1970s India had over 600 million people (today it is over a billion), with large portions of the population living in urban areas. Going out to a wall in front of someone's house in the city to relieve oneself was not a good thing.

Another reason for poor public hygiene was that local governments just didn't work well. It was their responsibility to collect garbage, build and maintain public latrines, and engage in similar activities. Unfortunately, corruption and apathy on the part of the municipalities, coupled with a perpetual shortage of funds due to widespread tax evasion, made proper attention to public health very difficult.

Poverty and ignorance were also a contributing factors. Many of the urban poor did not have access to latrines nor did they understand the importance of public hygiene.

My reflection upon public hygiene was interrupted as the bus pulled up in front of the General Post Office (GPO) in Abids. Abids was particularly busy at this time of day. So I had to forcefully push against people to exit the bus, and then push my way through the crowd at the bus stand. When I first moved here I found this difficult, but I learned that pushing people or being pushed by other people in crowds meant nothing. No offence was ever intended.

It was a hot day, and I was in quite a state after the day's excursion. I needed a bath. I quickly collected a change of clothes, and went to the bathroom. I thought to myself, "Yes this is a bathroom". In the US, the term "bathroom" seldom applied to places where you could actually take a bath.

Raising a fire in the outdoor water heater was not practical this late in the afternoon, but that was no trouble. The electricity was on, so I could get hot water from a "Geyser". This was a small electric hot water heater that heated the water as it flowed through.

Slowly I filled the big brass bucket with hot water. I estimated the temperature by how quickly the water flowed through the heater. One's normal tendency would be to put your hand into the water to feel how hot it was, but this could be very dangerous with a Geyser. They were not well made, and electric shocks were common - sometimes fatal.

When I was satisfied with my bucket of hot water, I sat on the raised stone block in the centre of the bathroom and proceeded to have a complete bath.

As I bathed, I reflected upon public and personal hygiene in India. There seemed to be a curious contrast between the abysmal state of public hygiene and the almost obsessive attention to personal hygiene. The number of times that Indians bathed varied from community to community, but for most people once a day was considered the minimum. Some communities, such as the brahmin communities, had a reputation for taking several baths a day.

Hygiene became codified into the religion. Mixing health practices and religion was not peculiar to India, for we also found this in the Western traditions. For instance, the nature of diseases such as trichinosis were unknown to the Jewish rabbis of old, but they understood that if you did not eat pork, you would be in a better state of health. In the same way, Hinduism and Islam prescribed hygienic practices as part of the religion. This was long before the nature of diseases were properly understood.

My reflections began to take a different turn as I thought about communal attitudes toward bathing. In particular, I started thinking about how Hindus looked at the subject. Many Hindus considered this to be the most important part of their rituals. The ancient scriptures provided very detailed procedures. For instance, the best time to take a bath was deemed to be 4:00 a.m. The number of times a person should bath in a day was also covered. It should be once for unmarried people, twice for married couples, and three times a day for renunciants and religious people. The variations on bathing were discussed in ridiculous detail, such as how one should bath in a flowing stream, lake or other body of still water, the differences in bathing in morning, noon, or night, and similar considerations. But scriptural considerations aside, most Hindus took one to two baths a day.

I remembered reading about the *Kumbha Mela*. This was a public ritual where people congregated in sites that were considered especially holy and bathed with the purpose of cleansing their souls. The most popular river for this was the *Ganga* (Ganges) at a place near Allahabad. Dates and times were fixed by astrology, but the most auspicious was the *Maha Kumbha Mela* which occurred once every 144 years. Obviously few people could ever attend this, so the *Purna Kumbha Mela* (every 12 years), or the *Ardh Kumbha Mela* (every six years), was more accessible. I could not know it at the time, but the upcoming 2001 *Kumbha Mela* would have a record sixty million people in attendance.

I started to compare the Hindu and Islamic approaches to bathing. I remembered a friend once told me that in Islam too, personal hygiene was considered to be very important. One portion the Qur'an says: "Truly, Allah loves those who turn unto Him in repentance and loves those who purify themselves."

In Islam, there were three types of cleaning. *Ghusl* was a complete bath, *wudoo* was when one washed only parts of the body. Under rare circumstance when water for bathing was not available, there was the *tayammum*, which was washing with sand or some other relatively clean earth.

There was a popular misconception that Muslims only took baths on Friday. This misconception ignored the fact that Islam required them to take a bath for a variety of purposes. Furthermore, washing any exposed part of the body was mandated before each *namaz* (prayer). This should be done five times a day. When one considered that these were just the ablutions required by faith, and were done in addition to baths done for non-religious reasons, it was clear that this popular misconception was unfounded.

Suddenly my reflections were interrupted when I dropped brass vessel. I was using this to scoop up warm water from the bucket and pour it over myself. As I picked it up, I could hear sounds coming from outside. Outside the bathroom was an eight foot wall. From just the other side of the wall, I heard the neighbour woman calling one of her sons. They were a Konkani Christian family.

"Ah yes," I thought to myself. "If there are communal differences toward bathing, what would the Indian Christian approach be?"

From a religious standpoint, Christianity did not have very much to say about bathing. True, the baptism was a form of ritualised bath. But it is well known that in Europe, during much of its history, bathing was considered to be an un-Christian thing to do. However, the majority of Indian Christians were relatively recent converts, and as such, they retained their Hindu traditions. Once or twice a day seemed to be about average for an Indian Christian. But unlike their Hindu ancestors, their bathing was motivated by culture and not religion.

I was amazed at the communal stereotypes that people embraced. Hindus were accused of being unclean because they sprinkled cow urine as a cleanser, and in extreme cases took baths in cow urine. They were also accused of being unclean because they were uncircumcised. Muslims were accused of only taking a bath once a week, while Christians were accused of being unclean because they ate pork and did not take baths. Most of these accusations were derived from extreme examples within their respective communities, and did not reflect the norm. I didn't see any appreciable difference in personal hygiene from community to community.

My reflections then took a turn towards etiquette. I thought about how hygiene influenced the way that people interacted.

One of the most important points of etiquette concerned the use of the right hand versus the left hand. The equation of the right hand with correctness, and the left hand with impropriety has a long history, even in the Western world. For instance, the English word "sinister" is derived from the Latin word *sinestra* for "left." The English "right" also means both "correct" and "true." Words like "righteousness" absolutely scream of value associations of right and left. In India the use of the right or left hand assumed a very special significance. The right hand was used for eating and writing, while the left hand was reserved for personal sanitary activities. In other words, since toilette paper was not used, it was the left hand that was used for washing oneself. This affected social interaction to the extent that one never gave anything or accepted anything with the left hand. To do otherwise was a great insult. I committed this *faux pas* early in my stay, and was immediately rebuked for it. I learned my lesson!

I finished my bath. As I was dressing I looked into the mirror, and thought to myself. "I'm starting to get a bit shaggy," It's had been a while since my last haircut. I told myself that the next day I should probably go and have it cut. With those thoughts I finished dressing and went about the rest of my activities.

Chapter 27
Grooming

The next day came, and I found myself in the barber shop. It was only fifty feet from the Kirtane house. It was modelled after Western barbershops. By Indian standards of the day, it was a posh affair. This posh quality was possible because of its close proximity to Abid's and its upscale shopping clientele. This barbershop had the typical two-tone walls, upon which were mounted mirrors and cabinets. The proprietor was Christian, but he was not local. He may have been either Goan or Anglo-Indian, but he was not Telugu, and certainly not a Hindu. Among Hindus, being a barber was synonymous with being low-caste, and no amount of poshness or financial success could completely overcome this stigma.

The barber prominently displayed a line of electric razors, none of which were ever used. Frequent power outages coupled with the difficulty of obtaining replacement blades precluded their common use, so they were displayed for decorative purposes. This barber did his best work with nothing more than a simple comb, scissors, and a bottle of water to spray on the hair.

It was very boring having my hair cut. As I sat there listening to the continuous "snip... snip... snip..." of cutting hair, my thoughts turned to barber shops and grooming.

Barbers for men were very popular in India, and have been for centuries. But in the 1970s, barber shops tended to be modest affairs. Before the British, a barber may have just had a customer sit on a rock and be given a shave or haircut with only the simplest tools. This was still the custom in rural areas.

But beauty parlours for women were rare. I couldn't know this at the time, but in decades to come, Western style beauty parlours would become very popular. But in the 1970s women's grooming were matters for social interaction. The purpose was not so much to make a girl look beautiful, but more for close female family members to get together and spend time gossiping and interacting. Oil baths, oil massages, eyebrow threading, applying depilatory pastes of turmeric (*haldi*), applying *mehendi*, and doing hair, were especially popular activities. These were usually attached to some other function. The most intense female grooming activities preceding weddings.

I happened to glance at a magazine, and was intrigued by an advertisement. It was in Telugu so I couldn't read it, but the back cover was dominated by an advertisement for a skin whitening cream called "Fair & Lovely."

I was particularly struck by the use of skin whiteners. Indians were amazingly colour conscious, and women took extreme measures to make their skin as fair as possible. The market was saturated with a variety of commercially available preparations that promised miraculous results. Obviously the reality was far short of the advertising, but there were a number of surprisingly effective preparations. The safest of these were based upon sun screens. Sun screens blocked the UV light which stimulated the production of pigmentation. When one blocked this, then the skin became fairer. Unfortunately, not every commercial preparation was safe. Many preparations bleached the skin, and often caused chemical burns.

My reflections upon personal grooming were brought to an end when my haircut was completed. I paid the barber, grabbed my *joli*, and left.

I exited the barber shop, and happened to see a family of monkeys that was moving through the locality. They scarcely paid any attention to the people passing below. The monkeys rested in the giant tree by the Troop Bazaar bus stand, slowly, purposefully, picking fleas from each other's fur. I suspected that a large number of these fleas were imaginary, but it didn't seem to matter. It was the simple act of grooming that was important.

Monkeys grooming themselves

My attention shifted to an auto that was parked in front of the barber shop. Its driver was negotiating a fair with a potential passenger. Although the auto had a government mandated meter, both drivers and passengers tended to look upon this as a mere suggestion.

Monkeys, autos, traffic, people running back and forth, everything seemed like a typical day, but then I saw a pushcart (*bandi*) that was full of small, square, multicoloured kites. He was surrounded by excited children and youths, each wishing to make a purchase.

"Ah yes," I thought to myself. "In three days, it will be Sankranthi." Sankranthi was a mid-winter festival that was famous for the sport of kite fighting.

Chapter 28
Lalitha's Doorstep

It was 5:30 in the morning. This was Sankranthi, so Lalitha was cleaning her house. It wasn't just ordinary house-cleaning, but a major job. It is said that the purpose of this intense cleaning was to invite Laxmi (goddess of wealth) into the house. But Lalitha tended to look at things from a modern viewpoint. Although she was a devout Hindu, her world views were that these cleanings were for hygienic reasons and that ascribing religious reasons was merely a way to make sure that the populace engaged in theme.

The hygiene in Lalitha's home, like most Indians, was more stringent and demanding than found in the West. But considering the abysmal state of public sanitation, it was a much more difficult proposition. Basic house cleaning was a daily routine, and she washed the floors weekly with strong antiseptic detergent.

Probably one of the most important hygienic practices in a Lalitha's home was the prohibition of shoes. In India, one simply did not go into anyone's house with shoes on. This was true whether one was dealing with Hindus, Muslims, or most Christians. Lalitha knew a very few Christians who walked around their houses with shoes on. This always annoyed her. She felt that it was a Western affectation with contrarian overtones, and served no purpose.

But at the moment, she was concerned with something else.

Lalitha knew that attending to the area in front of her house was a public reflection of her family's cleanliness. Long before Louis Pasteur discovered that dirt and dust carried germs, Indians realised that suppressing road dust was a way to ward off disease. Washing the area in front of one's house was the logical thing to do to maintain some type of cleanliness. But there was a problem, the area in front of your house WAS dust and dirt. It made no sense just to wash dirt. You had to lay something down on top of it, otherwise washing was pointless.

The area in front of Lalitha's house was covered in concrete. Lalitha's husband had only put down this slab last year. It was not a decision that was entered into lightly, for this was expensive.

The reasons for cement being so expensive were manifold, but primarily tied to corruption. It was almost impossible to get a license to construct a cement factory, because the bribes that one had to give were extraordinary. Even after obtaining the necessary permits, a hefty percentage of the factory's earnings went to local politicians just to keep them at bay.

But cost was not the only reason why many people could not put down a concrete slab. Many houses opened directly onto the road. In such situations, laying down a concrete slab would be deemed to be "encroachment" and could lead to problems with the municipality.

But Lalitha and her family had a slab, so now was the time to attend to it. She carefully took a small bucket of water and a crude brush, and started washing. The brush was nothing more than a bundle of reeds that were bound together to form a crude handle. A small bright red plastic strip, was artfully woven into the end of this handle. This gave an artistic touch to an otherwise crude and mundane household item. The very short handle forced Lalitha to bend deeply as she cleaned.

Lalitha reflected upon a simple point as she cleaned the slab. In Hyderabad, there were two things that you could lay down in front of your doorstep to suppress road dust. One was concrete, and the other cow-dung. During the 1970s, both approaches were equally used. Concrete was the way that most people preferred, because it was better during the rainy season. But this was not always practical.

Bovine-dung was an effective, economical, and time-honoured alternative to concrete. Cow dung was preferred, but water-buffalo dung was also acceptable. Lalitha recognised this as she saw her neighbour laying down fresh dung for the day's festival. The neighbour girl had a bucket that was filled with a slurry of dung and water. She applied it quite liberally. But people did not lay down fresh dung every day. One did this only for special occasions such as weddings and holidays.

Lalitha had heard of Westerners who were taken aback by this custom, but she knew that they didn't really understand. Cattle and water buffalo were so dissimilar to humans that transferring diseases from bovines to humans was a relatively rare occurrence (tetanus probably being the most notable exception). Therefore by human standards, dung was surprisingly clean. Furthermore, when the manure hardened in the sun, it was remarkably similar to particle board. It was hard enough that it could be easily swept with a broom, but not so hard that children could injure themselves in a fall. It actually made the area safer for the children by covering up rocks. It was economical, eco-friendly, and was very effective at suppressing road dust.

But Lalitha didn't have time for these reflections. She just finished scrubbing down her slab, and now it was time to move to the next step.

Lalitha grabbed small handfuls of a white dust and skilfully drew designs upon the freshly washed slab. These patterns were variously referred to as *rangoli* or *muggu*. The material from which it was made varied from one part of the country to another, but in the Hyderabad area, it was generally mixture of rice flour and lime (calcium oxide/calcium carbonate). Normally, this was a simple pattern and served no function other than to welcome guests. It also showed to the community that she was attentive to domestic hygiene. But today was different. Rather than draw a few quick simple designs upon her slab, today it had to be more elaborate and artistic.

It was nearly dawn as Lalitha finished her elaborate *Sankranthi Muggu*. The sun darted its rays above the horizon, painting the sky in glorious hues of blue, orange, and red. There was the sound of people coming, going, and attending to their morning duties. The air began to fill with the aroma of sambar, *iddli*, *dosa*, burning wood, and kerosene. Zamistanpur was coming to life on this fine Sankranthi morning.

Drawing *rangoli* (*muggu*) upon freshly laid bovine dung

Lalitha was satisfied with her work, but there was no time to reflect upon it. There were a thousands other things to do in preparation for the day's celebration.

Chapter 29
Grand Hotel

"When you bend over like that, it is easy for someone to cut your head off." That was the explanation that was given to me for the deep way that one had to bend over when passing through the impractically small door in the gate of the Kirtane compound. Apparently this was some sort of defence in ages past that was retained in contemporary constructions.

But this morning the history of Indian architecture was the last thing on my mind. A week had passed since Sankranthi, and everyone moved on to other matters. But I was neither concerned about Sankranthi, kites, nor vestigial aspects of architecture, for I was on a quest. I exited the compound through a small door in the gate, made my way past the large tree in front of the Troop Bazaar bus stop, past the barber shop, and across the busy street which connected Bank Street to Abid Circle. I walked into a place called "Grand Hotel".

The ambiance of this establishment was anything but grand. The two-tone walls had long ago been obscured by a black coating. This started as hair oil from numerous customers who had leaned against the wall. But to this oily base was added smoke and pollution. Grand Hotel was often unlit due to power outages, but even when the electricity was working, it was still perpetually dim. There was a cabinet in the front of the cafe that was full of *samosas*, *khaara biskits*, buns, and other snacks. The front room was crowded with *rikshawallas*, students, and a general variety of people who had come in off the street for a cup of *chai*. As I passed through the front section, they gazed at me quizzically, as though I had just stepped out of a spaceship. *Goras* (white people) were an extreme rarity in Hyderabad, and for them to see one actually coming into this restaurant was a novelty.

Undaunted by this intrusive display of curiosity, I made my way toward the back. Grand Hotel was laid out like most Irani hotels in the city. There was a front section that was frequented by people who only wanted a cup of tea and possibly a light snack. Since it was not unusual for Indians to drink five cups of *chai* in a day, this section was always full of people. But there was also a back section which was reserved for people eating full meals.

I exchanged *salaams* with the proprietor sitting behind a desk. He was a man of about forty years of age. He was of Persian extraction, so he had a considerably lighter complexion than most of the population of Hyderabad. He had a dark moustache, a shock of black hair, and was wearing a bush shirt. He sat at his desk and passed out small aluminium tokens to the waiters as they took food from the kitchen. These tokens represented the various dishes that the restaurant had to offer. At the end of the day, the tokens would be counted up, and this would let the proprietor and waiters keep track of the sales. This system worked even if the waiters were illiterate.

I made my way back to the "family section." This was a place where there were cubicles. It was laid out in this manner so women could remove their *burkhas* and eat in privacy.

Suliman, the waiter came over to my table. He was no stranger, because I had been a patron of Grand Hotel for two years. After we exchanged a few *salaams*, he took my order.

"*Mereko ek mattan-rost, do tanduri roti, aur ek dabbal-ka-mitha hona,*" I said. This was actually an order for goat meat, two breads, and bread-pudding. This was absolutely horrible Urdu, but it did reflect the local dialect. To use a more posh form would have been construed as being pretentious and serve no useful purpose.

Thoughtfully I absorbed the ambiance. A cat scurried beneath my feet, this was always a good sign. On festival days when the price of goat meat skyrocketed, I was always suspicious if I didn't see these cats. Sometimes after a particularly heavy meal, I was overcome by a strange desire to chase mice. The cubicle had green walls with a peculiar jewelled glass incorporated into the sides. There were dull brown wooden seats covered with DecoLam. Interestingly enough, the cubical had a white marble table-top. This posh element seemed curiously out of place in the humble ambiance of Grand Hotel; but it reflected the fact that for generations, quarries and stone works were an important part of the local economy. Consequently, marble was available at a surprisingly low cost. A fluorescent light on the far wall made a feeble attempt to illuminated the room. Next to this light perched a gecko. Its stillness was periodically punctuated by blinding bursts of speed as it went for one insect after another.

The perusal of my surroundings was interrupted by a small boy of about ten years who came in and plunked a couple of glasses of water onto the table. He did not use a tray, but instead had several of his fingers thrust deeply into the water. (Oh well, at least it was his right hand). Suliman came and scolded the boy for no discernible reason. He was always berating the boy, but then the proprietor was always berating Suliman. It seemed that the only reason for this constant scolding was to maintain the social hierarchy.

After a while Suliman brought my food. In spite of the humble ambiance, this place had some of the finest food that I have eaten in my life. For the next hour, I was in heaven.

Reflections on Hyderabadi Restaurants

All good things must come to an end. I finished up the last of my *double-ka-mitha*, when the waiter, Suliman came to collect the money. The cost came to 12 rupees (less than two dollars.) I gave him a 20 rupee note.

Indian Bank notes were very well thought out. They were colourful to discourage counterfeiting. Furthermore every note had a size which was relative to its value. For example a five rupee note was bigger than a two rupee note but smaller than a ten. This simple arrangement was necessitated by the high rates of illiteracy in the country. There was a clear window on both sides of the bill, so that when it was held up against the light, a watermark was clearly visible. In spite of all of these provisions, counterfeiting was common. No one had really any idea as to how many "*jali*-notes*" (counterfeit currency) were actually in circulation.

I sat there waiting for my change, and had a chance to reflecting upon many things. I saw a variety of people come in and out. I observed their animated discussions from afar. I noted their different preferences as to food. It started me thinking about the different types of restaurants in Hyderabad.

The restaurant culture in India was very different from that of the West. In the 1970s, few Indians ate out. There were various reasons for this. For many people, it was a reflection of communal dietary restrictions. Since you never knew the community of the person in the kitchen, and you never knew the particulars of how the food was prepared, people were naturally wary. Another reason was that the system of health inspection for restaurants was dysfunctional. Eating out put one at risk of contracting any of a number of diseases, including hepatitis. Still another reason why many people didn't eat out often was cost. If you found a restaurant that was clean and reliable, it tended to be expensive.

A curious aspect of India's restaurant culture was in the use of terms. Any cafe or restaurant was referred to as a "hotel." Apparently in the old days, hotels were the few places outside of the home where prepared food was available.

There were several types of restaurants in the Hyderabad area. Typically there were the Chinese, Udipi, Irani, and Andhra.

The Chinese restaurants were not too dissimilar to the Chinese restaurants of the West. Just as Chinese food in the US morphed into a genre that had little connection to the food of China, so too Indian Chinese food acquired its own unique form. If you can imagine American Chinese food with lots of crisp noodles and the amount of jalapeños and spices kicked up several notches, then this is a pretty good description of Indian Chinese food.

Chinese restaurants had a somewhat dubious reputation in those days. These restaurants almost always had a license to sell beer, therefore in many people's minds a Chinese restaurant was synonymous with a bar.

There were also the Udipi restaurants. Many years ago, the brahmin community in the small Karnataka town of Udipi discovered an economic niche. Since brahmins were only supposed to eat food prepared by another brahmin, finding food while they travelled was difficult. They took advantage of the situation by setting up eating and lodging establishments around the country. They had a captive clientele. They knew that most Hindus could eat there, and brahmins absolutely had to.

They started selling Udipi brahmin food all over India, it didn't matter whether it was Kashmir or Kanya Kumari. The local populations quickly accepted this style of cooking and it became very popular.

The Irani hotels were another common class of restaurants. They were cafes that were historically owned and managed by ethnic Iranians. I can testify to the fact that the people behind Grand Hotel were from Iran, because our paths frequently crossed at the police clearance office. (All foreigners residing in India needed to maintain proper police clearance). The proprietors of these Irani hotels were all raised in India, but when time came to take a wife, they went back to Iran, got married, then returned to India with their brides. When their wives became pregnant, they sent them back to Iran for delivery. After the baby was born, mother and child returned to India to rejoin their husband. The custom of sending pregnant wives back to their parent's house for delivery was common in India, but its consequence for this community was significant. Regardless of how many generations passed, they retained their Iranian nationality.

The Andhra hotel was also common in Hyderabad. Superficially this was very similar to the Udipi hotel, but the spices in the dishes reflected Andhra tastes. Another difference was that the proprietors of these restaurants were not brahmin, therefore meat dishes were usually available. These were referred to as "military meals." Although superficially the meat curries might appear to be similar to some of the meat curries found in the Irani hotel, the spices in them were very different. Furthermore, in the Andhra hotels, these were usually served either on a banana leaf or *thali* style (on a very large metal plate). Such dishes included rice, sometimes *puri* or *chapati*, *rasam*, *sambar*, several styles of curry, yoghurt, *papadams*, and usually a sweet. This was never the case in Irani hotels where everything was *a-la-carte*.

These reflections were suddenly interrupted when Suliman came with my change. I gave him a big tip. Over the years I always gave him a big tip, in return he always gave me substantially larger portions. This arrangement was never actually verbalised, it was just understood. It was a universal way of doing business. I grabbed my bag and made my way to the door. The light on the street was absolutely blinding. I had been in the dim cubicle for an hour, so it took me some time to adjust to the daylight.

Chapter 30
The Paanwalla

I was dazed from the sunlight, but staggered to the *paanwalla* that had set up a stall right outside of Grand hotel. This stall was probably no larger than three feet by four feet and roughly five feet tall.

The *paanwalla* was an institution in India. I will put to you that it was not the *mandir* or the *masjid* that was the centre of the community, but that it was the *paanwalla*. Everybody went there when they wanted *paan*, cigarettes, snuff, newspapers, or cheap *filmi* magazines. But more importantly, people went there to find out what was going on in the locality. If you wanted to know who was getting married, or who was having a baby, this was the place to go. But it wasn't just the ordinary information that was obtainable, this was the place to go if you wanted to know who was having marital disharmony, whose daughter was running around with whose son, or who the income tax authorities raided last week.

The *paanwalla* was unassuming but loaded with money. The entire business was on a cash basis, so everything was on the "number-two account." Their unassuming character assured that the income tax authorities seldom raided them. But when it came to performing marriages or other expensive functions, they never seemed to be short of funds.

But the *paanwalla* was not defined by magazines, cigarettes, nor matches. He was defined by *paan*.

At its simplest, *paan* was a leaf of the *paan pata* creeper (*Piper betle*) upon which a small amount of lime (calcium carbonate/calcium oxide) was rubbed and a small piece of betel nut (areca nut) was placed. The leaf was then rolled up and eaten. This description might satisfy the minimum requirement, but no self-respecting *paanwalla* sold it this way. Invariably, other ingredients such as *katta* (a powder made from the extract of a tree used to give a deep red colour), tobacco extracts, jellied rose petals, coconut, fennel seeds, and an assortment of commercially available, yet secret, mixtures were placed.

There was a misconception that *paan* was psychotropic. If there was any psychotropic action, it was comparable to a small glass of iced tea. This misconception stemmed from the fact that many intoxicants found their way into *paan*. The most common was an extract of tobacco known as *qimam*. On occasion one found *bhang* (a type of hashish). Naturally, if you ate this you would feel its effects. Yet, when these intoxicants were excluded, the basic *paan* had essentially no effect.

Paan settles the system after a big meal. Anyone who has eaten a full meal of Indian food knows that the combination of spices and chilies is itself a very stimulating experience. *Paan* has the almost immediate effect of eliminating the bloated feeling that can result from over-eating. I have been told that this last action was the result of something in the *paan* that causes the pyloric sphincter to open, thus partially emptying the stomach.

Today, there is a worldwide interest in Indian food, but *paan* has not been part of this. The reason may be because *paan* is an acquired taste. It was once described as "an assortment of building materials wrapped in a leaf."

All was right with the world. I had nice full stomach of non-vegetarian food, and a mouth full of delicious *paan*. Now I was off to the bank to change some money.

Chapter 31
Sports

Something didn't feel right. I came to the Bank of Baroda as I had done so many times before, but this time things weren't the same.

There was a guard standing at the entrance. He had a very dark complexion and wrinkles deeply etched into his face. He was probably about fifty years of age, but he looked a hundred. He was wearing khaki shorts and a khaki shirt. Propped up against him was a large, 12 gauge, double-barrel shotgun. It was an antique and I doubt that it ever had any shells in it. But that was fortunate for him, because if he ever tried to shoot the thing it would probably have exploded in his face.

I entered the main room on the ground floor. It was large and divided into numerous cages, each roughly ten feet square. In every direction, there were stacks, stacks, and still more stacks, of bundled, and ageing papers. If they ever needed to retrieve something, they would never be able to do so. A few tube lights suspended from the enormous ceiling vainly attempted to illuminate the cavernous room. It was a midden heap of financial information. The bank was a living fossil - a throwback to Victorian era banking.

I was there to exchange some money. The normal procedure was to take traveler's cheques and go from cage to cage, signing papers, giving, and receiving chits. In the penultimate step I was issued a large brass token. This token had a number permanently stamped on it. When my number was called, I would go to the final cage where a teller would exchange it for my money.

The process was slow, and generally took about an hour. But on this day, things had virtually come to a halt. One employee had not-so-surreptitiously smuggled in a transistor radio, and was playing it as loudly as its small speakers would allow. From every corner, a mantra could be heard, "*Skor enta? ... Skor enta? ... Skor enta?*" (What's the score?) Periodically there was a burst of activity (but not in banking). Everyone shouted joyously and discussed in Telugu, Hindi, and English what had just been announced on the radio. There was a major cricket test match going on, and all attention was on the game.

Since the bank was running at a snail's pace, I had plenty of time to reflect upon Indian sports. Cricket was the king of the spectator sports. But in those days, people would have none of these twenty20 games that would finish in a few hours. No, people wanted the full deal. They wanted games that went on for days. When there was a major international match going on, all of Hyderabad was crippled as work came to a standstill.

Whenever a major test match was going on, the streets were filled with pre-pubescent boys playing cricket using less than regulation equipment. Wooden slats were often used instead of bats, and balls of every type were substituted for cricket balls. In the absence of balls, even rocks were used. The items employed to substitute for wickets defied imagination, but piles of rocks were common.

Cricket madness assumed totally different dimensions when India played Pakistan. Hyderabad, with its large Muslim population, was on edge even at the best of times. But during these matches the city was particularly tense. This was due to the tendency of Indian Muslims to be fans of Pakistan. These matches became symbolic of India's Hindu/Muslim communal tensions.

Cricket may have been the undisputed leader of spectator sports, but there were a number of other games that people commonly played.

Billiards was also to be found. This was of course the British variety, not the American pool. Billiards was generally restricted to the clubs, and only played by the most affluent.

Carrom was a poor-man's billiards and was also very popular. It was played on a wooden board of about three feet square. It had pockets in each corner. Instead of balls, small wooden discs somewhat similar to checkers (draughts) were employed. Talcum powder, boric acid, or any similar powder, was sprinkled over the board to reduce friction, whereupon these sliding disks were propelled around the board. The object was to knock appropriate disks of different colours into the pockets.

One game that was peculiar to South Asia was *kabadi*. It was a kind of tag consisting of two teams. Each team sent a person over to the other side who wrestled with the opposing side while chanting "*kabadi, kabadi, kabadi,....*" the object being to keep chanting and return to the other side.

The most interesting game was *gilli danda*. This was played with two sticks. One functioned as a bat and another smaller one was somewhat analogous to a ball. The smaller stick lay upon the ground while the larger one (the bat) struck it. Upon being struck, it leapt into the air. Immediately, one swung the larger stick and (ideally) hit the smaller stick propelling it forward. The object of the game was to see who could hit the smaller stick the furthest.

My reflection on sports was suddenly curtailed when my number came up. It was time for me to get my money and leave. I had other work to attend to this afternoon, but this day was going to be especially good from a food standpoint. Not only did I enjoy a nice non-vegetarian meal for lunch, but I was going out to eat in the evening as well.

Chapter 32
Hyderabadi Food

The auto noisily crept along the crowded Chikkadpally road. It was sundown, and many people avoided the heat of the day by waiting for this time to go out and shop. Chikkadpally was especially popular for shopping so it was completely packed.

My guru-*bhai* Shekhar and I had been invited to his distant aunt's house for dinner. His aunt was Lalitha who lived in Zamistanpur. I wondered what the particulars of this relationship were. From Shekhar's conversations I gathered that Lalitha was a Telugu while I knew that Shekhar was Maharashtrian. But the term "Auntie" was thrown around so freely in India that this relationship could be anything.

But we had to pass through Chikkadpally to get there, and at the rate we were going this was going to be difficult. We slowly made it past the main shopping area, and past the theatres. The matinees just finished and they disgorged hordes of people. My eyes burned under the assault of diesel exhaust. The air was filled with the din of poorly maintained motors, autos honking, and an unimaginable number of people all talking together. We were able to progress only slightly faster once we hit Ramakrishna Studios. After what seemed an eternity we made it to Lalitha's place.

We left the auto at the gate just in front of her house, and were immediately greeted by Lalitha and her two children. After a few polite exchanges, we entered the house, where we greeted her husband who had just finished taking a bath after coming from work.

There was some chitchat. Lalitha and her daughter then retreated to the kitchen to continue the food preparations while her husband engaged us in conversation. But I was not paying attention to the conversation, for I was distracted by the delicious aromas coming from the kitchen.

Indian cuisine is probably one of the world's most sophisticated, varied, and difficult of the culinary arts. In a traditional Indian household, about half of a woman's work was involved in attending to the meals. I asked Lalitha why Indian cuisine was so involved.

"Food is very important in defining communities in this country," Lalitha said. "We can look at a dish and immediately tell you what community it represents. Many communities have extremely strict restrictions on what they can eat. For instance many Hindus are vegetarian and most Muslims can only eat food which is *halal*. Food is one of the things that we look at when choosing a son-in-law or daughter-in-law. Furthermore, food forms an important part of every religious and social function."

"Since food is used to define communal identities, it has also been used to break communal identities," Lalitha's husband continued. "In the past, missionaries converted entire villages by throwing bread into the drinking water. The principle being that once they drank water that was contaminated by the food of non-Hindus, the people were then considered to be outcasts. They could then be easily converted by the missionaries."

"My neighbour is a Sikh, and they use communal eating in order to cement their own identity," Lalitha continued. "In the Sikh religious congregations, the entire community cooks, distributes food, and eats as one. This is known as langar. There is no attention to caste, social position, or the ancestry of the people involved. Sikhism is a relatively young religion so one finds the descendants of upper caste Hindus eating food that may have been prepared by the descendants of untouchables or Muslims. This is not merely a case of historic irony, but a deliberate decision intended to break previous caste associations and cement the bonds of the Sikh community."

The conversation moved on to other subjects. But my stomach started to impose its own wishes, "*grr... grrr... grr...*" it went.

Lalitha's family belonged to a non-vegetarian Hindu community. Her family had been living in Hyderabad for as long as anyone could remember, so they were definitely *mulki*. As such they ate very typical Hyderabadi food.

After what seemed an eternity, Lalitha and her daughter came with the dinner.

I noticed that Lalitha and her daughter did not eat as they served us. This was not a universal custom, but I had run across it before. This time I raised the question.

"I suppose there are several reasons," Lalitha answered. "The simplest reason is because it is easier to serve the food and attend to the guests if we wait. But there is another reason. In olden times food was not always as plentiful, so it was important that the men be well fed."

I was somewhat taken aback by her statement, but I made a point not to let it show. During the 1970s the US was in the midst of a major surge in feminism. Since I was of a progressive bend, I tended to support this. But as usual I tried to keep a poker face and enquired further.

"There is a saying," Lalitha continue. "If a baby starves, it is unfortunate because a baby has died. If mother starves, it is worse because the mother and her dependent children die. But if a man starves, then it is a tragedy because then the whole family dies."

There was a logic in what she said. Once more I humbly had to admit to myself that my views and upbringing could not always be relied upon.

We washed our hands and prepared to eat. Washing the hands was necessary because Indians ate with their hands.

There were two items that were a permanent fixture for any dining table. One was an extremely small bowl filled with salt, and the second was a larger bowl filled with pickles.

Indian pickles had nothing in common with Western pickles other than the name. They were made by taking unripe fruit, most commonly mango, lemon, or *amla* (Indian Gooseberry), then drying them in the sun, and pickling them in a combination of mustard oil, dry red chilies, and salt. Additionally, there were a variety of spices added. Now the number of permutations on these ingredients defied imagination. Every community had its own particular style. In many cases, individual families had their own recipe. One might almost say that the pickle was to Indians as the tartan was to the Scottish when it came to communal identifications.

Salt, known as *namak*, was also very significant. Sometimes it was almost synonymous with food. This showed up in many common expressions such as *namak haram* or *namak halal*. If I ate in someone's house, it was automatically felt that there was some small karmic debt that I owed that person. As long as I maintained respect for that person, I was said to be *namak halal*. This literally translated to "faithful to one's salt." Conversely, if after eating in someone's home, I was later found to be gossiping about that person, or in some other way showing disrespect, then I would be considered *namak haraam*. This meant "to be unfaithful to one's salt." In Indian society this was considered to be a very bad personal shortcoming.

There was one small bit of etiquette about salt. If I was in a dinner situation, I was told never to take salt directly from someone's hands, nor give it to someone's hand. It was the common belief that to do this meant that those two people would get in a fight. I had to always place the salt down on the table in front of them, then let that person pick it up.

My reflection on pickles and salt was immediately interrupted when Lalitha brought in the food. It was a large platter of *biriyani*. Without a doubt, this was the most famous food of Hyderabad. *Biriyani* was a concoction of meat, usually either goat meat or chicken, spices, and basmati rice. The entire thing was baked for a long time in a vessel. It was eaten with a little gravy known as *shorba*, a watered down yoghurt sauce, raw onions, and occasionally sections of lime. Even though *biriyani* was made elsewhere in India, no one could match the skill of Hyderabadis.

Lalitha's daughter then came in with *mirchi-ka-salan*. This was a pepper curry, another famous Hyderabadi dish. It was made by taking large jalapeños and cooking them in a thick yoghurt sauce, which was heavy on spices. If this sounds hot, it was!

Almost immediately Lalitha came in with a vegetable, it was *bagara bangan*. This was still another dish that was greatly associated with Hyderabad. This was an eggplant (aubergine) curry. The key of course was in the *bagara*. In Andhra cooking, *bagara* was when you took a spoon and put some oil in it, heated it, and when the oil was hot you dropped in some spices that were immediately cooked. This *bagara* was then added to whatever you were cooking. In Andhra cooking, a spoonful of *bagara* was enough for the entire family. In comparison, the spices that were cooked into the *bagara* bangan were many orders of magnitude greater than just a single spoonful. This made for a very rich and exciting vegetarian dish.

As we enjoyed ourselves, Lalitha's daughter came in with the dessert. It was *double-ka-meetha*. This sweet was so linked to Hyderabad that most other Indians had absolutely no idea what it was. It was an Indian bread pudding. The term *double-ka-meetha* literally meant "sweet made from European white bread." It was similar to a not-so-common Indian dessert known as *shahi-tukde* (literally "royal pieces"). (Today, this sweet is on the verge of extinction.)

The evening was drawing to a close. It was getting to be about 10:00 at night, and if we waited any longer it would become difficult to engage an auto for the trip home. So Shekhar, myself, Lalitha, and her entire family leisurely strolled to the auto stand. Although Shekhar and myself were the only ones leaving, it was customary for Indians to accompany their guests as far as possible. (Years later, my wife would humorously suggest that it was to make sure that we left).

Shekhar and myself engaged an auto. We had to pay extra because it was late at night, but this was expected. Shekhar dropped me off at Troop Bazaar and then continued to his home.

Later that night, I was ready for bed. I was well satisfied by a delicious non-vegetarian meal. But I lay there reflecting on food. I wasn't just thinking of what I liked or didn't like to eat. Instead, I was thinking about the part food played in society. Maybe Indians were right in giving so much importance to it. I could now see the place it had in defining a community. With these thoughts I drifted off to sleep.

Chapter 33
Alcohol

It was a few days after the dinner with Lalitha when Shekhar and I were at a *paanwalla* near his house. We were just chatting and eating some ground betel nut (*supari*). Slowly, a man of about fifty came down the lane accompanied by a youth who was about twenty. From their interaction, the youth seemed to be the old man's son. The man was a bit unsteady on his feet and then suddenly - THUD - he collapsed on the roadside. The son quickly negotiated a cycle rikshaw, and with the aid of passerbys, loaded his father into the cycle rikshaw, and went home. I was intrigued by the fact that the emotion of the son was more of embarrassment than of anxiety. Even Shekhar was more amused than concerned.

"What was that all about?" I asked.

"It's nothing, the man was just a *sharaabi*, a drunkard," replied Shekhar.

"But how much did he have to drink in order to pass out like that?" said I.

"Not that much," Shekhar replied, "At the *kallu* compounds they mix chloral hydrate with the country liquor."

I was not a stranger to Indian alcohol, but this was something I had to think about. I decided to bring the topic up with Ram in our next meeting.

The Bombay Bar

It was about 8:00 one Thursday evening when Ram, Dhananjay, his cousin Suhas, and myself were sitting in the Bombay Bar. This bar was located just a short distance from Nampally station. It was very dim, almost to the point of being dark. It was laid out with individual cubicles that held about four people comfortably. We were ensconced in our cubicle with several beers and some snacks, so this seemed like a good time to bring up the topic of alcoholic consumption.

"David-*bhai*" said Ram. "You've got to understand how drinking in this country works. There are two things to remember. The first is that drinking is looked down upon. The second thing to remember is that there is a lot of alcohol consumed here. If this seems hypocritical, it is."

"Many of India's attitudes toward alcohol are linked to the British," Ram continued. "When the British were here, they drank a lot. The men had their whiskies and their pale ales, the women had their sherries, and all of the British had their gin and tonics. The latter was not an option, but a matter of life and death. This was their daily source of quinine, without which they would quickly feel the debilitating effects of malaria."

"Today India's middle and upper classes drink the British style drinks in order to appear posh. Look around you David-*bhai*, every cubicle here is filled with people who are drinking their beers and subconsciously reliving the British Raj. But at home, their women are pretending not to know where their husbands and sons are at this moment. The women don't care that they are off drinking, they only care about what others may talk. The only reason that they don't drink at home is because if word got around, they might have a hard time getting their sons, and especially their daughters married off."

"Have you noticed that this place is divided into cubicles. It is so that a father and his friends can be in one cubicle and a son and his friends may be in another cubicle, and no one will know."

Reflections on Drinking

I began to realised that there was much truth in what Ram said. But I also learned that the situation was a bit more complicated than Ram's sweeping generalisations. I found that the situation varied from community to community, family to family, and even from one individual to another. Still, I could see that attitudes tended to divide according to economic class and community.

Socio-Economic Class and Drinking

There were three different attitudes toward drinking. There was an upper class, a middle class, and a lower class approach.

The upper class approach toward drinking was inherited directly from the British. The very wealthy were open in their consumption. This was especially true when they were "at the club." During the British raj, there were several clubs in the Hyderabad area. The Nizam's Club, Lady Hydari Club, and the Secunderabad Club were noteworthy. Drinking at the club was a social statement of having arrived. Of course this type of socialising was denied a poor, single, young music student like myself.

The middle class approach to drinking was much closer to the picture painted by Ram. It was one where there was an official condemnation of it, but it was a condemnation that was widely ignored. Many of the middle class drank in bars and in Chinese restaurants.

But drinking in the lower socio-economic classes was very different. The drinks, the social circumstances, and the attitudes, all reflected a very different lifestyle and mentality.

There were several deshi drinks that the lower classes indulged in. The most common was shendi, or toddy. This was made by taking the sap of a palm tree and letting it ferment. A much more potent drink was *araak*, this was a distilled country liquor. There were several varieties, but the local drink of choice was *gudamba*.

We did not drink these local brews. I am sure that class connotations may have figured into the equation, but the main reason we avoided them was because they were dangerous. In the urban areas, they were invariably laced with chloral hydrate. Furthermore, they were occasionally adulterated with methanol or methanol-containing products such as French polish. The result of drinking such spurious liquor was often fatal.

One can't discuss drinking in the lower classes without talking about the *kallu* compounds. This was a Hyderabadi institution, but like some other "old institutions," it was seldom discussed in polite society. A *kallu* compound was a small enclosed space with a variety of benches. There was one or more stalls from which *shendi*, *gudamba*, or whatever country liquor a person wanted, could be purchased for a very small sum of money.

Caste, Community, and Drinking

Attitudes toward drinking were not completely aligned with socio-economic position. There were also communal attitudes.

Sometimes whole communities prided themselves on an open acceptance of alcoholic consumption. The Anglo-Indian and Goan communities were noteworthy in this regard. Members of the military also openly embraced alcoholic consumption.

But there were also communities that looked down upon alcoholic consumption. The most well known were the Muslim communities, but brahmins also looked down upon this. I never encountered an ancient scripture that said brahmins were not supposed to drink, but somehow this idea came about. But for both Muslims and brahmins, this did not stop them from drinking, it just meant that they had to be more discreet about it.

Drinking and Food

One of the most interesting things about the Indian approach toward drinking was snack food. It didn't matter whether one was in an upscale club or a humble *kallu* compound, there was always food. In the upscale establishments, it might be potato cutlets or mutton chops, but in the *kallu* compounds it was usually simple *khaaras*, or *mirchi bajis*.

Winding Down

It was the end of another day in Hyderabad. This was November, and the night time air was cool enough that I needed a sweater. The sky was crystal clear and Orion could be seen high in the sky. It looked to me to be more like giant butterfly than a celestial hunter.

I was with a good friend named Kamlakar on the roof of his house in the fashionable area of Adarshnagar. We were talking about a number of small unimportant things and drinking Kingfisher beer. As he poured a big glass, I mentioned that I was going to be spending the next day with Krishna Giri. I asked Kamlakar if he wanted to join us. He apologised and said that due to work he would not be coming. The conversation drifted to other topics.

We poured some more beer and relaxed under the Deccan night sky. The soothing brew worked its magic, and as Alnitak, Alnilam, and Mintaka ascended to dominate the night sky, all of the cares of the day ebbed away.

Chapter 34
Tobacco

"What is this?" I asked Krishna Giri as he pulled out a couple of small bundles wrapped in newspaper.

"It is *zarda paan*," he said as he put one in his mouth.

I put one in my mouth too, and almost immediately I felt my throat close up and my head start spinning. I had to spit it out or I was going to be very sick. I do not think that I had it in my mouth for more than about 30 seconds. This was my first contact with tobacco *paan*.

This made me curious, so I started to look up some things about tobacco. From my readings, I found that Indians have consumed tobacco for several centuries. Small amounts started showing up in South Asia soon after the New World opened up. Not long after that, India started growing its own. However, about 400 years ago, the Portuguese began to import large quantities of tobacco that was cheaper and better than the local varieties. By the seventeenth century, it was the major import coming through Goa. It is said that during this time, virtually everyone in Goa was either smoking or chewing tobacco.

But the cigarette was introduced by the British. Consequently it grew in popularity as the British increased their presence. By the 1970s, cigarettes were as popular in India as they were in the West.

Cigarettes were interesting, but not a major concern of mine. As a matter of fact, I didn't even think about it, until one Sunday morning when I was waiting for a bus to go from Hyderabad to Secunderabad. It was a warm and comfortable morning. Since it was Sunday, there was very little traffic. Unfortunately, the bus schedule was also reduced, so I had a lot of time on my hands.

I sat in the GPO bus stand passing the time, when I happened to see a large billboard just opposite Abid circle. This billboard was a large advertisement for Charminar cigarettes. Then I noticed other ads for Gold Flakes, and Charms. I began to reflect upon the tobacco situation in India.

Indians smoked the local cigarettes, but they really wanted the imported ones. American brands had a certain novelty, but the most sought after was the Dunhill. Since Dunhill opened his first shop in the upscale Duke Street area of London over a century ago, this brand had a reputation for being posh. It is not clear when Dunhills were first imported into India. But in the waning years of the British Raj, this brand had a mystique among the officers and wealthy British residents there. This mystique was accepted without question by the wealthy Indians, so Dunhill cigarettes became a mark of great prestige.

Dunhill may have epitomised poshness, but the most humble cigarette was the *beedi*. A *beedi* was nothing but a leaf of the *tendu* tree (Coromandal ebony or *Diospyros melanoxylon*) into which a small amount of the roughest, lowest-quality tobacco was rolled. It was then tied with a small piece of thread at the centre, and then baked in an oven to drive off the moisture. This thread marked the point at which one stopped smoking. To accommodate the fact that the *beedi* was only smoked half way, it was slightly conical in shape, so that most of the tobacco was in the front end.

There were strong gender associations surrounding the *beedi*. It was rare to find women smoking them, yet they were usually made by women. It was a cottage industry in the villages and was a common way in which women supplemented their family income.

Cigarettes, *beedis*, and other tobacco products were purchased from a *paanwalla*. Even the Hindi term for a cigarette was *dhumra-paan* or the "*paan* which is smoked." But not all tobacco was smoked, for edible forms were also popular. One of the more common forms was snuff which was scented with a variety of strong, yet pleasant fragrances. Some of the more exotic forms of tobacco included *zarda*, *khaini*, and, *qimam*. *Qimam* was a scented extract which was extremely potent and highly addictive. It was seldom eaten as-is, but usually mixed in with *paan*. This *paan*, known as *zarda-paan*, was very popular. Somewhere in the city my future father-in-law was eating 14 *zarda paans* a day!

There were also various types of *gutkha*. *Gutkha* is almost impossible to describe. There must have been a dozen varieties, all made with secret recipes. They were made of grated or powdered betel nut (areca) to which was added tobacco, lime (calcium carbonate/calcium oxide), various scents, and a variety of other ingredients. In order to give the *gutkha* more "kick," it was often processed with a copper rich clay. Unfortunately, this made the betel nut/tobacco concoction even more carcinogenic.

My reflections upon tobacco came to an abrupt halt as the bus to Secunderabad pulled up to the bus stand. Often times busses didn't even stop, but merely slowed down enough to allow passengers to run and jump onto the moving vehicle. There was no time to do anything other than grab my *joli* and dash for the open door.

The bus headed towards Basheer Bhagh. Just as it passed the Gandhi Medial College, it passed a *paanwalla*. I knew that this particular *paanwalla* sold more than just *paan*. I knew that he also sold cannabis.

Chapter 35
Drugs

"Did you do drugs back in the 1970s?" I am frequently asked by youngsters today. That is like asking a cat if it likes to sleep - of course we did drugs back then. I am not going to gloss over this, but simply "tell it like it is," or at least "like it was."

Cannabis

In the 1970s, cannabis was the king of the illegal drugs. This was true both in India and in the West. In India, there were several common ways that cannabis was consumed. These were in the form of *charas*, *ganja*, and *bhang*.

Charas was the Hindi/Urdu word for hashish. It came in a variety of forms, but usually was either a stick or a ball (*goli*), which could either be smoked or eaten. *Ganja*, on the other hand, was simply the dried leaves and flowering tops of the plant. This was usually smoked.

One common way of smoking either *charas* or *ganja* was in a *chillam*. A *chillam* was a conical pipe usually made of terracotta. The inside base was formed by dropping a small stone into the cone. This made a base that was patent enough to allow for the smooth flow of air, yet also allowed easy cleaning. A wet piece of cloth was usually wrapped around the base to act as a filter. One smoked the *chillam* through the hands, and not directly through the base. This both afforded a degree of hygiene as well as acted as a "carburettor" which allowed you to mix whatever proportion of smoke and fresh air you desired. The *chillam* was greatly preferred by the *sadhus*, and was as much an icon of their sect as their trident, ash covered bodies, and dreadlocks wrapped upon the top of their head. For the *sadhus*, *charas* and *ganja* were integral parts of their religious practice.

I have to admit to partaking of this type of thing on more than one occasion (*Bom Shankar!!!!*... where was I?... oh yea.... I am writing a book... far out man!) Now, as I was saying, I must admit to partaking of this sort of thing on more than one occasion. But in the circle that I was moving, there was a much more common way of consuming "mother nature's own." For this, ordinary cigarettes were procured. The tobacco was painstakingly removed in such a way that the cigarette papers were left intact. A small amount of tobacco was retained and mixed in with the marijuana, and in an equally painstaking fashion, it was put back into the cigarette. The cigarette was loaded almost to the end, then it was twisted in a way that we have all come to expect of a joint. Except it had a filter at the other end.

Another way in which cannabis was consumed was in the form of *bhang*. This commonly came in two forms. One form was a deep dark paste. If you can imagine a Charleston green coloured Play-Dough (Plasticine), then you have a good idea what it was like. This type of *bhang* was commonly put into *paan* or cooked in sweets. The other form was a greenish, sweet, milk drink.

I will tell you how it was made. But before I do this, I must make a small disclaimer. Kids, don't try this at home. These instructions are presented for information purposes only! (Remember when we used to have a First Amendment to protect writers? I thought it was pretty nice, but that was before extraordinary rendition, Guantanamo, and all that other stuff. Perhaps the First Amendment has gone the way of buggy whips, vacuum tubes, cars you could repair yourself, and TV worth watching. But I digress...)

Bhang was made in this manner: First, one took a quantity of marijuana, also known as *bhang ki pati*. Ideally these leaves would be fresh, but dried worked just fine. It is important that the seeds and stems be removed.

You placed the leaves in a pan of water and brought the whole thing to a boil. In a commercial setting, a small copper coin was placed in the pan as well. This imparted a small amount of copper salts to the mix which gave it more "kick." Unfortunately, doing this could make you sick. The universally held opinion of connoisseurs of *bhang* was that this practice was to be discouraged.

We boiled the leaves for a while (err... I mean THEY boiled the leaves for a while). When the leaves became nice and soft, you threw the water away. Then you strained it carefully through a fine linen cloth to remove all of the water. I know that discarding all of the water is counter-intuitive, but it does make sense. Remember, the active ingredients are not water-soluble, but lipid-soluble. This is an important point that we will return to later.

Next one took a flat stone and a smooth stone (or a mortar and pestle) and ground the mixture. This was a very tedious process.

At this point you could do one of two things. If you wanted a plain paste suitable for *paan* or cooking, you simply continued grinding. When it was ground to a smooth paste, it was finished. However, if you intending to make a milk based drink (*bhang ki thandai*), it was good to add a few black pepper corns. The reason was that the boiled leaf just sort of slipped around, but a little black pepper was very abrasive and made the job of grinding much easier. It was also one of the spices that lovers of *bhang ki thandai* have come to expect.

When the entire thing had a smooth consistency, you added a small amount of cardamom and almonds. It was important to remove the outer shell of the cardamom. Then you continued grinding. When it was a fine paste, you added some rich whole milk along with sugar. Using a good, rich whole milk was not just a question of flavour, it was necessary to give it kick, since the cannabinoids would dissolve in the milk fat. The whole was briefly brought to a boil to make sure that everything was smooth, creamy, and well mixed. Finally, it was taken off the heat and chilled in a refrigerator. If a refrigerator was unavailable it could be put on ice.

When you were ready to consume it, you simply poured it into a glass and garnished it by liberally sprinkling some roughly ground peda (a rich milk based sweet) over it. It could be further garnished with silver leaf (*chandi ki warq*). Voilà, it was done!

At least this is what I have been told you are supposed to do;-)

The most obvious question that comes to anyone's mind is, "Was the consumption of cannabis illegal?" This is actually a hard question to answer. Its legality varied from place to place and year by year. But even when it was illegal, it was considered to be such a small matter that no one really bothered. Although I read of cases where people were arrested for selling, I never heard of anyone being arrested simply for possessing a small amount of cannabis.

I encountered the legal distribution of cannabis in Delhi back in 1977. I was there visiting a very close friend of mine who was living in California, but was back home visiting his family. We decided to check out some of "mother nature's best", so we went to Old Delhi. After a few inquiries, we were directed to a small *mulghi* on a medium sized street. This *mulghi* was reminiscent of the *kallu* compounds that I had encountered in Hyderabad, but it sold *bhang* instead of country liquor. It was fully licensed by the government, so there was no question about its legality.

One thing that struck me about this particular *mulghi* was its low-key operation. There was only one small sign in Hindi advertising its nature of business. This low key quality was in direct contrast to the signage in front of most of the other shops. For these other shops, the signs were in English, *Punjabi*, and Hindi, usually with the addition of crude yet brightly hand painted pictures of whatever their wares were. The latter was both a graphic device, as well as a means of advertising to the illiterate.

Bhang was sold in small packets. These contained *bhang* in the form of paste, rolled into a ball, wrapped in a small square piece of plastic, and then later enfolded into a sheet of paper roughly seven inches square. The whole thing was quickly and skilfully folded and the ends inserted into the folds of itself to form a functional package.

The social acceptance of cannabis consumption was contradictory. I would describe it as being legal, but generally frowned upon. It was not considered to be evil, dirty, or bad in of itself. The attitude was, "You should not do this because OUR people do not do that." The obvious corollary to this was that "OTHER" people did. Now just who were these "other people?" A few that came to mind were Rajasthani business communities, many rural agricultural communities, and Western hippies.

For certain religious functions, the consumption of cannabis was not frowned upon, it was *de'rigeur*. One of the most notable was found on the occasion of *Mahashivaratri*. This was a night which was set aside for the worship of Shiva. When one performed prayers, a small amount of sacramental sweets was given. This was known as *prasad*. The *prasad* of lord Siva was often *bhang*. One simply did not turn down *prasad*. To do this would be a rejection of the bounty of the Lord. Another situation where the consumption of *bhang* was socially tolerated was during the springtime festival of *Holi*.

But things have changed since those days. In 1985, the Indian government passed the "Narcotic Drugs and Psychotropic Substances Act." This criminalised every aspect of the growth, distribution, and possession of cannabis across the entire country. But, it appears that the enforcement of this law is inconsistent.

LSD and Other Western Drugs

In the late 1960s and 1970s, LSD was the drug for the young, the hip, and the sophisticated. But I never encountered LSD or the other Western drugs when I was in India. The reason was simple, they had to be imported, and the only way you could find them was through someone who had contacts along the "hippie trail." Although I did not encounter them, I knew people who had. There was definitely a mystique concerning this drug among the Westernised youth. It was an experience that marked them as being separate from their peers. Still, this was a very small percentage of the Indian youth.

The Opiates

The most consumed opiate in India was simple opium. India produced very large quantities. It was referred to in Hindi, Urdu, and a number of other north Indian languages as *apheem*. There were significant legal as well as illegal systems for its production and distribution. Just a generation before I arrived in India, it was available legally, but by the 1970's, the sale was greatly restricted - at least on paper.

It seems that everyone had a story to tell about opium. I knew one elderly lady that was involved in an unfortunate incident. When she was about seventeen, she was entrusted with the care of a young infant. As was common practice in those days, she gave a small amount of opium to the infant to make it sleep while she went out to take care of some work, but when she came back, the infant was dead. She had inadvertently overdosed it. At one time, giving opium to infants was a common practice. It was given to make the babies sleep while the mothers worked in the fields, and it was also given as a treatment for diarrhoea. Most of the elders that I talked to knew of similar cases of infants being overdosed, so it seems to have been relatively common in the old days.

Opium addiction too, was at one time relatively common. In the past, it was only slightly more frowned upon than being addicted to tobacco. Even the *Nizam*, the last ruler of the independent principality of Hyderabad, was an addict. Most people could tell you stories of relatives who were similarly addicted, but by the 1970s this was largely a thing of the past.

Among my generation, one would find people who occasionally dabbled in a bit of opium or even heroin. But this was not common.

One synthetic opiate that was ready for abuse was pethidine. Pethidine was known in the US. as Demerol, but the term Demerol was completely unheard of in India. Pethidine was the drug of the medicos, because medical students, nurses, and doctors had virtually unrestricted access to it. Most people could tell stories of people they knew becoming addicted to it.

Arrows of Red and Gold

Arrows of red and gold fired from the archer of the sun, exploded their priapic jism of light across the sky above Naubat Pahad. The evening sky was fluid, spotless, devoid of the *dagh* of clouds. The next hill resounded with the cacophony of humanity, coming and going, being eaten by the *Balaji mandir* only to be disgorged a short time later. But that was the other hill. This hill was bathed in the pure light of the universe, clean - vibrant. The light of the universe dissolved all barriers, light - light - light. The barriers separating the mind from the body - dissolved. The barriers separating the body from the hilltop, dissolved. All separateness, all integrity - dissolved - dissolved - dissolved. Only the light of the mind, the mind of light, remained.

Chapter 36
The Hippie Trail

She danced with the utmost abandon. She had none of the reserve that was expected of an Indian girl. As she danced, she and her equally scandalous friends passed a *chillam* (clay pipe) filled with marijuana. Then they all began to sing, "*Dam maro dam, mit jaye gham, bolo subbha sham, Hare Krishna Hare Ram... Hare Krishna Hare Ram.*" Roughly translated, it went, "Take toke after toke, and your cares will go away, then chant from morning to evening, *Hare Krishna Hare Ram... Hare Krishna Hare Ram.*"

People sat staring at the spectacle. They were horrified yet mesmerised by the images on the screen. It was the film, *Hare Rama Hare Krishna*. This was Zeenat Aman's first big hit. She was a natural for the film. With her good looks, non-Indian body language, and slight *phirangi* (English) accent, she played it like no one else in Bombay could.

This was 1978, and I was in my second year living in India. Dhananjay and myself just left the theatre and got on his scooter and were making our way back home. Although the film was released several years earlier, it was still relevant to the situation in India.

This film reflected the social phenomenon of hippies in India. During the 1970s, there was an influx of Western hippies, and Indians were baffled, concerned, and confused by them.

Most of these hippies came through the "hippie trail". This ran from Western Europe, through the Middle East, and finished up in India. One's journey could begin in London, Paris, Frankfurt, or a dozen other cities. From there, it was to Istanbul, Tehran, Herat, Kabul, Peshawar, Lahore, and then to India. Once in India, it again branched out to different places.

The hippies employed different forms of transportation. Some made this trip by car or van. Many people used public transportation such as trains and buses. The journey from Europe to India lasted weeks, sometimes months.

The purpose of the trek was manifold. Many traveled to see new and exotic locations. For many, it was a journey of self-discovery. Some went to meet new people. Many went in search of spiritual wisdom, and many went because of cheap drugs.

I heard stories of problems that people encountered along the way. Run-ins with the law were common, and in some cases had dire consequences. However, most of these occurred in places like Turkey, Iran, Afghanistan, and Pakistan. Once the travellers arrived in India, it was as though they had found the promised land.

If they were inclined toward Tibetan Buddhism, many went to Kathmandu in Nepal. Tibet fell under Chinese control after the failed Lhasa Uprising in 1959. Its borders were sealed and thus it was completely off-limits to the hippies. Nepal formed a convenient substitute due to the large presence of Tibetan refugees. Once they arrived in Nepal, they found inexpensive living, a generally tolerant population, cheap drugs, and a mixture of Buddhist and Hindu surroundings.

Many on the hippie trail pursued a spiritual goal that led to Benares and the banks of the *Ganga* (Ganges). Some drew their inspiration from Allen Ginsberg's trip to Benares that he made just a few years earlier. Benares was more tolerant than many other places along the hippie trail (e.g., Kabul, Istanbul), but not as tolerant as other places in India. Possibly for this reason, Benares did not have the same power to hold hippies. That isn't to say that it didn't attract members of the counterculture. I met a number of people over the years who went to Benares, immersed themselves in the Hindu culture there, and later became respected Hindu scholars.

Benares may not have been able to attract and hold the more hedonistic members of this fraternity; but Goa certainly could. In the mid 1970s, Goa was just entering its second decade as part of India. It was a former Portuguese colony that was taken over by the Indian government in the "police action" of 1961. Because of its history, it was culturally very different from the rest of India. Goa offered the incoming hippies a relaxed, tolerant populous, clean, white beaches, warm weather, and cheap drugs. Spiritual enlightenment and self discovery be damned, Goa was for non-stop partying!

My reflections on hippies in India were immediately curtailed as we drove the scooter up to our house. Hyderabad was well off the hippie trail so I seldom saw any. But for that matter, I seldom saw any Westerner at all the entire time that I was there.

Chapter 37
Films and Radio

"Practice... practice... practice... how long am I going to bang away at these tabla?" I thought to myself, "The more I practice, the worse I get." These thoughts permeated my mind like maggots in a dead mouse. I was approaching burn-out, and clearly needed some diversion.

"Let's go see a film tonight," I said to Dhananjay. "The last film we saw was *Hare Rama, Hare Krishna*, and that was nearly two weeks ago."

"Sounds good to me," He replied.

We went straight for the *Deccan Chronicle* to see what was showing. All of the theatres in Hyderabad posted their showings in this paper. There was the Sangeet, Ashok, Saagar Talkies, Liberty, and a host of others. We discussed the matter a bit, then decided to go to a second show at the Zamrud. It was the old Manoj Kumar film Shor. Although it was an old film, I had never seen it before. Still for both of us, it was clear that this was just going to be another "time pass" film.

These were the days before cable, satellite, or other forms of popular entertainment, even TV was a rarity in Hyderabad. There were only two forms of mass entertainment, one was radio and the other was cinema. Of the two, the cinema was the undisputed leader in popular entertainment. Throughout the middle portion of the twentieth century, Indians of every age went to see films. Whether it was a posh air-conditioned theatre in a city, or a humble shed in a village, theatres were always bustling with activity.

The day passed uneventfully, we had our supper, and then Dhananjay and I got on his scooter and drove the short distance to the theatre.

The Zamrud was a holdover from theatres a generation earlier. It was an anachronism even in the 1970s. It was a moderately-sized theatre with thick velour curtains. These curtains, along with the rest of the theatre, had seen better days. It was advertised as an air conditioned theatre, but in the case of the Zamrud, this was stretching things a bit. Even when the AC was working, they only had it turned on for short periods.

The Zamrud observed the *purdah* system. This was a separate section that was curtained off for the ladies. This allowed more traditional women to go there and get out of their *burkhas* away from the prying eyes of male members of the audience. When the lights went out, the curtains opened allowing the women to view the show. At the end of the showing, the curtains closed, the women put on their *burkhas*, and then left.

Most theatres in Hyderabad were very different from the old decaying Zamrud. They prided themselves on their modern conveniences and modern architecture, or at least, what was modern for the times.

Theatres were strictly divided by class, and one chose a section according to one's social position. In the very front of the theatre was the *rikshawalla* or *barah-anna* section. The name *barah-anna* section was derived from the fact that in the past, tickets could be purchased for 75 *paise* (12 *annas* hence the name *barah-anna*). But when I was there, tickets generally cost about two rupees. This section was usually frequented by students and the poorer sections of society. More to the centre of the theatre was the general seating, in the mid 1970s, these seats cost about five rupees. At the very back and in the balcony were the first class tickets, this cost about eight rupees. Our social position dictated that we sit in the middle section.

We arrived very early and settled into our seats. Almost as soon as we arrived, they started showing trailers for some upcoming films. They dazzled us with tantalising excerpts from *Amar, Akbar, Anthony*, *Khoon Pasina*, and *Dream Girl*. They were trying to convince us that our lives would not be complete if we did not see these films.

Films were generally of four varieties: English, Hindi, Telugu, and Malayalam. The English films were a curious collection of Hollywood films, British films, and English dubbed-European films. Although these were sometimes major releases, they were more often a curious collection of Hollywood "B" films that for some inexplicable reason had been submitted for approval to the Indian administration for distribution in the country. There were the Hindi films, which were the most popular form of entertainment. There were also Telugu films, which in Andhra Pradesh, were sometimes more popular than Hindi films. Finally, there were Malayali films, from the south Indian state of Kerala. Although there was an insignificant number of Keralites in Hyderabad, Malayali films were the soft-core porn of India in the 1970s.

The newsreels started. These were blatant propaganda for whichever party was in power, so no one ever relied upon them for news. People went to the BBC radio to find out what was happening in the world. Nevertheless, I always enjoyed them because I liked to listen to the background music. These were usually by Vijay Raghav Rao. I always felt that he was one of the most underrated geniuses of Indian music. For some reason, he retreated to the relative obscurity of composing, writing, and recording background music for government newsreels.

Then the film started. The movie progressed in a predictable manner, then at some appropriate cliffhanger, the move cut to the intermission.

The interval (intermission) was an important part of the film experience. Half the people came in during the newsreels and trailers, so this was the first time you could actually see the whole audience. There was always someone there that we knew. Hawkers came up and down the aisles selling potato chips, popcorn, and soft drinks. There was also music playing on the theatre's sound system. For some inexplicable reason, instrumental versions of early sixties surfer music was particularly popular. As the music played, there was a slide show of advertisements. Although many of the advertisements were exactly what you would expect in a theatre (e.g., soft drinks, snack foods), some seemed a bit obscure by Western standards. These were for such items as immersion pumps for bore wells, voltage stabilisers, cement, fertiliser, and wet grinders. There was always a fair share of public service announcements too. These were the usual call for road safety, ads urging the public to practice family planning, immunise one's children, but there was one ubiquitous slide about a big reward for anyone who could alert the authorities to a case of smallpox.

The interval ended, everyone returned to their seats, and the film resumed. For another hour, the film ebbed and flowed in a forgettable *kichadi* of human emotions. Then about midnight the show finished, and we all went home.

I have no recollection of the story of the film Shor, but then, I really don't need to. Every Indian film was just a different permutation of the same formula. There was always comedy, tragedy, romance, exotic locations, one rape scene, several fight scenes, and a number of song-and-dance scenes. Furthermore, they had to have the original "item girl" Helen, dancing what were considered to be a highly erotic cabaret numbers. The films were implausible to the point of being stupid, but lots of fun. They were two-and-a-half hours of sheer escapism, presented in a completely unapologetic fashion.

Performers taking a break on a sound stage in Madras where a film is being made.

Indian films were produced in three major centres: Madras, Bombay, and Calcutta. By all means Bombay was the important film centre, producing Hindi films in quantities that dwarfed the other two centres. Calcutta and Madras tended to produce only films in the regional languages. Today, the Bombay film industry is referred to as "Bollywood," but in the 1970s this term was unheard of.

Fan Publications and Film Songs

The influence of the films did not stop in the theatres, it was everywhere. One area was fan publications. I was amazed at the attention most people gave to fan magazines such as *Stardust* and *Filmfare*. These were loaded with the titillating details of the decadent lifestyles of the Hindi film *glitterati*. Much of the content was completely fabricated, but no one seemed to bother. Sordid details of extramarital and premarital affairs were great for an actor's or actress' career. It was totally unimportant whether it was true or not. The old adage "there is no such thing as bad publicity," was as true for the film stars of Bombay as it had been for the Hollywood film stars a generation earlier.

But the most pervasive aspect of the *filmi* culture was in the broad appeal of film music. Every film had to have at least half a dozen songs. It was never clear whether the songs were there to sell the films, or the films existed as mere vehicles for the songs.

There is a lot of discussion about the connection between Indian cinema and film songs. Scholars wax eloquently upon the long connection between the theatre and music. (Or at least they believe their inscrutable writings are eloquent.) The connection between music and the theatre was documented in Bharat's *Natya Shastra* about two-and-a-half millennia ago. And historians absolutely lust over the importance of the Marathi theatre and its influence on the early days of the Bombay film industry.

The historical connection between the theatre and music is true, but I doubt that this ever crossed the minds of India's purveyors of popular culture. The producers, directors, and other hacks of the Indian film world, were motivated by simple mercenary considerations. Since the first days of the early "talkies," much of the responsibility of carrying a film to commercial success rested on the shoulders of the music director.

A film had to have a hit song to bring the audiences into the theatres, but the public had to be able to hear a song before it could become a hit. The obvious vehicle to promote them was radio, yet, this was not always so easy to do.

Radio

In the 1960s and 1970s, India was in the midst of a culture clash, and radio was on the front lines of this battle. Government controlled All India Radio (AIR) had broad influence over public tastes. This effected the commercial success of films, and the professional careers of many artistes. Therefore, AIR programming policies were very important to the film producers. But, the public and private sectors of India's entertainment business had very different views on what should be played.

All India Radio represented the public sector of the Indian culture market. All India Radio was commonly known simply as AIR, but was sometimes awkwardly referred to by the neologic Hindi term *akashavani*. After independence, the various privately-held radio stations were nationalised and brought under a single system. This system was expanded, and by the middle of the 1950s, all of India had access to radio broadcasts. AIR was engaged in uplifting the various segments of society by presenting entertainment and educational programming that highlighted themes of social importance. There were countless songs and dramas dealing with family planning, the divisive forces of regionalism, communalism, and other issues of the day. Unfortunately, such programs often turned into blatant propaganda bolstering whatever party was in power at the time. AIR was clearly attempting to model itself after the BBC and took the "high road" to programming.

However, the common people were not interested in the high road. All India Radio's fare of classical and traditional music, mixed with radio dramas of "social significance," was not what the people wanted. The common people wanted mindless film music, and the commercial entities in Bombay wanted to give it to them. If AIR would not broadcast these songs, then another way had to be found.

This alternative radio was in the form of Sri Lanka Broadcasting Corporation (a.k.a. Radio Ceylon). Radio Ceylon realised that there was money to be made by pandering to the more vulgar artistic tastes of India. If the Bombay film-*wallas* were prepared to spend money to get their music aired, Radio Ceylon was prepared to do it for them.

The 19-Second Loop

Regardless of which station people listened to, radio had a way of penetrating people's homes and private lives in a way that the films could not. Sometimes, the aesthetic impact was deeper than anyone could imagine. For instance, AIR did not use a test tone, but a tape loop of flute and tanpura. This little loop played itself over and over. It was hypnotic. It penetrated one's soul. Like the *suprabhatham* emanating from the temples, or the pre-dawn azaan which called the faithful of Islam to prayer, this small plaintive flute was ubiquitous. It was the backdrop for morning life in India. It was the soundtrack of people brushing their teeth. It was the background score for people cooking *iddlis* and sambar. It was a symphony of people taking baths, it was the sound of kerosene stoves being raised to make the morning *chai*. Just as the "beep, beep, beep" of the BBC burned its way into the very psyche of the British people, this little hypnotic melody burned itself into the soul of an entire generation of Indians. It is something that the modern, post-liberalisation, MTV generation of Indians, will never be able to relate to.

"Yeh Akashvani, Hyderabad Kendra Hai."

Chapter 38
Quietude of the Tree

The 19 second loop finished, AIR's daily programming commenced. But few people heard it.

The 32 year old mother in her faded cotton *sari* did not hear it. She was too busy getting her children ready for school.

The *rikshawalla* in Sultan Bazaar, didn't hear it. He was too busy with a passenger.

Neither did the shopkeeper in Chuddi Bazaar hear it. He was too busy opening his day's account book.

But the tree heard it.

The big, ancient, gnarly tree in front of the Troop Bazaar bus stand heard, saw, and knew everything.

But he never moved, nor did he ever say anything.

How much better was quietude.

He saw the Chief Minister's motor brigade go by, but never offered respect.

He saw the prostitutes plying their trade at night by his trunk, but never passed judgment.

He saw the legless beggar, pushing his way along the road, but offered no assistance.

He knew that all the running here and there, *idhar-udhar*, meant nothing.

All of this activity was nothing more than a protracted *tadapna* of death.

How much better was quietude.

With roots thrust deeply into the earth,

He drank from the breasts of *Ma Bhoomi*.

And his branches reached up toward the heavens,

To bathe in the clean rays of the morning sun.

Life was good.

How much better was quietude.

It was much better than the pointless scurrying of these little creatures.

Now this pathetic little American exited his useless little abode to make last minute arrangements for a pointless trip he was going to make.

Why?

Where would this trip take him?

From one place to another?

Neither place being better than the other.

Silly creature.

How much better was quietude.

Chapter 39
Sauda Baazi

Sauda Baazi was the time honoured custom of haggling in the market place. It was more than mere business, for both seller and buyer cannot feel satisfied unless this has taken place.

But I wasn't feeling satisfied. I was in Sultan Bazaar picking up a few things for a trip to Orissa that I was going to make with a good friend of mine. All of this haggling took time, I was never very good at it, and I certainly never enjoyed it.

But as bad as I was, at least I had the satisfaction of knowing that somewhere out there was someone worse than I. This visitor to India became a legend, inspiring generations of travellers to the East by his ... er... skill... in the marketplace.

It seems that this traveler was in a bazaar in some long forgotten town somewhere in northern India. After looking around a bit, he stumbled upon a knick-knack which caught his fancy.

"How much is this?" he enquired of the merchant.

"Oh *Sahib*, I see that you have a very fine eye," said the merchant. "This exceptional piece is yours for a mere forty rupees."

The traveler remembered a simple trick that he was once told. If you didn't know how much something cost, a safe thing to do was to cut the price in half, and then proceed from there. "Forty rupees is way too much for this. I'll give you twenty for it," said the traveler, well satisfied that he was getting the hang of the art of haggling.

"*Aare Sahib*," said the merchant, "There's no way that I can let you have it for that amount. But since you are obviously a gentleman, I can let you have it for thirty rupees."

Now the traveler was really starting to enjoy this haggling. "No, that's impossible, that's way too much, I will give you ten rupees."

The merchant was dumbstruck. He had absolutely no idea how to respond to this. Tentatively he replied, "*Sahib*, earlier you said twenty rupees. Ok, it's yours for twenty rupees."

But the traveler was not listening. He was so focused that he was oblivious to what was going on around him. He replied, "No that's outrageous. I will only give you five rupees for it.

Now numerous bystanders gathered and watched the *tamasha*. Some made comments in Hindi about the clueless *phirangi*, who had wandered into the market place. These had no effect upon the traveler since he knew no Hindi. However, others made comments about how useless the merchant was for getting involved in something like this. These stung the poor merchant, who said to the traveler, "*Tik hai Sahib*, five rupees it is!"

"No, No, No, I will give two and a half!" said the traveler.

At which point the crowd started going wild. In great embarrassment the merchant said. "*SAHIB* - IT IS FREE. PLEASE TAKE IT AND LEAVE!!"

A hush overcame the crowd. Everyone waited in anticipation of what was to happen next. After what appeared to be an eternity the traveler said -

"Let me have two."

Chapter 40
Politics of Disruption

"Kazipet, what kind of place is this?" I thought to myself. "I don't know anyone here, I didn't want to come here, and I see no immediate possibility of leaving this place."

26 hours ago, my friend and I left Secunderabad station for a pleasure tour of Orissa. After all of this time on the train, Kazipet was as far as we had gotten, a mere 78 miles (127 km). The reason for our abysmal progress was because the railway signalmen suddenly decided to go on a strike.

We didn't bother getting reserved berths, because we thought we were only going to be on the train for a few hours. We should have arrived in Vijaywada the previous evening, but we had not figured on the strike. Because of which, we had a miserable night as fifteen people tried to sleep in a compartment that was designed to accommodate eight.

So there we sat in the bogie of the train. It was a typical Indian railway car. It had a British Victorian sense of design, but a Russian Gulag sense of aesthetics. It was divided into compartments that were roughly ten feet square. The floors of the bogie were made of cement and were painted a deep dark brown. The walls were covered in a tan, industrial grade DecoLam (Formica). There were three banks of seats covered in a dark, thick, and uncomfortable Rexene (Naugahyde). At head height were permanently open bunks where one could sleep. These were suspended from the ceiling by pairs of metal bars. Upon these bars were Rexene covered chains which looped downwards, and then back upwards to connect with small metal hooks. The purpose of these chains was to suspend a middle berth which could open out at night. However in the daytime, these chains served no purpose except to swing to-and-fro and rattle, thereby adding to the overall din of the railway journey. There was a crudely painted red steel handle that was suspended from a steel cable buried within the walls. These were above head level, just between two barred windows. This was the handle that would be pulled for an emergency stop. Below this handle was a warning in Hindi, Telugu, and English about the legal penalties of pulling the handle without just cause.

A series of numbers crudely stencilled upon the walls mockingly indicated the seat and berth numbers. These numbers meant absolutely nothing. This bogie was designated as a second class unreserved compartments, so there was no assigned seating. Each compartment was designed to hold eight people, but there were approximately fifteen people per compartment.

There were two electric fans mounted on the celling. Curiously, they both actually worked. Although they shook and rattled in the most horrible fashion, they did give a small degree of relief from the Deccan heat.

Somehow through the strike we made it to Kazipet. This was a curious place. It became a major railway junction during the *Nizam's* time. This itself was inexplicable, because Kazipet was in the middle of nowhere. Even after a century, there was still nothing going on here except the railways.

But the purpose of the railways was to move people and goods. Yet we were going nowhere.

I was with a very close friend of mine named Rajagopal. I originally met him by way of his brother, who was residing in Houston. He was a brahmin whose family hailed from a district which straddled Andhra Pradesh and Tamil Nadu, so it was somewhat questionable as to whether his ethnicity should be considered to be Tamilian or Telugu. He was tall, well over six feet, and bore a resemblance to the film star Amitabh Bachchan. This resemblance was consciously accentuated by his habit of wearing hair cuts that were popularised by Amitabh.

Rajagopal and myself decided to get some relief. We left the train and headed away from the station. Not far from the station we came upon the *Janata Bar and Cafe*.

We entered the establishment and immediately ordered a round of Rosy Pelicans. This was a typical Indian lager, nearly indistinguishable from its closest competitor, Kingfisher. It was a fine, yet moderately light brew. At least it was light when compared to Khajuraho. The beers came very quickly. Given our great thirst and the unbearable heat, they were like mana from heaven. While refreshing ourselves, Rajagopal and I started talking about a number of subjects. One of which was the politics of disruption.

The railway signalmen's strike was part of a larger political culture of disruption and obstructionism. During the 1970s, strikes and agitations were so common that they strained the entire economy. But India's love affair with political obstructionism was by no means a recent phenomenon, it went back to the Independence movement. During the freedom struggle, many people rejected violent confrontation with the British. For some people the rejection of an armed struggle was motivated by ethical concerns, but for most people it was a question of pragmatism. Great Britain had one of the largest, most well equipped armies in the world, and an armed conflict was exactly the kind of thing they could deal with. However, the British were completely clueless as to how to deal with obstructionism from the non-violent *Satyagraha* movement. This worked well against the British.

But by the 1970's the politics of obstructionism was not working. India was entering its fourth decade of Independence, and a seemingly endless stream of strikes was making life difficult for the average Indian. But it had become permanently lodged in the political culture.

"It's all really simple," said Rajagopal, "For any politician, this is the easiest road to success. It's a very difficult job to address our country's problems and come up with workable solutions. However, it is much easier to find someone or something that you blame. You then oppose them by organising strikes and marches. It doesn't actually solve the problem, but it does build a political base."

"But the most disruptive and dangerous political tool is the riot," Rajagopal continued. "It is called *gadbad* in Hindi. Sometimes these are spontaneous uprisings of communities against some wrong, but riots can also be done for economic or political gain. This is very unfortunate, because it results in poor people dying so that the rich and the influential can become more wealthy and more influential."

"How can any political or economic benefit come from a riot?" I asked.

"Let's start with a simple example," replied Rajagopal. "You are the PM in Delhi and you represent a particular party, but a state is ruled by an opposition party. Your supporters tell you that in the upcoming elections you're going to have a problem. You can wait for some incident to occur, or you can create an 'incident' related to some long standing communal tension. After this, you give money to *dadas* on both sides of the communal divide to incite the people to riot. People then start to die, there can be hundreds of people dying," he said.

"So what benefit comes from having a lot of people die?" I asked.

"Well it works like this," he continued. "When things are out of control, you impose 'President's Rule.' As Prime Minister you can do this. This allows you to suspend the state government, thus empowering your own hand picked and loyal Governor to take over. You then throw all of your political opposition in jail by accusing them of inciting violence. Since the normal rules of due process are suspended, you don't have to actually prove this. During 'President's Rule', your political supporters have complete reign over the state, while your opposition is either in jail or severely hamstrung by security measures."

"So here is the end result," he continued. "You may have killed hundreds of innocent people, sometimes thousands, but you wrested its control from your political opponents. Indira Gandhi, was a master of this gambit."

Evening was coming to Kazipet. It was beautiful. The arid, dusty, Deccan terrain was bathed in the golden glow of the setting sun. There wasn't a cloud in the sky. This, along with the Rosy Pelicans, should have put me in a good mood. But the thought of political machinery that was oiled with the blood of the innocent, was simply too abhorrent to accept. But these things did not need my acceptance. They simply "were," and existed for their own right.

Chapter 41
Music Festival

"How long before we get there?" I asked Shekhar in the train.

"We still have a few hours to go," Shekhar replied.

"It seems that I'm spending all of my time on trains lately," I said. "It was just a couple of weeks ago that I got back from Orissa."

This was true. Two weeks earlier I was stuck in Kazipet, but the "lighting strike" seemed to end as fast as it started. Rajgopal and myself continued on to Orissa. From there we had a good time; we saw Konark and Bhubaneshwar, then returned to Hyderabad. Now Shekhar, Shaik Dawood, Sayeed, a couple of other guru-*bhais*, and myself, sat in a train bound for Ambajogai in Maharashtra. It was a narrow gauge railroad, so it went very slowly, and it rattled and shook in frightful manner.

"You know, the place where we are going used to be part of the old Hyderabad state," said Shekhar. "Marathwada was the old Marathi speaking area which was merged with Maharashtra in the 1950s. The music festival we are going to, the *Marathwada Sangeet Sammelan*, had been held almost every year for a very long time."

I looked out of the window of the railway compartment. The train passed though areas that were largely uninhabited. The soil was too sandy and rocky for there to be significant agriculture and there was very little rainfall. Here and there weathered rock outcrops thrust up from the barren ground. These formed great abstract stone sculptures, moulded by the forces of nature as though they were child's plasticine (play-doh). But the land was not completely deserted, for numerous rock quarries supported the local economies.

A few hours later we arrived in Ambajogai. This was originally known as Mominabad. In spite of its small size, it was intellectually and culturally vibrant. There were an unusually large number of schools, colleges, temples, hospitals, and a very large auditorium.

We were received at the railway station as though we were royalty. We all packed into cars and headed off to the Swami Ramanand Teerth Medical College.

The front seat of our car was occupied by two men. The person in the driver's seat was a driver by profession. He didn't know any language other than Marathi, so it wasn't possible for me to engage him in any conversation. But the other man was about forty years old and was clearly the driver's employer. He spoke English, and after some conversation I found that he was a professor at the engineering college.

After a short time we pulled up to the hostel of the medical school. The school was built just a couple of years earlier, so its layout and architecture were contemporary. It had a typical institutional feel to it, but it was an "Indian" institutional feel, one that is absolutely impossible to place into words.

"Is this where we will be staying?" I enquired of the professor.

"Yes, it is," he replied.

"But where are all the students?" I asked.

"They've been given holidays and sent away until the *sangeet sammelan* is finished," replied the professor.

I was impressed, that was taking ones music seriously. I tried to imagine this happening in the West. The thought of closing a medical school for a week just so one could give lodging to a number of musicians and their students seemed unfathomable.

Shekhar, myself, and two other guru-*bhais* were put in a room. After a bath and a change of clothes, I rested in my bed. This was the first day of the *sammelan*. It was late afternoon and performances had already commenced. But no one seemed concerned or anxious to go to the auditorium. It was going to continue for several more days so there was no hurry. So I lay there in bed resting and reflecting upon music festivals.

Sangeet Sammelan

My mind went back to the expression *sangeet sammelan*. This literally meant a "convention of music" and implied a music festival. The *sangeet sammelan* was an outgrowth of the old music competition. In ages past, kings occasionally had music competitions to choose court musicians. Artists came from far and wide to participate. The stakes were very high. Established court musicians stood a chance of losing their patronage, while the challengers knew that if they won, they could be made the new court musician. This would provide financial support for them, their family, as well as their students. It is said that these competitions were followed by people with the same intensity that today we might follow major sporting events.

But competition was not a central theme for modern *sangeet sammelans*. Since the end of the 19th century, the exchange of musical ideas was the main objective. Because musicians gathered from all over the country, this sort of thing was greatly encouraged by the Independence movement. It fostered a sense of national identity. Even after Independence it was still encouraged, because it fostered national integration.

Tea Time

My contemplation of music festivals was interrupted as we were called to tea. We all went down to the dining hall. It was a large hall with the same institutional feel, I found this interesting and not unpleasant. While living in Hyderabad, I had become used to public buildings being old converted royal mansions rather than buildings specifically designed for institutional use, so this was an interesting change.

I got some *chai* and a small amount of *chudwa*, and sat with Shabbir and Shekhar. The dominant discussion centred around who was at the *sammelan*.

Social structures at the hostel were clearly demarcated. There were several big name musicians, and each one had about half a dozen students. But everyone was suddenly in unfamiliar social situations. Therefore there was a "closing of the ranks," as each musician and his students contracted into well defined cliques.

Shaik Dawood, myself, Sayeed, and my guru-*bhais* formed one such clique. I was never quite sure what the relationship between one clique and another was. Since I didn't know who were on good terms or who had "bad blood" between them, I just tried to keep a low profile.

My contemplation of the social structures was suddenly interrupted by a man who came into the dinning hall.

"The car is here to take people to the auditorium," said the man.

We quickly finished our *chai*, then Shekhar and myself followed the man to the car. We reached the auditorium and entered to find a vocal performance in progress. This was a very enjoyable performance by some upcoming artist.

Although the vocalist was very good, I found myself overwhelmed. I tried to sort out everything that was happening around me.

The most fundamental thing that I need to know was the timings. There didn't seem to be any official starting time. Each day the performances usually began about 11:00 or 12:00 in the morning. They continued through the afternoon, night, and generally stopped about 4:00 in the morning.

There was also a lot of backstage politicking going on. Much of this was concerned with the allocation of performance times. The prime times were always the last performances of the day. They generally started about 2:30 a.m and finished about 4:00 a.m. These were given to the big name performers. The least desirable slots were in the daytime. Theses were usually allocated to the students.

My thoughts concerning this unfamiliar environment were interrupted when the vocalist stopped. There was a lull in the musical activities as a sitarist prepared to take the stage.

The Sitar

The sitarist was young, probably no more than about 22 years old. He wore a *khurta-pajama* made of a homespun yet expensive cotton / silk mix. The sitar straddled his lap as he carefully adjusted the myriad of strings. The tabla player looked on patiently as the sitarist occasionally blew upon a small metal reed pitch-pipe to maintain his sense of pitch. I looked at him, and at the sitar, and reflected upon how the instrument was laid out.

Most people were baffled and confused by the sitar. This was not any weakness on their part, because it was almost as though someone intentionally designed a stringed instrument to confuse people. If you looked at the strings, it was not intuitive as to what any of them did. At first glance the instrument was somewhat reminiscent of a guitar, but the strings were arranged in such a way that playing chords was impossible. The sitar was actually a melodic instrument that was closer to a flute or clarinet than a harmonic instrument like a guitar or mandolin.

The layout of the strings made sense when one realised that they were divided into three functions. There were the melodic strings, drone strings, and sympathetic strings.

The melodic strings were the most important. Although most of the playing was done on a single string, there were two to four strings upon which the artist could play a melody. The drone strings on the other hand, were strummed to provide rhythm, but their height above the frets precluded any type of melody. The melody and drone strings together accounted for only seven strings, but these were the main ones. Yet the majority of the strings were sympathetics and were placed under the frets, thus precluding any type of melody. It was rare that they were even strummed. The number of sympathetics varied from instrument to instrument, but thirteen was a common number. These strings functioned as a reverberator.

There were other aspects of the sitar that were also interesting. The sharp, almost electronic quality of the sound was due to specially designed camel bone bridges that rested upon the faceplate. At first they appeared to be flat, but upon closer examination one could see that these bridges had a carefully controlled contours. These contours set up a rattle when the string vibrated, thus increasing the harmonic richness. Furthermore, both the main resonator and the secondary resonator were made of gourds. The fact that they were made of gourds was accentuated by decorative leaf motifs adorning the instrument.

sitarist

The sitarist finished tuning, the tabla player quickly tuned the drums. After a very short introduction by the M.C., the sitarist began to play.

The Audience

There were probably about a hundred people there. This was a respectable number of people for this time of the afternoon. But the auditorium had a far larger capacity, so it looked almost empty.

It was the quality of an audience, and not the quantity which was important for a classical Indian performance. This was certainly a quality audience for they really knew their music. In terms of community, virtually everyone was Maharashtrian. Some people were obviously not wealthy, but others appeared to have substantial means. But regardless of their socio-economic class, everyone was very serious about their music.

I would soon find out how serious the audience actually was about the music. Most people would come and go throughout the day. People took off from their work. Some people brought blankets, food, and their whole families, with the intent of camping out in the back of the auditorium.

People sat rapt as the sitarist slowly developed the *rag*.

The Rag

The *rag* was the melodic portion of Indian music. This was sometimes transliterated as *raag*, or *raga*, and wasn't easy to describe in Western terms. In some ways it was similar to the Western concept of the mode.

Western music most commonly used a single mode. If we recall the *Do, Re, Mi, ...* , that we learned in elementary school, this was the mode which was most used in the West. But if we took this and altered the distances between the notes, we could come up with different modes. This was the basis of the *rag*.

But the mode was only the starting point for a *rag*. To this we needed to apply certain melodic compulsions and restrictions. In other words, some ways of moving around in this mode were forbidden, while other ways were to be emphasised. It was all very arcane, and even in India most people didn't understand it.

Suddenly, the sitarist shifted to the next movement. For this, there was a fully developed rhythm known as *tal*. This required the tabla player to join in. The tabla player began to play against the sitar in a very fast and flashy fashion. But after an appropriate period he introduced a small cadence (*tihai*), and then settled into a clean accompaniment.

The Tal

The tal was easier to understand. This was sometimes transliterated as *taal* or *tala*, and represented the rhythmic forms. Many of the elements of the Indian *tal* were analogous to elements found in Western rhythms. If we looked at popular music (e.g., C&W, rock, alternative, folk) we found that there were three levels of structure. There was the beat, the measure, and the cycle. Most people understood beat and measure, but non-musicians sometimes had a hard time understanding the cycle. It shouldn't be difficult, you could take a song and start listening to the bass line. Most popular music had patterns which repeated every 8, 12, or 16 measures. Indian *tal* also had the same basic structure.

However, there the similarity ended. Western music placed the emphasis on the measure, while Indian music placed the emphasis on the cycle. This simple difference had profound implications. Since Western music emphasised the measure, it was very rare to find it change. That is to say that if a song was based upon a four-beat measure, every measure would have four beats. But in Indian music, having measures of different lengths was normal. This was called "mixed measure" in Western terms.

I watched the sitarist and the tabla player for the next 45 minutes. They were not considered to be anywhere near top ranking musicians. Still, I was impressed.

After a small break the next group came on. This was a *Carnatic* performance. This highlighted the fact that there were two systems of Indian classical music, one in the North and one in the South. The North Indian system was known as *Hindustani Sangeet*, most of the performers at this *sammelan* represent this system. But *Carnatic Sangeet* was found in the South, and was a bit unusual for this *sammelan*.

Shortly after the South Indian vocalist started, Shekhar and I were summoned to a waiting car. They were taking us back to the hostel for suppertime.

"I'm hungry," I said as I sat before a large metal plate. Upon this plate were quickly placed *chapatis* (flat bread), rice, and nearly half a dozen small metal bowls (*katori*), each filled with curries, yoghurt, and a sweet. I was satisfied, but one of my Muslim guru-*bhais* started swishing the dal around and looking displeased.

"*Ye kya hai?*" he asked in a disgusted manner.

I knew what he was referring to. This was a purely Maharashtrian meal, and the dal was a thin *amti* which was so popular in this state. But my guru-*bhai* was used to the richer *moghali* style *dal* like Hyderabadi Muslims ate. I was in my second year of living in a Maharashtrian household, so I was used to *amti*.

I know that hostel food in India is infamous for being poor quality, but ours was very good. But this may not have been the same food as the medical students ate. During the entire trip, the only aspect of the food that I was not satisfied with was the *paan*. I was use to a rich, Hyderabadi style *paan*. But in Ambajogai, I never had anything other than very light ones. It was barely more than a *sada paan*. It was so insubstantial that it made a *ram-pyari* seem absolutely luscious and royal in comparison.

Dawaa

After supper, myself and two senior musicians were trundled off in a car to an undisclosed location. I asked where we were going, but was given the somewhat enigmatic answer that we were going for some *dawaa*. I knew that *dawaa* meant "medicine", but I didn't grasp the significance.

We came upon a house which was typical for upper-middle-class Indians. This turned out to be the home of the engineering professor that we had met earlier. I had a delightful time there, although proper *maryaada* meant that I adopt a somewhat low profile in the presence of these senior musicians. They were discussing several topics, one of which was the allocation of performance times. Another topic was the *dawaa*. As we were leaving, the professor gave a few bottles of country liquor to the senior artists. They seemed very satisfied with their "medicine", and we were taken back to the auditorium.

This incident with the *dawaa* underscored something that I had run across before. I knew that the professor could have offered rum, whisky, or any of a number of more expensive drinks, yet instead he gave some cheap *araak*. Many people didn't like the expensive drinks. Since these were not laced with chloral hydrate, many complained that they just didn't give enough "kick".

We went back to the auditorium. This time there was an obviously important person in the audience. He wore a rich silk *shirvani* and a very expensive turban. He was the titular head of the *sammelan*. Shabbir informed that he was an old raja. Although he lost his power after Independence, he was still wealthy and well loved by the populace. As I was very much a novelty at the *sammelan*, they made a point of introducing me to him.

I enjoyed the rest of the evening, but I just couldn't stay awake until the end. So I went back to the hostel about 2:30 a.m.

The music festival continued through the next few days. There was a constant routine of shuttling back and forth between the hostel and the auditorium. This went throughout the day, except 4:00a.m.-10:00 a.m. when there were no performances.

Over the next few days the organisers allocated the performance slots. Shabbir, Sayeed, Shekhar and my other guru-*bhais* gave their performances.

Then I got my slot.

Chapter 42
Performance

"I am going to make a fool of myself in front of hundreds of people," I thought to myself. I was given a prime slot to play a tabla solo. This was 2:00 a.m. on the last day of the *sammelan*. I really wasn't happy about this, but I couldn't let anyone know this. I knew that I got this slot because I was a American, and thus a sort of a novelty act. Being a novelty act didn't bother me, but I had only given a tabla solo in public a very few times. I certainly wasn't qualified.

I spent whatever free time that I had back in the hostel practicing. But the hustle and bustle of the hostel was not conducive to good practice.

The day of the performance came, and I was feeling nervous. The day's activities went as the previous days' had gone. Then night came. Many of the biggest performers of Indian classical music were there. Midnight came - I was tired, but the musical performances continued. Then one o'clock in the morning came, and I was very sleepy. Two o'clock in the morning came, this was my allocated time. The previous performers had all taken longer than allocated, so the entire schedule was delayed. But I had been up since breakfast at 7:30 a.m., I couldn't stay awake. I went to sleep there in the auditorium. About 3:00 a.m., I was awaken by Shabbir.

"David-*bhai*, it's time to get ready," said Shabbir.

I woke up. Sleep instantly left me as the adrenalin kicked in. I knew what was coming.

I sat on stage with my tabla. I stared out into the blackness of the hall. This may seem paradoxical considering that there were so many bright lights. But it was because of the bright lights shining in my face that I could see almost nothing except blackness. Vaguely I could just make out people in the front rows. I knew there were about 800 people in the audience. Was I going to make a complete fool of myself in front of all of them. On one side of me was Shaik Dawood on the harmonium, and on the other was Sayeed on the *sarangi*. I gave a few taps on the tabla with my small hammer to tune it, then indicated that I was ready to start. After a few words from the M.C., we were ready.

Shaik Dawood and Sayeed started off with a slow *lahera*. A *lahera* is a small repetitive melody which is used to accompany tabla solos. These melodies were compose in such a way that the first beat, known as the *sam*, was very prominent. When the first beat rolled around, I started.

"*Dhin - Kra Dhan Dha Ti Dha TiRaKiTa......,*" I played on the tabla. I continued through this introductory form known as a peshkar. It came to its conclusion and I moved to the basic *Teental - "Dha Dhin Dhin Dha...."* Next, I started a very famous *kaida* that every tabla student knew: "*Dha Ti Ta Dha Ti Ta Dha Dha Ti Ta Dha Ge......*" It would be more correct to say that the theme was known to every tabla student, because the actual variations differed from one teacher to the next.

I played the first variation....

I played a couple of more variations...

Then it hit me... I was lost! I was drawing a complete blank ... but I couldn't stop or let anyone know that I was lost. So I randomly assembled phrases from the *kaida*, all the time I was listening to the *lahera*. When the *lahera* indicated the *sam* (first beat), I instantly moved to a familiar variation, then continued from there. When a resting point came, I looked over at Shaik Dawood, then offstage at Shekhar and Shabbir. They had somewhat bemused looks on their faces. I continued with *gats, parans* and the usual material, and then ended my solo. Everyone appeared satisfied.

After the program was over, Shabbir asked me what I played. I made some evasive reply. But the basic response was that they were pleased. Even though it was a knowledgable audience, there were probably only five people in the entire auditorium that knew that I had been in trouble. These were Shaik Dawood, Sayeed, and three guru-*bhais*.

This underscored a very important point about Indian classical music. Performances were based upon improvisation. What I did may not have been elegant, but it was within the accepted form of a musical performance. In many ways Indian music could be thought of as being similar to jazz. Just as jazz music was improvised around a precomposed "head," in a similar way Indian classical music was improvised around a precomposed theme.

After my performance, Bhimsen Joshi came and sang until 5:00 in the morning.

We returned to the hostel and had a few hours sleep, then we were back on the train to Hyderabad. I thought about my performance during this trip. Was it brilliant? By no means. Was it of a calibre to match the other prime-time performances? No way! But I think my performance was competent for a student, and everyone seemed satisfied. But I didn't have time to concern myself with these thoughts; I had to go back to Hyderabad and get back to my usual routine.

Chapter 43
Socialising

A small insect circled the fluorescent light. Round - and round - and up - and down.....suddenly ..... SNAP! A gecko perched on the wall, appeared to defy gravity as it lunged forward snapped the bug in its mouth. This same micro-drama of life and death repeated itself every few minutes.

Gecko on the wall

I returned from my trip to Ambajogai, and immediately immersed myself into my usual routine of practice. But I couldn't spend all the time practicing, so Dhananjay and myself, went to visit his cousins. His first cousins, Suhas, Meena, and Kalpana Kirloskar, lived in an upper story of their parents' maternity hospital in Basheer Bagh. Dhananjay and Meena were playing ping pong. I was never interested in sports, so my attention became fixed on the gecko and its small ecosystem that surrounded the florescent light.

The most popular pastime for Indian youth was socialising. One could spend hours just visiting friends.

But socialising usually incurred some type of expense. Going to the cinema, going to restaurants, and similar activities, couldn't be done for free. The concept of "going Dutch" was unheard of. Where it was normal in the West for people to go out socially, and have each individual take care of his/her own expenses, this was just not done in India. One person would always pay the whole bill. However, there was an unstated tab that everybody was keeping. I might pick up the bill today, but another member of our group would pick it up the next time. In this fashion, it just went around and around.

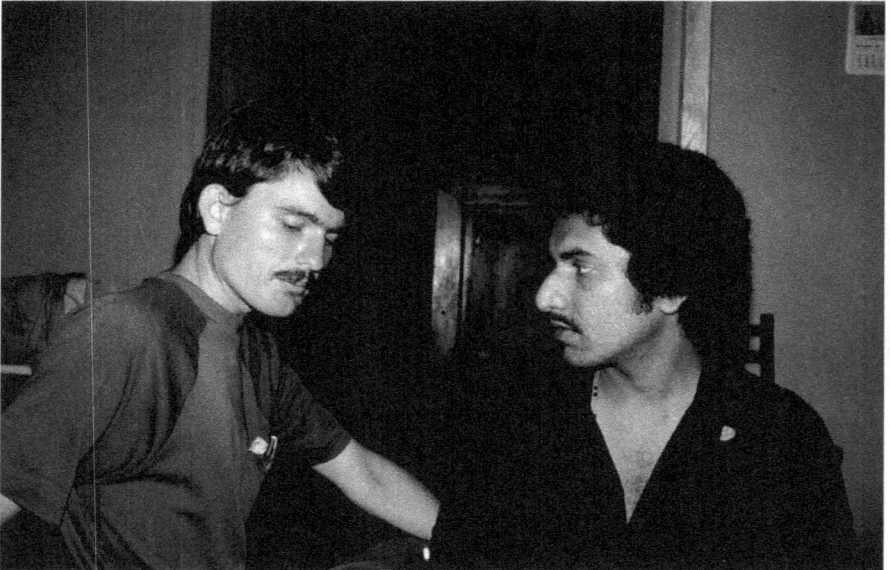

A little "down time" to socialise with my good friend Krishna "Dumbu" Giri

We spent a good deal of time in conversations. This raises the question as to what topics could be discussed. I actually encountered fewer topics on the taboo list in India, than I did in the US, but I suspect that this was not universally true. Among females, elders, and less "modren" communities, there were probably more restrictions. The only sensitive topics I found were those that related to the communal identifications of members of our group. Such topics were seldom brought up even among close friends.

Girls and Dating

There was no open dating. Although I cannot speak for larger cities like Bombay and Delhi, I can say that I never met a family in Hyderabad that would allow their daughters to go on a date. That's not to say that this sort of thing didn't happen, for it did. But it was done on the sly. It was done so secretively that it was almost as though this was a part of their life which was kept tightly locked away in a Godrej *almirah*, locked away so tightly that none could see it.

The only social interactions that were tolerated between the sexes were at the homes of the more "modren" families. In such families, boys and girls socialised freely. Of course, adult members of the families and servants always kept a watchful eye on what was happening, so no hanky-panky ever went on. This type of family was not common, but it was to be found in the upper social strata.

One may wonder about the marriageability of the girls involved. After all, moving freely with members of the opposite sex, even under tightly chaperoned conditions, was considered by many people to be scandalous.

As I reflect upon it years later it is interesting how everyone turned out. In some cases, the boys and girls went on to have traditional arranged marriages. (Although we were in our early twenties, any unmarried person was considered to be a boy or a girl). However, a few cases resulted in Bollywood-style love marriages, complete with familial objections and all the accompanying melodrama. But in a surprisingly large number of cases, it was neither a traditional arranged marriage, nor was it the Bollywood style love-marriage, but a peculiar sort of in-between. This was where the youths developed some sort of attachment, and then contacted their elders who fixed the marriage. It worked like a traditional arranged marriage, with the difference being that the boy and girl knew each other before the marriage, and had substantial input in the process. Although I couldn't know it at the time, I would have no such luxury. I would not meet my wife until the day of the marriage proposal.

But whatever our experiences were, they paled in comparison to one man. When Mohammad Hanif Shah married, he could not have foreseen the consequences.

Chapter 44
Communalism

Mohammad Hanif Shah was on top of the world. His wife Heena was expecting a child, and discussions were going on for a naming ceremony. He was a hard-working man, and a very open man who was unconcerned whether a person was Hindu or Muslim. In fact, his young wife was born a Hindu, her name at birth was Hema Bhatnagar. At the time of marriage, she converted to Islam and took the name Heena. In India there is a saying, "*Jab miya biwi razi, to kya karega kazi*?" (When a man and his wife are in agreement, what can any third party can do?). The implication being that when a man and his wife were in a harmonious relationship, outsiders should let things be. Unfortunately, members of Heena's (Hema's) family did not agree. At about 6:30 one morning, they called Mohammad to a public place for a discussion. The discussion turned heated, and shortly thereafter, he was grabbed, a gun was put in his mouth, and he was shot. Mohammad Hanif died on the way to the hospital. He was only 28 years old.

It is hard to imagine that this sort of thing still goes on, but it does. In India feelings of caste and community run deep.

Communalism forms the fault lines that divide and weaken Indian society. Communalism, like racism and sexism, employ negative stereotypes about other communities, while overemphasising the accomplishments of one's own community. Just as racism was a constant unhealthy undercurrent in US society, communalism exerted its force on every aspect of social interaction in India. This was displayed in the form of objections to intercaste marriages, employment biases, and in extreme cases, death, carnage, and disruption of civic life during times of communal conflicts.

Communalism and Communal Strife

But what did "communal conflict" mean? Sometimes this referred to clashes between "upper caste" and "lower caste" Hindus. Sometimes, it referred to conflicts between members of different linguistic groups. But in the Hyderabad area, it could only mean one of two things. On occasion it referred to Andhra/Telangana conflicts, but more often referred to Hindu/Muslim problems.

Hindu/Muslim Conflicts

Hindu/Muslim frictions were the deepest and most divisive aspect of life in India. It ran the entire width and length of the country, but was especially pervasive in Hyderabad. A look at Islam's introduction into India gives us a clearer picture of the history of this conflict.

Islam first made its way into India in a very peaceful manner. It was spread by way of merchants following the trade routes from the Middle East. The first *masjid* in India was the Cheraman Perumal Juma *Masjid*, built in South India in 629 CE. This was even before Islam had firmly established itself in Saudi Arabia.

Unfortunately in the public's mind, the peaceful spread of Islam was greatly overshadowed by the actions of later conquerers such as Mahmud Ghazni (971-1030CE). It was he who brought parts of the Punjab under his rule. If he had merely looted, as was the habit of kings in those days, things would not have been so bad; however, he made a point of destroying the places of worship of the Buddhists, Hindus, and Jains. Although he later declared them to be ahl al-kitāb, ("People of the book"), thus affording them some protection, by then permanent scars were left in the psyche of India's non-Islamic communities.

The relationship between later foreign Islamic invaders and the Hindu population of India was varied. Many Islamic invaders initially brought northern India under their control using the same tactics of desecration and plunder as Mahmud Ghazni. But during the Mogul period it reached a point where a very large Hindu population was under the control of a very small Islamic ruling class. During this period, the Islamic rulers adopted a conciliatory approach toward their non-Islamic subjects. I suspect that this respectful attitude was more a question of political common sense rather than any enlightened worldview. Considering the fact that the Islamic population was greatly outnumbered by their non-Islamic subjects, to do otherwise would not have been wise. (The first Mogul to abandon this liberal attitude was Aurangzeb. Not surprisingly, his reign is considered to be the end of the Mogul period).

In the 1970s, the relationship between India's Muslims and Hindus was tense. Although the abuses of India's Hindus at the hands of Muslims were far in the past, people had very long memories. To Hindus, events nine centuries earlier were regarded as though they happened yesterday.

In 1947 India became a Hindu-dominated country. Although it was officially secular and a number of legal concessions were given, India's Muslims still perceived themselves as an embattled community. This caused many changes in their mindset, one of which was to exhibit feelings of kinship toward Muslims in other parts of the world. (Interestingly enough, it didn't erase *sunni*/*shia* tensions at home).

"Float Like A Butterfly, Sting Like Bee"

This sense of kinship that Hyderabadi Muslims felt toward other Muslims was shown to me on one occasion. Once, I went with my teacher Shaik Dawood and a couple of other people to see a movie. It was a documentary on the boxer Mohammad Ali. Curiously, this was an English movie, and I knew that Shaik Dawood didn't know any English. I was a bit surprised by the way that they were identifying with Mohammad Ali. After all, he was an American boxer with very little in common with Indian musicians. But the sheer fact that he had embraced Islam created a bond in their minds. Furthermore, Mohammad Ali's struggles against the draft and his open condemnation of the criminal position of Amerika (sorry, I mean America) in regards to the war in Southeast Asia, became a metaphor for their own perceived struggle in a Hindu-dominated country.

Holidays, Festivals, and Intercommunal Relations

I was always impressed by the way that holidays promoted interactions between disparate communities. Some observances promoted inter-communal harmony. Unfortunately many observances were an invitation to communal frictions.

Joyous celebrations generally produced positive interactions. Hindus and Muslims often went to visit their Christian friends on Easter and Christmas. In the same way, many Hindus and Christians visited their Muslim friends on *Eid* and *Bakr-Eid*. People from all communities participated in Sankranthi and Diwali activities. Unfortunately, holidays did not always bridge communal divides, sometimes they had the opposite effect.

Muharram was the most volatile time. This was a month-long period of mourning for *Shia*, Muslims. My ustad would not teach during *Muharram*, because music was considered to be inconsistent with mourning. The more conservative elements of this community felt that everyone should refrain from any type of merriment. Was it reasonable to expect India's Hindus to refrain from having weddings, or any other joyous events during this month? Of course not! So when Hindus were engaged in some celebration, while the Muslims were observing *Muharram*, it was a recipe for a communal riot.

But there was also *jaise ko taisa* (tit-for-tat) when it came to the Islamic celebration of *Bakr-Eid*. For Muslims this was a joyous event, but the sacrifice of goats was typically done very publicly, often in the lane in front of their dwelling. I am sure that even in the West, if your neighbours dragged a goat into the street in front of their house, and slit its throat, this would provoke some type of commotion. Conservative vegetarian Hindus invariably found this appalling, and it inflamed Hindu nationalists.

Some of you may be saying to yourself, "Wait a second. If a Hindu fundamentalist is unable to tolerate the sacrifice of a goat, how could he possibly bring himself to harm another human being?" I assure you that in the middle of a communal uprising, a vegetarian Hindu fundamentalist is just as capable of killing a Muslim, as an Islamic fundamentalist is capable of killing a Hindu.

Most Hindu celebrations were not contentious affairs. As long as they did not fall on *Muharram* there was usually no trouble. But there was one event that was problematic. This was the Ganesh procession which occurred during the time of *Ganesh Chaturthi* (late August to early September). During this time, a statue of Ganesh was taken to a body of water and thrown in. In most cases this was an innocent religious observance. Unfortunately, these were sometimes organised by right-wing Hindu fundamentalists in such a way as to intentionally provoke communal tensions. In some cases these activities had to be closely monitored by the authorities.

It is impossible to generalise about clashes between Hindu and Islamic religious holidays. The Hindu calendar is solar based, so they will occur roughly the same time each year. But the Islamic calendar is lunar based, therefore these holidays may be at any time of the year.

Communal Conflicts in Hyderabad

Hyderabad had a long history of communal tensions. The first officially documented case of inter-communal rioting was in 1938. The first time that curfews were imposed was in 1947, when the *Nizam*'s private army known as the *Razakars*, revolted over the deposing of the *Nizam*. After that, things were relatively quiet until the 1960s, when there were many communal uprisings. In this period it was sometimes Hindu/Muslim conflicts, but at other times it was Andhra/Telangana agitations. Thereafter there were occasional outbreaks of communal tension.

One outbreak that was particularly noteworthy was the Rameeza Bee incident, but more on this later.

Chapter 45
The Jume'raat Epiphany

Sayeed, ordered two cups of hot *chai*. I didn't normally drink tea at night, but this evening was different. I just arrived a minute earlier and met with Sayeed at the Hotel Simla. Hotel Simla was a very typical Irani hotel located in Nampally just a few hundred yards from the railway station. It was very crowded.

Although the table where Sayeed and I were sitting was not large, there was another unknown person sitting there as well. Indians had a very different sense of personal space. Having total strangers crammed up next to you as you sat in any public place was very normal. The only reason we didn't have yet one more person sitting with us was because one of the chairs was occupied by Sayeed's *sarangi*. It was packed away along with his bow and other paraphernalia in a large Rexene bag. This bag allowed him to take it on his bicycle anywhere he went.

Most of my Hindu friends would not eat in Hotel Simla. Even the non-vegetarians among them were always concerned that they mixed beef with the goat-meat. I was completely unconcerned about this, so I had no hesitation eating there.

I met Sayeed because from there we were going to an all night *mehafil*. A *mehafil* is a gathering where there is music, poetry, and sometimes dance. The *mehafil* was well known to all Indians as a narrative device used to introduce "item numbers" in Hindi films in the 1940s and 1950's. I had seen these films, but this was to be my first time to attend one. I was looking forward to it.

After we had our *chai*, we went outside to our bicycles, and rode off into the hustle and bustle of the Hyderabad night. I didn't know where the program was to be held, hence the need to meet with Sayeed. We made our way towards Mozamjahi Market. We passed the Exhibition Grounds where each winter manufacturers, clothiers, and a variety of businesses from all over India came to sell their wares. To the left and right we passed numerous iron merchants with their stocks of scrap material. The streets were in relative darkness for there were no street lamps. But the darkness was punctuated by the sharp, piercing light from an arc welder, who assembled steel jalis (grills) for people's homes. Here and there a person could be seen repairing punctured tyres. Another person had placed a cloth on the ground and was selling *kumkudakailu*, these were small nuts which the less affluent used as a substitute for shampoo. All of these activities were done on the footpath and extended as far into the street as safety would allow.

But this hubbub of small commercial activities was drawing to a close. It was about 8:30pm and people were closing down for the night.

About two-hundred yards before reaching Mozamjahi Market, we stopped at a petrol bunk (gas station). There were three men there, and Sayeed introduced me to them.

We stood there talking a bit, but my attention was actually on the petrol bunk. This was similar to others in the area. There were two pumps, yet only one was working. In front of this single pump stood a boy about 10 years of age. He was wearing khaki shorts and a white t-shirt. At least they used to be khaki and white. The clothing, like the boy, was covered in a black mixture of motor oil and pollution. The lad dispensed petrol to a mass of motorcycles queuing up to the pump. I use the term "queuing" in a more figurative sense, because there was nothing about the process that remotely resembled a queue.

There was a cross-section of Hyderabadi society waiting for petrol. There was a Muslim man who was about 30. He was dressed in the neutral fashion of a Western style shirt and pants. The only indication of his religion was his *burkha* clad wife, who sat side-saddle across his Lambretta scooter. She had a small infant in her arms that could hardly have been more than three months old. Even though it was not cold, the infant was bundled up with a cap and wrapped up in a way that must have been very hot. There was another

216

Telangana boy of about eighteen on a small moped. There were *Marathi* brahmins, scheduled caste Andhra Hindus, Gujarati *baniyas*, and a host of other communities. Usually they inhabited different worlds. Their different worldviews, customs, and etiquette, coupled with deep rooted suspicions kept them perpetually apart. Yet here in this petrol bunk, in some very small way they shared the same world.

My perusal of the petrol bunk was interrupted by another person coming in. There was some more chitchat, whereupon I was told that this group had been meeting every *Jume'raat* (Thursday night) for some years. Slowly we made our way to a room in the back.

The room behind the petrol bunk was not big, but it was stuffed with 50 people. Everyone sat on the floor. The floor was covered by old rugs, blankets, and any other material that the owners had. In principle, it was there to provide a clean place to sit. However, I doubt that they had ever been washed, so it was questionable how clean they were. Still, this room was in the back of a petrol bunk, so I could only imagine the state of the concrete floors underneath.

Everyone in attendance was male. Virtually all of them Muslim. The very few Hindus there were obviously *mulki*, so they were considered to be OK - not like those "other" Hindus.

The evening was very enjoyable. Sayeed played. I played to the best of my ability, although I was still very much a beginner on tabla. Everyone was very gracious and appreciative.

I thought back upon the nature of *mehafils*. They were private affairs. Whether they were upscale *mehafils* in the *kothas* of the nineteenth century, or more humble ones in the back of a petrol bunks, they were closed to all except a small circle of *shaukeens*. Yet here I was in the middle of all of this.

Then suddenly I had an epiphany. I realised that I had a mobility in Hyderabadi society that no one else had. Whenever Indians met, there was always an undercurrent of communalism. You could almost see people thinking to themselves "This person is a Muslim", "This person is a brahmin", or whatever. Centuries of communal frictions percolated just under the surface at all times. These created barriers which restricted how people could move and interact socially.

I was free to move in all communities! I was usually the first American that people had ever met. I did not belong to any Indian community, so there was no history of communal frictions. I was not British, so there was no leftover ill-will from India's imperial past. Hyderabad was well off the hippy trail, so there was no history here. Furthermore, this was before the days of globalisation, so the culturally insensitive, greedy, corporate Americans, had not yet made their way to India. I was a novelty, and I was the universal *mehman* (guest). As a *mehman*, I was given all courtesies that were possible to extend to a person.

Unwittingly I had been exercising this freedom of social mobility for some time, but now I recognised this consciously. I knew that this represented a unique opportunity for me to learn. If I used this freedom carefully I could get an insight into a broad spectrum of Indian worldviews. But with this sudden recognition came a certain apprehension. I could only expect the courtesies of the *mehman* to extend so far. I had to be very careful otherwise a misstep on my part could have serious repercussions.

Communal tensions suddenly became very real to me. I was close enough that I could see the dynamics of these tensions. But I was also close enough to get burned.

Chapter 46
Rameeza Bee

Burning - burning - burning - buildings burned not more than a few hundred metres from my house. I sat on the roof watching the orange sky pulsating to some inscrutable *danse de la morte* of political conflict. In this dance everyone had their part. The soldiers on the streets, the police barricaded in their stations, the youths with their Molotov cocktails, everyone participated in this grand and erie *danse macbre*.

My world contracted to the size of the Kirtane compound. With such a small sense of space, a person could have been hacked to death a hundred yards from my doorstep, and I would neither have known nor cared. It would have been as distant for me psychologically, as it is for a person to hear about some bombing that occurs on the opposite side of the earth. But the few times that I did venture out, what I saw made a deep impression on me. These small excursions made it difficult to continue dissociating myself from what was going on.

During the daytime when the curfew was relaxed, Meena Alexander and I went out to see what we could see. The streets were strewn with stones, and buildings were burned. Very few businesses could function in the four hours that the curfew was relaxed.

These surrealistic scenes moved all of us. Meena Alexander later used this as the central event in her novel *Nampally Road*. Now, I am relating it here. I doubt that anyone who lived in Hyderabad during this period was unaffected by these events in some way.

You must be curious as to how all of these things started. These were the "Rameeza Bee" riots that gripped Hyderabad in 1978. This was a popular uprising that was fuelled by strong Hindu/Muslim communal tensions.

It all began a few days earlier on March 29, 1978. Rameeza Bee, along with her husband Ahmed Hussain, went to a second show of the Telugu film *Yamagola*. After the show, they were coming back in a cycle rikshaw. At about 1:00a.m. near the Government Fever Hospital, they stopped the rikshaw so that Ahmed could relieve himself. At that point, constables arrested Rameeza on suspicion of prostitution. She was detained at the Adikmet police station, which was under the Nallakunta jurisdiction. While in custody of the police, she was raped by sub-inspector Surender Singh, constable Mohammed Sultan, and constable Mohammed Khaja. At about 6:00a.m., March 30th, she was taken to her home where the police took her husband Ahmed Hussain and another person named Imam Saheb back to the police station. At the police station, Rameeza Bee informed her husband that she had been raped. He became incensed at the violation of his wife, and got into a fight with the police. Obviously it was no match, and the police severely beat him. They took him back to his home about noon. The police broke into a box, took four hundred rupees, and then departed.

Ahmed was left in such a critical state from the beatings that his condition continued to decline. Under the advice of friends he was taken to the Government Fever Hospital, which was not far from their house. But this was to no avail. At about 4:00p.m., he was officially pronounced dead.

This sort of thing is reprehensible, but unfortunately it was not unusual in India. Yet this time the environment was ripe for a backlash.

His body was taken home that evening, but the matter was far from over. Members of the family and the community decided to take the body to the Nallakunta Police station and demand justice. The police were unresponsive. Thereupon thousands of people showed up to protest, and in anger they began stoning the police station.

The next day the situation escalated. Students at Osmania University boycotted their classes. A march on the police station was organised, but they never reached their destination. Before arriving, they were intercepted by the police with tear gas and *lathis* (weapons, made of large bamboo sticks sometimes topped with metal). This attack on the students outraged other students across the area, and in retaliation police were attacked wherever they encountered the public.

Rage from years of angst was unleashed. Rameeza Bee was backed by a number of leftist organisations as well as the local feminist organisation, *Stree Shakti Sanghatana*. She was also backed by the Islamic fundamentalist group *Majlis-e-Ittehad-ul Mussalmeen*, this was natural considering the fact that she was Muslim. But this last backing introduced Hindu/Muslim tensions.

The peoples' demand was simple, the police officers should be arrested for rape and murder. However, the response from the Inspector General of Police was that such an action would "demoralise" the police force. Needless to say, this enraged the populace even more. To make matters worse, the Chenna Reddy government (i.e., the state government) also refused to arrest the concerned policemen. Not only did the authorities refuse to hold the police accountable, they gave the police *carte blanche* to deal with the situation with a heavy hand. These actions created even further resentment.

This was when I realised that something completely out of the ordinary was happening. I followed the story in the newspapers, but things were escalating faster than the newspapers could cover them. Therefore the details were not very clear. The preceding points didn't emerge until the release of the Muktadar Commission's Findings many months later.

Unrest spread very quickly. Crowds as large as 22,000 assembled. The police station was attacked and set on fire. The police responded by opening fire on the crowds. According to "official" estimates, nine people were killed, and an undisclosed number of people were wounded. Over the next few days, tension spread to neighbouring districts. Agitations broke out in Nizamabad, and Karimnagar. There were protests in Visakhapatnam and Vijaywada. Virtually every part of Andhra Pradesh experienced tension.

The backing of the Islamic organisation *Majlis-e-Ittehadul Mussalmeen* signalled a change in the tone of the uprising. Where the tensions in other districts had the colour of a secular popular uprising, the involvement of the *Majlis* gave the Hyderabad agitations a different quality. It quickly changed from a police/community issue into a Hindu/Muslim conflict. For Hyderabad's sizeable Muslim population, it was now a case of Muslim subjugation at the hands of a Hindu dominated political structure. This was countered by Hindu fundamentalists who held the view that this was just a case of Muslims getting uppity over the minor abuse of a prostitute in their custody.

The riots went on for days. A twenty-hour-a-day curfew went into effect, and the army was called in to maintain order.

Ultimately, the situation came under control. The authorities finally submitted to allowing the arrest of the concerned officers. If this had been done immediately, perhaps many lives could have been saved. There are no reliable figures as to how many people were killed, nor is there any reliable information as to the extent of property damage. Curfews were lifted on a locality by locality basis. Our house in Troop Bazaar had the curfew lifted after about a week, but there were areas of the Old City (the area with the highest Muslim concentration) that remained under curfew for up to fifty days.

But the Rameeza Bee riots were like inkblot tests. Just as these test allow you to see what you want to see, in the same way, this uprising has been examined and re-examined by historians, each with very different interpretations. Marxists and others on the left tend to frame it in terms of a popular revolt arising out of years of class exploitation. Muslims tend to look at it as an uprising that occurred when people finally rose up against the inactivity of a Hindu-dominated political structure in response to an attack on members of their community. Feminists often look upon this as the birth of India's modern feminist political struggle. Hindu fundamentalists generally look upon it as an example of lower-class Muslims being stirred up over a relatively minor event in order to suit the political agenda of the *Majlis*. I feel that all of these points have validity, but attempting to fit this uprising into any particular ideology is pointless. It just happened!

Moving On

I was in my room as I had been weeks before. Then the room was dark except for the dim light of a kerosene lamp, now the electricity was on, and the fan was working. I was busy transcribing tabla compositions into a large ledger. Everything was back to normal.

Perhaps that was the trouble, everything WAS back to normal. The city was scarred by the incident, but Hyderabad bore the scars of centuries of kings, conquerors, and conspiracies. The Rameeza Bee incident was just one more. These scars never really went away, but buried themselves, often unconsciously, into the psyche of the people.

But I couldn't really spend too much time on these thoughts. Dhananjay came in and indicated that it was time for us to go. We were meeting Ram and Suhas for diner. So I closed my ledger and prepared to leave.

Chapter 47
The Emergency

"One of the darkest periods of Indian history began in 1971; but at the time, no one knew it," Ram said. This aroused my curiosity, so I waited to hear what he was referring to. But the conversation was interrupted by a waiter who came to our table.

Myself, Ram, Dhananjay, and his cousin Suhas were in Mohini's. This was a restaurant in Basheer Bagh which specialised in Punjabi food. The waiter had just come to take our order, so we had to wait to hear what Ram was going to say.

The ambiance was familiar. The lights were dim. There were two sections in which one could eat. There was a lower section where our table was, and there was a balcony in which families ate. A cassette recorder behind the proprietor's desk played. "*Kabhi kabhi... mere dil mei... Kheyal ata hai....*" Mukesh sang this for the 100,000th time. He died just a couple years earlier, but his songs kept right on going. It seemed as though Mukesh's ghost was locked in a prison of magnetic tape, and cursed to sing the song for all eternity. This was a curse to rival that of Tantalus, or Sisyphus. The waiter took our order and then went back to the kitchen. Yes, it was a familiar and comfortable environment.

It was the perfect place to carry on a casual conversation about politics. But with Ram political conversations were seldom casual. He was very knowledgable about the subject.

"As I was saying," Ram continued, "1971 was the the year that there were national elections. Indira Gandhi was the incumbent Prime Minister, and her party, the Congress Party, easily retained its majority in the *Lok Sabha*. The margin of victory was very high, so few doubted that the will of the people had been properly carried out."

"So what was the problem?" I asked.

Indira Gandhi

"There were widespread allegations of fraud and other irregularities," said Ram. "That was the problem. These allegations found their way to court, and in 1975 the Allahabad High court found Indira Gandhi guilty of 'misuse of governmental machinery'. The court declared that her election was null, and ordered her unseated from her *Lok Sabha* seat. Furthermore, she was banned from contesting any election for six years. This judgment essentially removed her from the position of Prime Minister."

"So then what happened?" I asked.

"She responded in a way that was typical of her style," continued Ram. "She refused to step down as Prime Minister. But her refusal to honour the decision of the Allahabad high court threw India into a constitutional crisis. Indira Gandhi continued to rule the country in spite of the fact that she had lost all legal claim to the position. Agitations for her to step down spread far and wide. Under pressure from Indira Gandhi, president Fakhruddin Ahmed declared a "State of Emergency." This went into effect at midnight on June 25, 1975, really June 26th for all practical purposes. Her party, which was the Congress Party, then passed a number of laws and constitutional amendments that brought the whole country under her control. All civil liberties ceased, the rule of law ceased, and Indira Gandhi ruled by decree."

My thoughts turned to the Emergency. I remembered it well, for it was only a couple of years earlier that I arrived in the midst of it.

"She ordered massive arrests," Ram continued. "The leaders of the opposition parties were the first to be rounded up. But then they worked their way down to the point where anyone suspected of opposing Indira Gandhi was thrown in jail. The exact number is still debated. Some say that 140,000 people were imprisoned, other estimates place the number of arrests at close to a million. Many of the arrested had no official charges, and an unfortunate number died in detention under 'mysterious circumstances'."

I placed Ram's words within the framework of my own experiences. Most of my experiences centred around All India Radio. No one dared to broadcast anything critical of her administration. The few who did so faced arrest and imprisonment. All India Radio, and *Door Darshan* (the government television network) were converted into propaganda machines.

I also remembered Indira Gandhi's "20-Point Program." All public buildings were plastered with posters advertising this. This was a series of reforms that were supposed to eliminate poverty and advance the country, neither of which happened. In retrospect it is clear that this was nothing but a public relations gimmick intended to generate popular support for her totalitarian administration.

"But the worst of all was that badmash son of hers," said Ram as my attention returned to his impromptu discourse. "Sanjay Gandhi was his name. He had no real position other than being the head of the Youth Congress..."

I had to mull over this last point a bit. I gathered that being head of the "Youth Congress" was somewhat comparable to being the head of the "Young Republicans" back in the US.

"... yet Sanjay Gandhi was the second most powerful person in the country. His whims became law. Around him no woman was safe, and no property was secure. Anything he wanted, he just took. If anyone needed any work done, they had to go through him to get to his mother. His most notable excesses were the expulsion of poor people from the slums near the Turkman Gate in Delhi, and widespread forced sterilisations as part of his family planning measures."

The conversation drifted on to other topics. Although the talk ended, the subject of Indian politics still echoed in my mind.

I arrived in September of 1976, and the Emergency ended in March 1977. Therefore I was in India for 6 of the 21 months that the Emergency was in force. One would think that this would give me a strong impression. Actually, my impressions were not as strong as they could have been. I had never seen any India except the one under Indira Gandhi, so I had nothing to compare it with.

I was only able to get a perspective on the the Emergency after it was over. All things considered, it was a mixed bag. Trains ran on time during the Emergency. (This was the same thing said about Mussolini). Public order was much greater. But that is the extent of any positive comments that I can make. Things could not continue under Indira Gandhi's despotic rule. It was often said that bribery and corruption in the bureaucracy was down. This may be true, but all that meant was that corruption from non-Congress Party officials disappeared. Within her own party, I feel that nothing changed.

When Indira Gandhi was voted out of power in 1977, there was great jubilation. Many people felt that Morarji Desai and the Janata Party would fix all of India's problems. Yet this didn't happen, and the Janata Party seemed to have no agenda other than opposition to the Emergency. Therefore, three years and two prime ministers later, Indira Gandhi was re-elected.

But how did all this happen? What was the political framework in which the Emergency was possible? What was the political history that led up to this? Perhaps most importantly, how can I construct a paragraph entirely of rhetorical questions?

That evening in bed, I thought about the discussions that we had earlier. I got into my *khurta* and *lungi*, tucked the mosquito net securely under all sides of the mattress, and was ready to go to sleep. I lay there reflecting upon the discussion we had earlier.

It occurred to me that politics played a part in every country's identity, yet it was probably more important in India. Possibly the only thing more important than politics, was the food that one gave pet dogs. Dog food? No - that was not right. I was very sleepy and my thoughts were became erratically connected. With that, my thoughts quickly became even more incoherent and I slipped into a deep,.... deep, ... oblivious sleep................................

Chapter 48
Indian National Identity

I was out of the house early. Normally, there was nothing going on Sunday mornings, but today I had a very specific objective. I remembered well the conversation with Ram the night before, and I was determined to get some information. I exited the gate of the Kirtane compound, and made my way past the ancient tree which stood at the Troop Bazaar bus stop, past the barber shop. There was a string of small shops, but these were all shuttered and closed. Most of the footpath dwellers had awaken, and started their day's activities. The morning air was clean. The streets were calm - almost quite. It was a stunningly beautiful Sunday morning.

I walked, zigzagging my way between the foot path and the dusty road. I chose my path to avoid obstacles. When I was on the footpath, the very ground itself provided obstacles. It was uneven at places because it was composed of a random mix of rough cut stones and cement. These had to be traversed with care, or I might trip. Most people walked in the street, but this had the obvious problem of placing one in danger of traffic.

At one point I came across an aged bullock. He was thin and weak, and had scars etched into the skin at the boney protuberances on his hips and shoulders. These scars were the only reminder of the years that he spent pulling a cart and plough. A spot of red *kumkum* adorned the centre of his light grey forehead. He lay there in the road opposite the Grand Hotel, completely unconcerned about the activity around him. His deep dark eyes stared into nothingness as he chewed his cud. His only other activity was an arrhythmic swishing of the tail to ward off flies.

The bullock had become too old to pull a cart. The owner was not able to continue feeding him, but he was unwilling to kill the beast. So the bullock was given to the temple. He wandered around the vicinity living off food that Hindus in the area would bring. He would do so for the rest of his life, but this might not be too long. Hyderabad had a large Muslim population who had no hesitation about eating beef. It was common for trucks to go in the middle of the night and round up these cattle as they slept. They were then taken to butchers and sold. The meat was poor quality, but it was cheap, and would feed some of Hyderabad's poor Muslims one day.

I left the bull and made my way to Abid Circle. This was a large traffic circle about twenty metres in diameter. There was a somewhat pitiful attempt at a garden in the centre of this circle. Its perpetually brown, nearly flowerless plants, struggled against the toxic exhaust of vehicles and the irregular attention paid by the municipal workers.

Abid's was surprisingly free of traffic that morning. Two policemen were sitting next to the book stall in front of the GPO (General Post Office). They were chit-chatting and relaxing since they didn't have anything to do. A few people could be seen going in and out of the *masjid* across from the GPO. The circle itself had a few people going around in bicycles, cycle rikshaws, and scooters.

I reached my destination, it was the Sunday morning book bazaar. The epicentre of this bazaar was the area in front of a posh *sari* shop known as *Meena Bazaar*. I saw scores of people sitting along the footpath in front of shuttered shops. They laid out books and were selling them.

There were second hand books on every topic imaginable. There were school textbooks, books on film songs, and religious works. There were books on social issues put out by the Communists. There were Western magazines interspersed with *Illustrated Weeklies*. For people who had more daring tastes, a few discrete inquiries would lead to copies of *Playboy* magazine which had been smuggled into the country. Everything was there.

But I was not there just to buy any book, I was specifically looking for history books. I knew that if I wanted to make sense of India's present political system, I needed to know something about its political past.

I bought several books and took them home to read. There was a lot of information on topics that were more than a thousand years ago. This was interesting, but clearly irrelevant to contemporary politics. The more relevant sections began with European involvement in South Asia.

After weeks of reading, several things became clear to me. For instance it was the European concept of "India" that was pivotal to India's political evolution. But this concept was a product of European ignorance. The British were generally oblivious to the complex ethnic, linguistic, and tribal identities of their South Asian subjects. They simply called South Asia "India", as if a single name could cover the multitude of kingdoms in this area. Even the name "India" reflected a British linguistic limitation. A very large portion of the British population could not say the "h" sound. Therefore, when they tried to say "Hind" (e.g., Hindi, Hindu) it came out as "Ind", which soon became "India".

This brought up a very powerful question. "If the concept of India was the result of European ignorance, then why did the Indian population embrace it?" I asked myself this for a long time, but no answer was forthcoming. As it turned out the answer was simple, it was a political necessity. But to understand why it was necessary, I had to go back to a time before "Indians" embraced the concept of "India."

In the middle of the nineteenth century, British imperialism was taking its toll on South Asia. A combination of meddlesome missionaries, economic iniquities, stifling tariffs, and annexations of territories by the British, created a lot of ill will. Tensions increased until the subcontinent exploded in the "Uprising of 1857" (a.k.a. "Sepoy Mutiny", or the "Indian Rebellion of 1857").

Initially, the uprising was very successful. The number of British in India was small, so they were very quickly killed, captured, or driven away. But after these initial military successes, the Indians found themselves in a "now what?" situation. There was no clear concept of an *Azaad-e-Hind* (Independent India), so everyone just sat around waiting for the British to send over troops. And that is exactly what happened. The Crown sent over forces and put down the uprising in a very brutal manner.

After the suppression of the Uprising, Great Britain decided that it was going to hold India under tight control. The reasons for this were complex and involved many economic considerations. Some of the reasons revolved around the need for cotton for Britain's textile industry. But there was also the need to expand markets for British manufactured goods. But in the process of consolidating India into the empire, Britain embarked upon an effort to Anglicise the subcontinent. The Indian Civil Service (now known as the Civil Services of India, of which the IAS is a major component) was expanded into a massive bureaucratic machine.

But this gigantic bureaucracy required many English speaking Indians. Therefore, English-medium schools were established throughout the subcontinent to fill this demand.

These European-styled schools with their emphasis on the English language had a profound impact upon Indian society. One of the curious consequences was that they unintentionally unified South Asia. Throughout India, the newly created middle class now had English as a common language. Furthermore, they shared a common set of worldviews imparted by this education. Two of these European concepts would have an important impact upon the history of the subcontinent. One of these was the concept of "India", and the other was the concept of nationalism.

The European concept of nationalism was becoming popular. This was the idea that an ethnic group was best served when they had their own nation. This was considered to be a great step forward, because it freed people from the whims and abuses of the old colonial system. The Indian intelligentsia readily embraced this concept.

But there was a problem with Indian nationalism. India was not like France, Germany, or Poland. There were Marathas, Punjabis, Bengalis and a host of other ethnic groups, but there were no ethnic "Indians." This placed nationalistic aspirations on a very weak foundation. The political intelligentsia realised that one of the reasons that the Uprising of 1857 failed was because there was no concept of a unified, independent India. They were determined that this mistake would not be repeated.

But the task of forging an Indian sense of national identity was not an easy thing to do. What was the commonality between the diverse ethnic groups? After all, the majority of the people (*janata*) did not have the benefits of a European-styled education, so the concept of Indian nationalism was too abstract for many people.

Many advocated using Hinduism to create a sense of national identity. Organisations such as *Brahmo Samaj, Rashtriya Swayamsevak Sangh*, and the *Arya Samaj* actively pursued this approach. Superficially, this seemed the most workable approach, but the more astute among the intelligentsia realised that this could be counter-productive. It automatically alienated India's sizeable Muslim populations. The Gandhians were particularly noted for their rejection of the concept of a Hindu nation, and strongly advocated for a secular state.

While the concept of a Hindu nation was rejected by the Indian National Congress, the damage was already done. Large numbers of Indian Muslims felt alienated, and they responded by supporting the All India Muslim League. This was an organisation that was created in 1906.

The Indian National Congress continued advocate for a secular state, while the Muslim League pushed for a separate Islamic state. Partition proved to be unavoidable, and in 1947 India and Pakistan were both born. This was a particularly bloody affair, one whose political repercussions are still being felt.

My readings cleared up many things, but they also created one very nagging question. If Hinduism was rejected as a mode of defining a national identity, then what took its place? Clearly language and ethnicity were out of the question. Music and arts were safe and used to a great extent, but they were not enough to create a strong visceral concept of national identity.

Then the answer hit me . The concept of "India" was based upon nothing... absolutely nothing at all! It was based entirely upon arbitrary borders imposed by the British!

This epiphany that "India" was based upon nothing, cleared up a lot of questions that I had encountered in my readings. I found it disconcerting that there was a disconnect between the facts and figures in the Indian history books, and the not-so-subtle underlying messages. There was an inordinate amount of time spent discussing the empires of old. But if you looked at the numbers and dates involved, they only covered a very small portion of India's history. These empires were aberrations and not the norm. Similarities between ethnic groups were exaggerated or fabricated, and differences were downplayed. It was clear that the biases in the Indian history books were attempts to foster the concept of India as historically being a unified entity, even though this was contrary to the facts.

But I also knew that my view was very unpopular. Generations of Indians were raised and indoctrinated to reject this. They were raised with a "circus hall of mirrors" approach to history, and they didn't see the disconnect between the subtextual messages and the historical facts.

I am the first to admit that acceptance of India's fragmentary origin is a very dangerous view. The political embrace of this must logically lead to regionalism and separatism. In South Asia, divisive political philosophies invariably create instability, riots, and the death of many innocent people. But unfortunately, it was the only objectively defensible view that could be derived from Indian history.

I didn't know it at the time, but in the coming decades the dubious origins of the concept of "India" would become irrelevant. An "Indian" ethnicity would be created, it would become self perpetuating, and strong. It would come to be reflected in Bollywood films and Mumbai film Hindi. It would be reflected in "Zee-TV", and Indian "MTV". Throughout India, the modern generation would acquire a common upbringing and a set of world views to a degree never seen before. The mavens of popular culture would accomplish what generations of political intelligentsia were unable to. In the end, it would not really matter that "Indian" culture was barely more than a century old.

Chapter 49
Relationships

I put down my copy of *A Brief History of India*, by Dr. R.C. Majumdar, as the train pulled into Secunderabad Station. Indian history was very interesting, and I had been pouring over theses books for weeks. But railway platforms were interesting too.

Krishna Giri, Seetha Devi, and myself were on our way to Madras. The trip was just beginning. We left Nampally station only a few miles back, but Secunderabad station was more of an alternate starting point for this train rather than a middle stop. Therefore, we were going to be here a while. There were a lot of passengers milling about the train platform.

Why would passengers wander about the platform when they knew they were leaving? Actually there were a number of reasons. To begin with, no one ever knew when a train would actually leave. This was openly acknowledged when timetables sometimes declared that a train would not leave BEFORE a stated time, rather than the worldwide custom of stating that a train would leave ON a time. Therefore, people would while away the time on the platform attending to other things.

On the edge of the platform, a young mother was assisting her two year old son in passing urine. He stood there bowlegged as all two year olds are. His mother pulled down his crude knickers as he passed urine from the platform. The small boy was obviously Hindu due to his lack of circumcision, and he had a black string tied around his plump infantile stomach. He was wearing a cotton shirt with crude and obviously unlicensed Disney characters printed on it.

Twenty feet away was a water fountain, where a middle aged Telugu man filled a plastic bottle with water. He was wearing *khurta* with a *kanduwa* draped over his shoulder. He also wore an impractically long *dhoti*, as was the fashion for *zamindars* and village heads. This may have been a mere affectation.

A hawker with a pushcart slowly moved up and down the platform chanting "Chips, Cool Drinks - Chips Cool Drinks ...."

A traveler engaged a ticket collector over the details of his ticket. The traveler's agitated demeanour was in sharp contrast to the disinterested detachment of the railway official.

Coolies rushed back and forth with luggage skilfully perched upon their turbaned heads. Their faded red turbans matched the coarse red cotton shirts that they wore upon their torsos. Conspicuous brass medallions declared to all that they were fully approved by the railways.

I fixed my attention on a group of people standing a few yards from the train. There were fifteen people there to say goodbye to just one couple. This was a common custom. Railway officials kept the situation under control by selling platform tickets. You had to buy one of these tickets so that you could accompany your friends and relatives to see them off. The rationale being that if one charged people to go to the platform, one could keep the number of people milling about to a controllable level.

I was well into my second year in India and became adept at assessing people's communities. This group of people were Gujaratis as evidenced both by the way the women wore their *saris* as well as bits of speech that would rise above the din of the platform. They had bundles of cloth that were clearly merchandise and not for personal use, therefore I surmised that they were in the cloth/clothing business.

But more interestingly was the easy way of telling the relationships of the people in the group. One could tell who was a daughter-in-law, who was a son, mother, father, etc. These relationships were virtually stamped upon their foreheads. You could tell by their speech, their demeanour, and their dress.

I reflected upon the nature of relationships. These were the foundation for their world views. Some relationships, such as the mother attending to her two year old son, were universal. Sometimes people played out dramas that were dictated by temporary relationships, such as the tense interaction between the ticket collector and the traveler. There were efforts to influence relationships, as evidenced by the impractically long *dhoti* of the man filling the water bottle. Even the coolies were placing themselves in temporary, but well defined relationships.

The Indian and Western approaches to relationships were fundamentally different. Where Western society was viewed as a collection of individuals, Indian society was highly structured, and people viewed themselves as being part of an extended, complex, and very ridged matrix. I too became part of this matrix.

My initial position in the Indian worldview was that of a *mehman*. The word *mehman* means "guest", this was a very honoured position. Every courtesy and consideration was extended to me. But my position as a *mehman* was not a permanently sustainable one. As time went on there were unconscious efforts to reposition me in a framework that was more sustainable. One key to this was the way I addressed other people.

Terms of endearment were important in defining relationships, and they were especially important in my integration into Indian society. After some time I started referring to people in terms such as *Ayi* (Marathi for "mother"), *bhai* (Hindi/Urdu for "brother"), *Pinni* (Telugu for "maternal aunt"), etc. These were more than mere terms of endearment, because they defined the manner in which I related to people.

I think that most Westerners may find this a hard concept to accept. How do you look upon someone as brother, sister, aunt, etc., who has no blood relationship to you? I might like to remind you that you probably look upon your pet as being a child in your family. This is not any type of psychopathology, but merely acknowledges that we are biologically indisposed to any visceral feelings of symbiosis. But traditional familial concepts easily accommodate these relationships with our animals. It is the same way in India with people. These people became my aunts, and uncles, and I became their nephew, brother, etc., because these were the most applicable relationships available within the Indian mindset.

Now this placed responsibilities on me. By adopting these terms and their implied relationships, it entailed certain obligations, responsibilities, and modes of behaviour on my part. I had to learn and observe these.

Sometimes terms of endearment created problems for people. Over the years, I met a number of people who were involved in love marriages. When the boy and girl first started to move together, typically they would refer to each other by terms such as *bhai* (brother) or *bahen* (sister). However, as the relationship turned amorous, these terms automatically raised feelings of guilt associated with incest, even though there was no actual blood relationship. Even after marriage, Indians who were involved in a love marriage have a high incidences of unusual interactions. This may be in the form of wives addressing their husband by name, unusual terms of endearment, and similar things.

"*Wooooooooooooooo... whooot...*" the train whistle blew. Within seconds the train started to move. This movement was quiet and barely perceptible at first, but quickly started to accelerate. Everywhere people ran to open doors of the bogies, and there was much commotion. The railway platform filled with a cacophony of goodbyes in half a dozen languages. There was an arrhythmic "*tak, tak, tak*" as the wheels encountered the transitions from one rail to another. The train gradually increased its speed as it moved on towards the *Rel Neelayam*. I knew that soon after the train passed Lalaguda, the gentle murmur would be replaced by a deafening roar.

My journey continued.

Chapter 50
A Chilly Morning

"This cycle rikshaw looks like it might collapse at any time," I thought to myself. But I was not in the mood to be choosy. I just wanted to get back to the Kirtane house with a minimum of fuss. The trip to Madras went fine. I returned to Hyderabad, but left Seetha Devi and Krishna Giri back in Madras. Now, I was standing in front of Nampally station negotiating a rikshaw.

"*Khali Hai Kya*?" I enquired of the *rikshawalla* to see if he was free. There was some negotiation, then we agreed upon a price. I knew that it was a rupee higher than it should be, but I really didn't care. The fact that I was a *pardeshi* in this city guaranteed that I would always pay more for things than a local. Besides, he was a poor man, and I didn't feel right about pushing the negotiations too hard. I was only going about four furlongs (1/2 mile), so it wasn't far.

It was a surprisingly chilly morning. This was one of the few times in the year that sweaters were necessary. Although it was barely sunrise, there were a few people on the street. They wore their sweaters, shawls, gloves, and caps, and were behaving like they had suddenly found themselves in an Antarctic winter. I found this amusing. For me, all I needed was a sweater, but I suppose we had very different standards as to what constituted cold.

Many people purchased their winter clothing from Tibetans who sold their wares on the footpath. These Tibetans were a displaced community. They came as refugees to India when the Chinese took over their country in the late 1950s. Even though there was an entire generation of Tibetans who had no knowledge of any country other than India, they could not vote nor participate in the political process. They showed up in Hyderabad during November and December and made their living selling woollen garments. During the rest of the year, they went back to the north.

The cycle rikshaw ride from Nampally Station to Troop Bazaar was very pleasant. It was very early in the morning, so there was virtually no traffic, no noise, and no pollution. I made sure that the *rikshawalla* folded the covering so that I had full access to the clean morning air. This covering of wood, bamboo, and Rexene may have been useful during the rainy season; but this time of year it was primarily for Muslim women so that that they could be obscured from public view. When deployed it made the rikshaw very cramped. What may have been comfortable for a five-foot one Hyderabadi lady, just didn't work with my five foot ten American body.

I sat there as the rikshaw slowly made its way home, and I reflected upon things. The journey back from Madras, negotiating rikshaws, handling all the small details of the journey, it all became very easy for me. Just a couple of years earlier, I would have found this very stressful.

"Did India change this much in a couple of years?" I halfway thought, but then stopped due to the absurdity of the proposition. No, India didn't change - I changed. I changed a lot!

I felt that my psychological integration into Indian society proceeded in three stages. The first stage was one of being overwhelmed. The second stage was characterised by a complete breakdown of my sense of self. This third and final stage of my reacculturation was one of stability. For me, this stage lasted from my second year onwards.

But what had changed? Why was I finding India so much easier?

The answer lay in my sense of self identity. I developed a triadic model of my self identity, this helped me keep track of the changes that I was going through. Before I moved to India, my sense of self was whole. But when I moved to India, I felt this shatter. These pieces began to reform themselves, but when they did, they came together into three loosely connected parts. On one hand there was my American self, this was a collection of roles, language, conventions, and worldviews that I acquired from childhood. The second part of my self identity was my Indian one. This too was a collection of worldviews, language, and conventions, but ones that allowed me to function in India. The third aspect of my self identity was my personal one. This was my core sense of self, one which was stripped of all role playing and conventions imposed by either society. This trifurcation of my sense of self was not easy, nor was it voluntary.

A variegated sense of self identity is not unusual. It is very common for individuals to have one persona at work and another at home. This is not a question of psychopathology, but merely a way of functioning within two very different environments. The only thing unusual about my situation was that the differences were much more extreme.

The first two years were the most difficult. I had a hard time during my brief trips back to the US. I was unable to carry on conversations with people that I had known for years, for there was no longer anything in common between us. Simple social interactions were an exhausting affair. Looking back, I think that it was difficult because my original sense of self had been broken down, but I had not yet developed a fully functional new one. Later it all worked out, and this marked the point that signalled the start of the third phase of my reacculturation.

My somewhat pointless self examination was brought to a stop as the cycle rikshaw pulled up to the ancient tree by the Troop Bazaar bus stop. I paid the *rikshawalla* and entered the gate of the Kirtane compound.

I sat down for a quick *chai*, whereupon Kamal handed me a chit. This small note was from Ram informing me that he would have to cancel meeting with me in the afternoon. There was not much explanation, only that something came up that he needed to attend to.

Chapter 51
Ram's Tea Party

Ram's family looked over the living room of Lalitha's flat. They wanted to find a wife for Ram, and Lalitha's family came well recommended. They knew that you could tell a lot about a girl simply by looking at her home environment.

A large black and white picture of a man was on the wall. The man's overall appearance was old. He had his hair cut in a way that no one in the 70's did, and he had a gigantic caste mark on his forehead. This picture had been very clumsily colourised by hand. Unfortunately over the years, all the colours faded except for the blue. This effect simply added to the crudeness of the endeavour. It rested only inches below the ceiling, and leaned out from the wall at a steep angle. A dusty garland fashioned from shavings of sandalwood adorned the picture and informed all visitors that this person was dead. Presumably it was the girl's grand-father.

There was a refrigerator in the living room. Although the kitchen was the logical place to put it, refrigerators were very expensive, so Lalitha's family wanted every visitor to see that they had one. It worked, Ram's family was suitably impressed.

Other items were on display. There was a Godrej *almirah* in the living room. There was also a table upon which was a "two-in-one", combination cassette player and radio. It was very large and obviously of Japanese manufacture. Since it was foreign made, it must have cost a lot of money. There was a small doily partially draped over it. It was hard to say whether the doily was there as a vain attempt to reduce dust, or to venerate this imported luxury.

A commercially available poster of infants adorned one wall. It was garishly coloured and the infants were grotesquely stylised, but most Indians considered them to be cute. This poster epitomised a common Indian aesthetic. It was kitsch presented in a totally unapologetic manner.

But Ram's family looked over the flat and they did not perceive it to be a cluttered collection of kitsch. In their eyes, it represented a reasonably well established and stable middle class family. It radiated the same middle class mores that Ram was raised in. If a match were to be made, this girl would probably have no trouble settling into their family.

Ram, his father, and mother, were in the living room of Lalitha's house in Zamistanpur. Lalitha sat with her husband, daughter, and son.

Many in the West find the concept of arranged marriage difficult to understand. However it all makes sense when one keeps a simple fact in mind. In the West, marriage is considered to be the union of two individuals, while in India, marriage is considered to be the union of two families.

But the fact that marriage was a community event, didn't mean that everything was conducted in the open. There was a need for secrecy. The reason for the secrecy was clear. Should the negotiations fall through, people in the community would engage in embarrassing speculations as to what was wrong with various parties. The negotiations were kept so secret, it was as though this part of their life was kept locked away in a Godrej *almirah*, where almost no one could see it.

"This really feels awkward!" Ram thought to himself. But he knew he shouldn't say anything.

"You know, my son has the highest sales in his division at work, isn't that right *Babu*?" said Ram's father.

"Yes, *Nana*, last month I turned over two lakhs in orders," replied Ram with feigned enthusiasm.

Ram looked at the girl sitting eight feet from him, but he was not impressed. He thought to himself, "She hasn't said a word. Maybe she can't speak. Maybe she's a deaf mute, and her family is trying to pass her off onto me so she will be my problem. Maybe her tongue was torn out by wild animals when she was a child." But upon careful reflection this didn't seem likely. She was probably just demure. But then it was more likely that she was just pretending to be demure.

"Ram is expecting to get an enhancement in pay within the next six months," said his father.

Ram nodded in agreement, but his mind was actually on the girl. "Look at that face. I've seen prettier faces on a camel," he thought.

"You know my daughter graduated with a B.Com in the top of her class," said Lalitha's husband.

"I'm now trying to get a job with the Tatas," said Lalitha's daughter.

Ram thought to himself. "Ok, so she's not a deaf mute. Actually she has quite a nice voice."

But there was another point that was understood by all parties with this last statement. Getting a Bachelor of Commerce degree was acceptable, but traditional families would be uncomfortable with their daughter-in-law pursuing a career outside the home. Lalitha's family was sending a signal that they were more modern and progressive in regards to their daughter's professional goals.

Lalitha and her daughter retired to the kitchen to prepare tea and snacks.

Immediately, all eyes in Ram's family focused on the girl. Did she limp? Did she seem healthy? Everything seemed to be ok.

The departure of Lalitha and her daughter signalled a lull in the activities. It allowed Ram to reflect upon the things which lead up to this tea party.

Getting the Word Out

The first efforts at finding a match for Ram took place some time back. Initially they tried the most common method, these were other marriages. At such functions, there were hundreds of people from Ram's community. In these marriages, the *mausis* (aunts) spent hours discussing who had marriageable children and examined the suitability of hypothetical matches. All manner of considerations were discussed. "She's too tall." "He's OK, but his features are not good." "He makes a lot of money." "She is much darker than him." Such discussions always resulted in ideas as to what would make a good match. Some recommendations made their way back to Ram's family, but they just didn't seem to lead anywhere. So the family had to look elsewhere.

They decided to contact a marriage broker. There have been professional matchmakers in India for centuries. In the past they were usually brahmin pandits who maintained lists of marriageable boys and girls. They made referrals based upon both astrological considerations as well as more mundane criteria. The nature of this business was evolving. In the old days, simple paper files were all that were necessary. By the time I was in Hyderabad, there was a publication that was nothing but matrimonial ads. These were all carefully organised by community and gender. There were also the matrimonial ads in the newspaper. Ram couldn't know this at the time, but by the turn of the 21st century, this business would move onto the Internet with sites such as Shaadi.com or BharatMatrimony.com.

It turned out that Ram's family didn't really need to contact a marriage broker. As soon as Shekhar discovered they were serious about finding a match, he remembered his distant aunt Lalitha. After a few initial discussions between Ram's father and Lalitha's husband, they decided that they should introduce the boy and the girl. That lead to the tea party.

The Tea Party Continues

Lalitha's daughter served tea and snacks.

"You know my daughter made these sweets by herself," declared Lalitha.

However, Ram thought they were uncannily similar to the sweets from G. Pulla Reddy. The marriage market was definitely governed by *caveat emptor*. However, Ram wasn't too concerned about the sweets, it just occurred to him that Lalitha's daughter really had a nice figure.

The parents too may have noticed that the girl had a nice figure. But they were taking this as being only a part of a number of basic operating parameters.

"I understand that your daughter is twenty-three," said Ram's mother. "Ram is twenty seven" she continued. This would actually correlate to twenty-two and twenty-six by American reckoning. This reflected the Indian habit of counting the year in which one was living, and not the years completed. But the important point was to emphasise that this was a comfortable age gap. In previous generations even a ten or fifteen year gap was considered to be acceptable, but by the 1970s, two to five years was considered to be the optimum.

There was more chit-chat, whereupon Lalitha's daughter got up to remove the cups and dishes. This time, Ram's family looked to see how tall she was. She should be shorter than him, but not by too much.

Both families eyed Ram and the girl carefully in regards to their skin colour. Indians were very colour conscious, and fair skin was always desirable in a mate. Obviously, it was not possible for both parties to be fairer than each other, so it boiled down to who had the upper hand in marriage negotiations. In almost every case, the boy's family had the upper hand. Since Indian families are patrilineal in their focus, the tendency was to seek girls who were fair. Therefore, with advancing generations, the family would become more lighter-skinned.

Ram's family was satisfied with the complexion of Lalitha's daughter. However, there was a touch of subterfuge in these regard. She had been using a commercial skin whitener called "Fair & Lovely" for some time now.

"You know my son is active at the *Ramakrishna Math*," said Ram's mother. This was not entirely true. He had been pressured to go since childhood, but Ram avoided it whenever he could.

There was always a tendency to portray one's own family as being slightly more orthodox than it really was. This was to convince the other family that yours was a respectable family. Still, most people didn't want to represent themselves as being too orthodox. This sort of thing could fail on two accounts. First of all, it was a pretence that would fail under the slightest scrutiny. Secondly, most people were smart enough to realise that with extreme orthodoxy came rigidity. brahmins were much more likely to exaggerate their orthodoxy than other communities.

"Did you see *Mukti*? What did you think about it?" Ram asked Lalitha's daughter.

"I really think that Mithun Chakraborty is an incredible actor. I think that he's going to go far," she replied.

The conversation continued on the topic of films, actors, and actresses. This was totally inconsequential, but it did allow them to relax a bit. Both Ram and Lalitha's daughter were temporarily relived of the pressure of being on display.

"She is easy to talk to, and she seems smart too," Ram thought to himself.

The relaxed atmosphere did not continue indefinitely. Ram's father enquired as to the *gotram* of Lalitha's family. Although they tried to slip it into the conversation in an unobtrusive manner the purpose was clear. A proper marriage should only be performed if their *gotrams* were different.

For Hindus, the system of *gotram*, also known as *gotra*, was a parallel caste system. But marriage within the same *gotram* was prohibited. This was in contrast to the caste system, where marriage within the same caste was the norm.

Although *gotram* deterred a certain number of consanguineous marriages, it did not address the root cause of inbreeding. The main cause of the problem was from the way that matrilineal lines were ignored in defining families. In other words, a man could not marry his father's-brother's-daughter because this was considered to be incest. But first cousin marriages on the mother's side were considered acceptable, because they were not considered to be in the same family. Not only was it considered to be acceptable, but these first-cousin marriages were actually encouraged, sometimes with unfortunate consequences.

The meeting became even more tense when Lalitha's father asked, "How do you feel about dowry." This topic was the most delicate part of the negotiations.

"We are not really concerned with dowry," replied Ram's father. "But I am sure that you may wish to make some gifts to the couple."

This was an evasive answer that meant absolutely nothing. It was clear that this topic would have to be put off for later.

"You know that our daughter studied *Kuchipudi*," said Lalitha as she pulled out a picture album showing a dance recital of her daughter. In the South, a girl should have some skill in music or dance. This generally was not a requirement for north Indian communities, and was often a disqualification.

Ram and the girl discussed different topics. Suddenly from an open window, the light of the setting sun reflected off the back of the girl's raven black hair. He noticed the graceful asymmetric manner that she, like all Indian women assumed when wearing *sari*. The sparkle from the brocade captured his attention, and led his eyes, ever so discretely, to the feminine contours of her blouse. Ram saw this and something inside him stirred.

"How could I have compared her face to a camel. She's actually quite attractive," he thought to himself.

Shortly before Ram and his family left Lalitha's house, his parents discretely asked Ram if they should proceed in the negotiations. He indicated that they could.

Ram's family asked Lalitha's family if they wanted to come over sometime for dinner. They waited, knowing the significance of the answer. They agreed - the talks would continue.

Chapter 52
The Hindu Marriage

"These are very beautiful girls," I thought to myself. A pair of attractive young girls stood at the entrance to greet the wedding guests. This was Ram's wedding, and the girls were Lalitha's nieces. They were about seventeen years of age and wearing full-*saris*. Their age and community was such that I suspect they were more used to wearing half-*saris*, but in their full-*saris* they still carried themselves well. They had their hair in a single plait which ran down their back, upon which was a string of jasmine flowers. This was a style that was normally reserved for married women. These made them appear older than they actually were. They welcomed the guests by sprinkling everyone with rose water from small, delicate, and intricately engraved silver gulabdanis.

I entered the *shamiyana* where the marriage was taking place. This was a very large tent, in many ways it resembled a small circus tent. Two large gnarly poles in the middle supported the covering. Its sides were green cloth and had the most garish appliqués of yellow and red patterns. There was a very thick, rugged, woven cloth covering the ground. It was originally red, but from long abuse it had faded to a rust colour. Florescent lights clung to polls in a tenuous manner, held in place only by a few turns of bailing wire.

As I entered the *shamiyana*, I saw many people I had never seen in my life. But I knew that even Ram had never met many of the guests. It was always a joke that complete strangers could walk into any marriage. If they were dressed appropriately and pretended that they knew people, they could eat their fill of fine food, give their *ashirvaad* to the couple, go away, and no one would ever be the wiser.

A handful of friends such as myself were from outside of Ram's community, but by and large it was a community event. This would be interesting, because each community had their own marriage customs. There might be hundreds of different styles of weddings in India.

Ram's was a fairly typical south Indian Hindu wedding. It had been going on for several days, and would continue for one more. This was in sharp contrast to Christian and Muslim weddings which tended to be only one day. Both Christian and Islamic weddings were essentially just the cleric asking the bride and groom if they wished to marry, and then asking if anyone in the community had any objections. Hindu weddings on the other hand, were extremely convoluted. They involved numerous aspects of Hindu worldviews on the nature of marriage, the nature of life, the universe, and everything. (No, the answer was not 42.)

Ram, Lalitha, and other members of their family were at the opposite end of the *shamiyana*. They sat upon a small stage known as a *mandapam*. This stood about two feet off the ground. At four corners of the stage were heavy wooden poles. Fresh palm leaves were woven around these pillars in an intricate fashion. These pillars supported a covering that was a bamboo lattice with flowers and leaves. Tinsel and metal foil floral decorations, placed at artistically appropriate places, decorated the entire *mandapam* and gave a nice *chamak*.

The whole area resounded with the most incredible din. Ancient horn speakers that were crudely wired to the poles, blasted the area with the chanting of the *poojari*. Lulls in the services were then filled with popular film songs. A generator too added to the din. The marriage was in a residential area, not an industrial one. Consequently, the electricity had already been shut off for a few hours. The roaring generator assured that the noise of the horn speakers would continue. But all of this racket was further augmented by the wedding musicians. Two *nadaswaram* players and a person playing a drum known as a *tavil*, sat upon separate dais about fifteen feet from the *mandapam*. There was hardly anyone who enjoyed Indian music as much as I, but the sounds which emanated from this band could barely be considered to be music. It was obvious that volume was more important than intonation. One would think that with all of this cacophony, it would make conversation impossible. But no, this did not deter the guests. Everyone was determined to ignore the wedding and carry on with their chitchat.

There was nothing unusual in the way that everyone ignored the wedding ceremonies. These climaxed a series of functions which had been going on for days. Maintaining the discipline of a Western wedding for anything more than an hour was simply not possible.

"David *bhai*", said Shekhar. "*Aao bhai* - Come sit over here."

I joined him at a corner. We sat upon the faded red cloth covering. There were hardly more than four or five folding chairs in the whole place. These were reserved for the oldest guests whose infirmities would not allow them to sit directly on the ground. All the attendees took off their sandals before entering the *shamiyana*, but there was still an uncomfortable level of sand scattered around. I didn't pay too much attention, because I realised that the arid Hyderabad conditions were such that sand got into everything.

"The *shaadi* started about 4:00 in the morning," Shekhar informed me. "But there were other functions over the last few days."

I remembered that there were three overall sections to Hindu weddings. The first section was a series of pre-wedding functions that were intended to prepare the bride and groom. These included such things as an official arrival of the groom, and a public declaration of the agreement of all parties for the match. Then there were the wedding ceremonies proper, this was what was happening when I arrived. Finally, there were ceremonies related to the groom's family taking the girl to their house.

Hindu weddings were a restaurant menu of activities. Families chose what activities they wished to incorporate and what activities they wanted to leave out. These decisions were based upon community traditions, the number of days the wedding took place, as well as individual preferences of the families involved.

I saw Ram sitting in the *mandapam* in front of me. He was dressed in a cream coloured silk *khurta*. He, his father, mother, Lalitha, her daughter, Lalitha's husband, and the *poojari* were all on stage with him. The *poojari* alternated between Sanskrit shlokas and Telugu explanations of what was going on. I knew neither Telugu nor Sanskrit so it was all inscrutable to me, but I did catch the overall theme. It was a *kanyadaan*. The term literally meant "to give a maiden", and implied that Lalitha's family was giving the bride to the Ram's family.

Another friend of Shekhar's came and sat with us.

"Did you hear what happened last night?" the friend said. "Two of Ram's uncles got into a fight."

"*Aare yaar*, tell me the *khas-baat*," replied Shekhar, as he pumped his friend for details.

"It seems that they were off drinking last night," said the friend, "After a while, they just started fighting." The conversation continued in *Hindlish* with a simple gist. When hundreds of people got together, it was unrealistic to expect that everybody would be in complete harmony. Sometimes marriages brought individuals together in the same way one might bring roosters together for a cockfight. In the case of Ram's uncles, there was animosity due to a dispute over the division of property at the death of their grandfather. Even though this was more than 30 years ago, the combination of alcohol and long standing frictions, produced a fight. The family tried to hush up the matter, but it was already a topic of much *bakwas*.

Even the drinking was done somewhat surreptitiously in Ram's community. In almost every Indian wedding, many of the men-folk go off in the evening for some drinks. Obviously with so many men indulging in this, one could not expect everyone to be controlled in their consumption. It was normal to find a few people drinking to excess, occasionally with embarrassing results.

Suddenly everyone's attention was on Ram. He got up from the *mandapam*, put on his shoes, and headed for the exit. Lalitha's husband, and son stopped him and enquired what was going on. He declared that he didn't want to get married! He was going to renounce the world, take *sanyas*, and go to the holy city of Benares. There was a lull in the chitchat as people started to pay attention. One would think that these declarations at such an awkward time would provoke great consternation, but this was expected, and was all part of their community's tradition. Lalitha's brother and cousins then explained that there were particular duties (*samskars*) that were attached to the various phases of one's life. They further informed him that to take *sanyas* now would be very inappropriate, because it was his duty to become *grihastha*, and assume the responsibilities of taking care of a family. After a reasonable amount of time, Ram then feigned acquiescence, and returned to the *mandapam*.

The rituals continued. Occasionally someone popped onto the *mandapam* and either brought something or took something away, all of this was under the direction of the *poojari*. The *tavil/nadasvaram* group periodically punctuated theses rituals by honking out some noise.

There was some commotion near the *mandapam*. This caused everyone to stop socialising and see what was happening. Ram, under direction of the *poojari*, tried to leave the *mandapam* to get something. But upon attempting to leave, he realised that Lalitha's nieces had stolen his shoes. Ram protested in great indignation, or at least mock indignation, because this too was all a tradition in their community. These girls taunted Ram and demanded an exorbitant amount of ransom. After much commotion, they agreed upon a sum of money, whereupon Ram was given his shoes back.

"Hey Shekhar," I asked of my friend, "What's the reason for all of this silliness?

"There are many reasons," Shekhar patiently replied, "Remember these are not just two people getting married, but two families. Marriage negotiations are very tense. There are many disagreements over the particulars of the dowry, wedding expenses, and things like that. These little games may seem silly, but they help diffuse tensions left over from these negotiations. But this isn't the only reason. There are a lot of games left over from the days of child marriages. In the old days, when the bride and groom were mere children, these games encouraged them to get to know each other. For instance, the bride and groom often pour rice over each other's head. Sometimes a ring or similar item is buried in a pot of rice and both the bride and groom stick their hands in to see who can retrieve it first."

"*Dam... Dam... Dam... Dam...,*" the *tavil* beat and the *nadaswarams* once again interrupted our talk. More rituals continued. Clarified butter was poured into a small squarish iron vessel that was located in the centre of the *mandapam*. This vessel was known as an istra, and the sacrifices to the fire god Agni were some of the oldest Hindu rituals.

After some time, the *poojari* placed the ceremonies on hold for a few hours. People began to mill about, some went outside to carry on their discussions.

They were preparing for lunch. Servants laid out long rolls of white cloth upon the faded red covering. Others went around placing banana leaves at even intervals in two rows across the white cloth. These banana leaves functioned like paper plates, they would be used once and then discarded. Other servants quickly followed behind with buckets of white rice, tamarind rice, *dal*, eggplant curry, and various condiments. People sat down on the ground and started eating. But the serving continued, as another person came around with a mixture of rice and curds (*perugu-annam*). Finally someone came by with a sweet mixture of vermicelli and milk, this was known as *payasam*.

There was an order to which the various dishes were served. Although the order varied from community to community, eating something out of order would always raise eyebrows. I suppose it would be comparable to a Westerner starting the meal with the dessert, then eating the main dish, then finishing up with a salad.

It was a very sumptuous lunch and all were satisfied... or at least most people were satisfied.

Some *mausis* were sitting just diagonally from me. Their conversation ebbed and flowed between English, Hyderabadi, and Telugu.

"Look how *kanjus* they are with the ghee!" One *mausi* said, complaining that she did not get enough clarified butter. "Last year at Krishnam Raju's son's wedding, the food was much better."

"I know," said the second *mausi*. "This wedding is ok, but that one was much better. If they had just asked me, I would have told them how it is supposed to be done."

I was taken aback by these comments. These were my friends. They had a lot of nerve to come here, eat their food, and at the same time make comments like this. But they were my elders, so I was in no position to say anything. Furthermore, I knew that it wouldn't matter how glorious the fare was, they probably would have made some kind of comment. There were always a few people like this to be found at any wedding.

Kawab-me-hadi was an expression often used to describe them. This expression literally meant "A bone in the kabob". The implication was that no matter how nice something was, there would always be somebody to spoil it.

We finished our meal and got up to make room for the next round of people to be served. The final order of business was to wash our hands. For this purpose, wash basins stood just outside the tent. These resembled free standing cabinets that were about four feet high. They were garishly painted, and had the name of the company emblazoned upon them. Spigots and small basins that were incorporated into their design were the only indication of their function.

The lunch break ended and servants cleaned everything. The afternoon ceremonies commenced. There were several things going on in this session, but only a few really important ones. Still these were the most important ceremonies.

One of the ceremonies was the exchange of garlands. For this, the bride and groom placed garlands around each other's necks.

Another important event was the tying of the *mangalsutra*. This is a pendant, or according to many communities a pair of pendants, which the boy tied around the girl's neck with a length of yellow thread. According to tradition, she must wear the *mangalsutra* as long as she and her husband were alive. (Although after a few days the thread is replaced by a gold chain, usually with black beads.)

Yet still another important part of the Hindu ceremony was the circumambulation. For this, the girl tied the end of her *sari* (the *pallu*) to the boy's garment. Together, they circled seven times around the fire.

The evening came and Ram was married. We congratulated the couple and then I returned to Troop Bazaar.

There were activities for the following day. These included the *appagintalu* (a.k.a. *vidai*) and revolved around the boy's family taking the girl to their home. In the past when people were married as children, the girl would have stayed with her parents until she "matured", at which point the *appagintalu* would occur. There may have been several years gap between the wedding and the time the girl went to her in-laws house. However the *appagintalu* simply evolved into the end of the marriage ceremonies.

But there was no need for me to go to this, this was really just a family function. My part in all of this was finished.

My Journey

I reflected upon my journey through life, especially my time in India. Ram's wedding especially resonated in my mind. Ram was just slightly older than I. Many of my friends were married. My younger sister was already married and a mother of two children. I was coming to the age where I needed to think about these matters.

Chapter 53
Finding a Wife

"We'll have to find a nice Indian girl for you," I heard elders say. I heard this right from my first week in India, usually in a joking manner. But as I neared the completion of my second year in India, it became less of a joke.

Ram's marriage caused me to think about the whole subject of marriage. I was approaching twenty-five, which was the average age for a boy to be married in those days. The topic frequently came up in discussions with others. During my stay in India, I realised that the whole dating system of the US didn't amount to anything. I had friends who had gone together all through high school, through college, then married, but divorced within a year. It was clear that getting to know your partner guaranteed absolutely nothing. Conversely, divorce was extremely rare in India. All Indian marriages were not necessarily perfect, but on balance it was clear that they were doing something right. Therefore, I decided that I would go for it.

Once I made it clear that I would consider an arranged marriage, the machinery was set in motion. Vinjamuri Seetha Devi and Dr. Kirtane were the main people in this regard. They immediately went to work in several different directions.

The Initial Meetings

I don't know how many initial contacts were made on my behalf. As was typical, most initial contacts never made it past the first step. The only thing that I had any knowledge about were those potential matches that were serious enough for me to have met the girl. If memory serves me well, there were about five girls that I met. Two of which I have only the vaguest recollection of, so I really have nothing to relate.

There was one girl I do remember something about. She responded to the ad that was placed in the *Deccan Chronicle*. She was a Tamilian Catholic girl. She was not a *mulki* Hyderabadi, but she spoke Urdu with a pure, "old city" accent. Her family had been in Hyderabad for a long time, and she was raised in the Charminar area. For some inexplicable reason, on the day of our meeting, she chose to wear a *sari* for the first time. She was obviously uncomfortable in it. To make matters worse, at one point as she was walking, she stepped on the leading edge of her *sari*'s hem and the whole *sari* came unpleated. I know this was very embarrassing for her. She had come to Dr. Kirtane's house without her parent's knowledge. In these matters it was very important to have the input, support, and involvement of the rest of the family. I didn't feel like getting into any situations that might be difficult, so we didn't continue the discussions. Nevertheless, I was very impressed by her independence. I hope that she did well in her life.

There was one other girl that really looked like the match would work. She was a Maharashtrian brahmin girl who was well known to a close friend of Dr. Kirtane. Her father was a widower living on the outskirts of Secunderabad. Meetings went on for a while, but ultimately this match did not develop due to objections from family members.

Oh well, we would continue looking. Besides, there were some prerequisites that needed to be attended to. One of which was a horoscope.

Chapter 54
The Horoscope

"*U-phoo*, some people have no common sense!" Dr. Kirtane exclaimed, "How am I supposed to get the car out?" She saw that there was no way around the crates which blocked her exit. These crates were filled with partially assembled bicycles. She honked her horn... she honked still a few more times. Finally, the proprietor of the cycle shop sent a *chokra*, to move the crates.

Dr. Kirtane and I pulled the Premier Padmini out of the compound and onto the road. The Padmini was not a fancy car, but it was in good condition. In those days, there were only two choices for cars. There was the Padmini and there was the Ambassador. The Ambassador was virtually a required vehicle for a politician, while ordinary rich folk often went for the Padmini. I say "rich" because you had to be rich to have any kind of car at all.

This morning we were off to the astrologer's house. No Indian marriage was attempted without a horoscope. Therefore, it was time to take care of this important matter.

We took off toward Lingampally. It was 8:00 in the morning, and although all of Hyderabad had been up for hours, there was very little traffic on the roads. But then why should there be? Only the schools, vegetable markets, and a few isolated businesses were open. Lingampally was not far from the Kirtane house in Troop Bazaar, but the layout of roads forced us to take a circuitous route.

We arrived at the house of the astrologer. As usual, parking was a challenge. We first dislodged a nanny goat and her kid who had ensconced themselves in our intended parking space, then pulled up to an electrical pole that was located in front of the astrologer's house. The house had a small veranda with a metal grill (*jali*) to separate it from the street. This *jali* was made of numerous small steel strips about a foot in length and somewhat less than an inch wide. They were bent in a variety of swirls and circles, but welded together in such a way that the grill assumed a large floral pattern. This grill was immediately on the street, so there was a cloth curtain on the inside. This provided both privacy, as well as a means to reduce the amount of road dust coming into the house.

We tried ringing a doorbell. It was a square block about one inch by two inches located at head's height. It had an ivory coloured, spring loaded, rocker switch mounted in it. In the middle of this switch was the image of a small stylised bell etched in red. Unfortunately, this doorbell proved useless, because the electricity had been shut off. This was normal. Still, our presence was already known to a person sitting in the veranda. He was a dark man in his late twenties, and was wearing a white undershirt and a printed *lungi*. He opened the door of the veranda. This door was made entirely of a steel grill in the same style as the rest of the veranda.

The person in the *lungi* had no connection with the astrologer. In Hyderabad, people made extensions to their property and rented them out in a haphazard fashion. He and his family rented the front portion of the dwelling while the astrologer's family lived in the back portion. I tried to imagine what it would be like in the West to have to pass through someone else's apartment just to access your own. I encountered this arrangement many times in India, but no one ever seemed to be bothered by it.

Dr. Kirtane and myself climbed a flight of stairs to see the astrologer. He was a thin but healthy looking brahmin in his mid fifties. He lived with his wife, grown son, daughter-in-law, and small grand-child. He knew Dr Kirtane, and treated her with a mixture of affection and great respect.

Dr. Kirtane explained the reason for our coming. He asked me the usual questions about both the time as well as the place of my birth. Then he looked at my palms. I doubt that the palms were relevant to astrology, but it was clear that he just wanted another perspective. After some more socialising, he told me to come back later for my horoscope and an analysis.

I went back after a few days, received an explanation of both my past lives as well as my prospects for the future, and was given my horoscope. It felt like I was being given a diploma. I paid the agreed upon sum and took the papers. This important marriage prerequisite was now taken care of.

There was a standard procedure for handling horoscopes while negotiating a wedding. Families exchanged either birth information or complete horoscopes, which were taken to their respective astrologers. It was the astrologer's duty to do two things. First and foremost, he had to select an auspicious date and time (*muhurtham*) for the wedding. Secondly, the astrologer gave an opinion as to the compatibility of the two horoscopes. In the old days, an incompatibility was sufficient to cancel the wedding plans. However in my lifetime, I never saw this happen.

Sometimes there was a problem (*dosh*) with a horoscope. Generally there was a *yagna* (religious ceremony), that could be performed to deal with the matter.

But during marriage negotiations any number of problems could arise. For instance, there were heightened intelligence gathering on both sides. Friends and family discreetly scoured the entire locality, hunting for any "dirt" they might find on the opposite party. Did the girl have any boyfriends before marriage? Did the boy drink, or have any other bad habits? Furthermore, there were tense discussions concerning dowry and other financial aspects of the marriage.

If something went wrong, a *dosh* in the horoscope came in handy. One could always claim that the boy, girl, etc. were all fine, but due to an incompatibility in the horoscopes, they needed to bring all marriage plans to a stop. This would not insult the opposite family, nor would it "air their dirty laundry" to the whole community. I saw this tactic used on more than one occasion. Unfortunately, I know of at least one case where it should have been used to cancel a marriage, but was not. The most notable was the marriage of Kundula Nagbani.

Chapter 55
Dowry

"Will these people ever stop tormenting me?" Nagbani thought to herself. "All they ever think about is money.... money... money."

Nagbani was a beautiful young girl with deep dark brown eyes, and jet black hair. Two years ago, she was like any other sixteen year-old. She attended school, joked with her classmates, and was very happy. She had loving and doting parents. When her parents came and told her that they were fixing a marriage with the Kundulas in the next town, she did not really think too much about it.

Nagbani first sensed that things were not going well during the marriage negotiations. These negotiations involved things such as marriage expenses, but more importantly, it involved the dowry.

Tradition dictated that she would enter her husband's home with three types of property. There was the *streedhan*. This was property that belonged to her. It was her insurance so that if something ever went wrong with the marriage, she would not be completely penniless. There was also the *saare*, or household items that were jointly owned. Finally, there was the *dahej*, known in Telugu as *katnam*. This was property that was given to the boy's family and would be retained by them even if the marriage dissolved. It was this latter *katnam* that was the cause of contention.

She sometimes wondered why her family had to give dowry. She had seen *Lambadi* women, and knew that in that community it was the men who had to give money to the girl's family. Yet throughout India, it was the general custom that the girl's side gave money to the groom's family.

Nagbani's future in-laws made demands upon her father that were hard to meet. But there was nothing that her family could do about it. Things had progressed too far to back out of the marriage. The wedding invitations had been sent. If they broke things off now, their family would become the laughing stock of the community. Besides, this sort of thing was common. Everyone assured her that once the marriage was done, everything would be okay.

But after she came into her husband's home, things did not improve. Her in-laws began to pester her. As per the original negotiations, Nagbani's family paid 50,000 rupees and 15 sovereigns of gold to her in-laws. They kept this locked away in a large Godrej *almirah*. But the major contentions were some of her father's agricultural lands and an outstanding debt of 35 sovereigns of gold. Her father did agree to put the agricultural lands in her name, but this did not satisfy the avarice of her in-laws.

"Are you going to sit there all day, you useless girl?" exclaimed her mother-in-law. "Wash those dishes."

Nagbani's mother-in-law was Kundula Annapurna. Right from the moment Nagbani moved into the house, she behaved as though it were her god-given duty to make life hell for the young Nagbani.

Nagbani's husband merely watched as his mother scolded and abused his wife. His name was Kundula Bala Subrahmaniam. He was not particularly bad, but he was very weak. He was definitely "tied to his mother's *pallu*."

"When I was your age I'd already given birth to a son," Annapurna said accusatively. "What have you done, you worthless thing?"

"*Chi - Anni kastalu!*" Nagbani muttered under her breath as she reflected on her cruel fate.

Nagbani's father had consulted a lawyer when he came to know of her problems. The lawyer told him dowry was theoretically illegal. Dowry was banned by the Dowry Prohibition Act that was passed in 1961.

But the system of dowry couldn't go away because it was linked to inheritance. Under Indian law, inheritance should follow a system of "partible inheritance," where property was equally divided among all the children. But in an agricultural economy like India, this didn't work. If every time a man died the property was divided, within a few generations the land became so small that it would not support a family. This guaranteed starvation! Everyone knew that having property pass undivided to one of the sons was the only way to be sure that it could sustain a family. Usually this was the oldest son. *Primogeniture* the lawyer called it. In this system, daughters inherited nothing. But dowry was a way that a girl could enjoy her portion of her father's wealth while he was still alive. Dowry was supposed to assure that a daughter's standard of living remained high even after marriage.

Yet, Nagbani did not feel that her standard of living was high. Everyday was filled with hellish abuse.

"Nagbani, what is this?" exclaimed Annapurna as she held up a stack of letters. "Have you been conspiring with that shameless family of yours?"

Nagbani was indeed in correspondence with her family, but in a very surreptitious manner. She wrote letters and secretly gave them to her neighbour. All of these were in Hindi, because her in-laws knew only Telugu. These letters detailed the abuse that she had been suffering.

"*Nee Amma* ..., Answer me! What have you been telling your parents?" demanded Annapurna.

Another fight ensued. This was not itself unusual except for one thing. This time Annapurna went to the kitchen, and brought out a steel container of kerosine. This she poured over Nagbani.

"*Babu*, you know what to do?" Annapurna ordered her son. Whereupon Nagbani's husband lit a match, and put it to her kerosine soaked *sari*.

The *sari* immediately burst into flames. Nagbani was overcome by terror and pain. The polyester *sari* melted in the heat, and clung to her young flesh as though it were napalm. She ran to the living room and collapsed on the floor screaming for help. The melting, burning polyester bubbled, turned brown, then black as it enveloped her body.

The room filled with smoke and the most horrible smell. It was a diabolic scent, reminiscent of burning plastic, kerosene, and the smell of burning flesh from the burning grounds.

As Nagbani lay in the living room screaming in agony, the neighbours came in. They immediately saw the situation, and demanded that Nagbani be covered with a blanket to extinguish the flames. But Nagbani's husband and mother-in-law just stood there, waiting for the fire to do its unholy work.

Finally the flames were extinguished. Nagbani lay naked on the living room floor. The fire had burned over 90% of her body. Much of her skin was a black crust. It was very difficult to tell whether this black crust was charred polyester or flesh, as the end result was the same.

"Please tell mother and father as I am telling you. My mother-in-law poured kerosene on me and my husband set fire. You tell father and mother about this. Don't fight. Anyhow, I am dying," Nagbani told her neighbour.

A short time later Kundula Koti Nagbani was dead. She was eighteen years old.

This was not an isolated event. Even today in the 21st century, it is estimated that up to five-thousand young brides a year are either killed or driven to suicide due to dowry disputes.

Chapter 56
Chandrakantha

"I think I know a good girl for you," said Vinjamuri Seetha Devi, "She's a very good singer and comes to AIR a lot." She and her sister Anasuya had been pelting me with names and descriptions of girls until my head was spinning. She asked if I wanted to go see her.

"Sure I'll go see her," I said. Although in all truthfulness, I wasn't really sure which girl or description I had agreed to go see. Still, I saw no reason to object, so we made arrangements to go to her house.

Seetha Devi, Sunandani Eypes, and myself, went to see her one afternoon in September of 1978. The girl's name was Nada Chandrakantha, and her family was living in the Risala Gadda area. The three of us made our way to her lane by auto, but left the auto about a hundred metres from her house. As we came down her lane, there were some pre-adolescent and early adolescent children playing marbles in the lane. With them was a girl of undetermined age wearing a peach coloured *sari*. Seetha Devi discreetly told me that she was Chandrakantha, the girl we had come to see.

Very quickly Chandrakantha, more affectionately known simply as Chandra, recognised Seetha and Sunandani. She got up and told her mother, who was sitting in the veranda in front of their house, that we were coming. Although there was nothing wrong with playing marbles in the lane, proper *maryaada* (respect) demanded that she assume a more dignified manner in the presence of elderly guests. So she got up, waited at the gate, and exchanged a few pleasantries with us. A small ruse was presented to them that we just "happened" to be in the area to meet someone else, but they were not home. As per Indian etiquette, we were invited into the house for *chai*, an invitation that we quickly accepted.

Chandrakantha (circa 1977)

Once inside, there was some idle conversation. During this time Chandra spoke some in Telugu, but hardly any English. I exchanged a few words with her. But it was clear that she had very little knowledge of English, only a smattering of Hindi, and no Urdu. Therefore, there was not really much conversation. At one point I was asked to show what I knew of tabla. They had a pair, so I sat down and played some for them. This appeared to impress them.

The only notable event during this first meeting occurred as we were leaving. Discreetly, Seetha Devi asked me if I was willing to pursue the matter. I saw no reason to break things off, so I indicated that everything seemed okay. Seetha Devi and Sunandani took Chandra's mother aside, and explained the real reason why we came. Immediately her mother's face became ashen in colour and she became very quiet.

I didn't have first hand knowledge of what transpired after the first meeting. It was only much later that I came to understand all the events which followed. When Chandra's father came home, her mother quickly hustled him off to the kitchen for some private discussions. He immediately left to send a telegram to the eldest son who was living in Bangalore. There was a lot of commotion, but no one told Chandra what it was all about. The next day the eldest son came, and this time another meeting was arranged. It was at this point, that Chandra realised that all of this commotion was revolving around her marriage.

This second meeting occurred at Dr. Kirtane's house. This was the first time that we were all there together discussing the match in earnest. After the meeting, everyone in Chandra's house was for the match with the exception of one person, Chandra. She was crying and saying she didn't want to get married, and asking why they were trying to get rid of her. But she was completely outvoted and ignored in all of the commotion of consulting the astrologer, printing wedding invitation cards, and all of the other details.

The position of everyone involved was understandable, but at times conflicting. Chandra had nothing against me, but in general she didn't want to get married. But the family was very concerned about her. One problem was her music. Their community was very conservative and previous potential matches had all demanded that after marriage she should give up public singing. Chandra's family, especially her father, was broad-minded and very supportive of her aspirations towards a musical career. I wanted her to continue singing, so this was a major plus point. The fact that I was not of their community was definitely not desirable. But the Protestant Telugu community was so small that matches outside of this immediate community were much more common than one would normally find. The fact that I was raised Christian, was deemed to be sufficient in their eyes. (This same viewpoint is common among India's Islamic communities as well.)

But there was a much more pressing concern in their family. Chandra was already twenty-four years old and by Indian standards, she was starting to be considered an "old maid". The family was concerned that as she got older and became undesirable in the marriage market, the amount of dowry they would have to pay would increase rapidly. They were very pleased that I was making no demands for dowry.

Chandra in sari

The Nadas

Chandra's family name was Nada. The name was derived from a village from which they came. They belonged to a Telugu Christian community. Before conversion to Christianity, her family belonged to a Hindu community involved in agriculture and weaving.

The immediate family consisted of ten people. There were the father, mother, and eight children, but only five of the children were living at home.

N. Samuel Sundaram and his wife N. Deva Krupavaram (circa 1977)

The head of the family was the father, Nada Samuel Sundaram. He was an exceptionally broad-minded individual. During World War II, he was stationed in the North. Therefore, he was proficient in Hindi, unlike many other members of his community. Due to his college education, he was also very proficient in English. By Indian standards of the time, he was well-traveled and well-educated. He had a sympathy for leftist politics. He had no particular love of preachers, but a respect for the writings of Chinmayananda. During the Second World War, he served in the military as a telegraph operator. From this position, he ultimately made his way into the Indian Post and Telegraph Department. He was one of the most honest people I have ever met. (This trait placed one at a disadvantage if you were working in any Indian government position.) Samuel Sundaram had an isolated position within his family. His world was a highly intellectual one. This made it difficult for the rest of his family to relate to him. He tended to retreat into books. He was a voracious reader, and was knowledgable in a variety of subjects.

The mother was Nada Deva Krupavaram. She was a typical housewife and mother from Machilipatnam. The only language that she had any proficiency in was Telugu. I doubt that she ever stepped foot outside of Andhra Pradesh. She was even hesitant about moving 150 miles (250km) from coastal Andhra to Hyderabad. In her mind, this was like moving to another country. She was good-hearted, nurturing, and matronly; but she never understood the intellectual world that her husband inhabited.

There were eight children. The eldest, Harry Arron, was an engineer living with his wife and daughter in Bangalore. He worked on Soviet-designed MIGs at the Hindustan Aeronautics Limited plant there. Savitri was the second child, she was married with three children and was living in coastal Andhra in the small town of Akividu. There was Moses, who was living with his wife, son, and daughter, again in coastal Andhra. That left five children at home. There was Jayant, who was a very accomplished keyboard player and composer. There was Chandran, a kind, warm soul, and then my fiancé, Chandrakantha. Younger to her was Jaidev, and the youngest of all was Suri. Both of whom were working for the Indian Post and Telegraph Dept. This was the makeup of the family that was to become my *sasural* (in-laws house).

The Nada family home in Machilipatnam

My Marriage

Chandra and I were married on November 9, 1978. This was just six weeks after I first saw her playing marbles in the lane in front of her house. It was an Indian Christian ceremony, so it was a mixture of Western and Hindu influences. There were about 600 people in attendance, so this was considered to be a very modest wedding by Indian standards. On that day when we exchanged garlands, exchanged rings, and I tied the *mangalsutra* to her neck, my life entered a new chapter.

That is how my married life began.

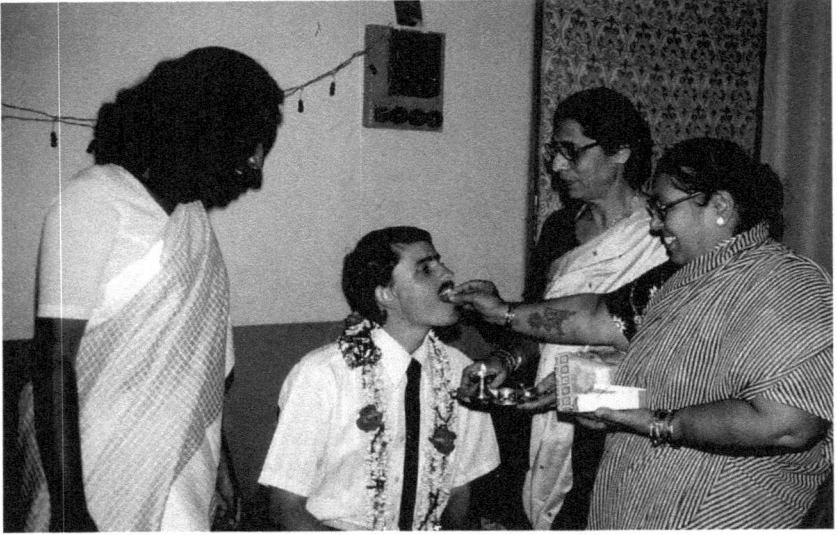

Preparations for my marriage, (lft to rt) Meena Alexander, myself, Dr Kirtane, and Gandi-*mausi*)

Tying *mangalsutra* to Chandra's neck

Chapter 57
Married Life

My married life began in a rather ordinary fashion. Chandra stood in the front of the hall, wearing her white silk *sari* with red border, while I tied the *mangalsutra* around her neck. From that point on we were married. There was the remainder of the ceremony, and some exchanges with the wedding guests, then it was off to Chandra's house for food and socialising. This went on for a few hours, then it was time to take Chandra away. There was some lighthearted exchange as Chandra's girlfriends refused to let her go until I paid money to them. In her community, this was the equivalent of holding the groom's shoes for a ransom. I distributed a small sum of money to Chandra's girlfriends, this freed us to go. Chandra, myself, and a couple of elderly ladies, sat in the back seat of a car, and made our way to a hotel where a room was rented for the evening.

The room for our *suhaag ki raat* was extraordinarily decorated with flowers. One of my closest friends, Krishna Giri had spent a lot of time on it. This floral decoration was a typical Bollywood cliche. But as impressive as it seemed, it looked much better than it felt. In the Bollywood films they never tell you the flowers have small bugs in them which come out and bite you in the night.

The next morning, we took a train to Agra and then on to Delhi. We were off for two reasons. Primarily, we were off to honeymoon in Agra and visit the Taj Mahal. We were also going to Delhi to see my mother off at the airport. After a few days, we returned to Hyderabad.

Honeymoon in Agra at Taj Mahal

We moved into a modest yet comfortable apartment in Mussarambagh. It is located next to Dilsukhnagar on the Vijaywada Highway. (The area where our flat was can be found on Google Earth at 17°22'15.48"N 78°30'55.16"E). Those who are familiar with Hyderabad may be surprised to know that in the 1970s, this was on the absolute outskirts of the city.

Mussarambagh as seen from my front door

I chose this location due to friends. In particular, there was the family of Tangirala Umashankar who was an old friend of mine from Texas A& M University.

The name *Mussarambagh* reflected a curious human habit of contorting unfamiliar words into something familiar. *Mussa-Ram-Bagh* literally means "The Garden of Moses and Rama". However, this didn't reflect the etymology of the name. It was at one time owned by a French arms maker and soldier who used to work for the *Nizam*. His name was "Monsieur Raymond", so quite naturally his estate was known as Monsieur Raymond Bagh. Unfortunately, this was completely unpronounceable to the public, so it was converted into the much more accessible *Mussarambagh*.

Tangirala Umashankar

Mussarambagh was so far from the centre of the city that transportation was sometimes a problem. It was especially difficult to get autos to go there at night. This was generally not a problem, because I had my World War II vintage Norton motorcycle.

I have had many motorcycles in my life, but I never enjoyed one as much as my Norton. I suppose I liked it so much because it had a character. If the character of the Norton could be considered to be a personality, it was definitely an eccentric personality. To begin with, it was not a shiny, pretty vehicle, it still had its original dull military green colour. The sound of its engine was like nothing I had heard before. When running at cruising speed, it did not buzz like most motorcycles do, but instead it emitted a *Dub... Dub...*

Dub..., sound. Furthermore, it was not a smooth rhythmic sound, for it had the most erratic pulse imaginable. When it was idling, it sounded like it was going to die at any instant. However, that was just its normal sound. It was a big vehicle, in fact, I might almost describe it as monstrous. The length from wheel to wheel was roughly that of a VW "bug". If it ever fell over, it was so heavy that it took two people to bring it to an upright position. It had an engine that was so powerful that I was never able to get it up to top speed. Even in the rare situations where I was on an open road, its lack of shock absorbers made it difficult to hang on once I hit 25 mph (40 km/h). But my Norton was not destined to be with me for long. On one of my visits to the US, Chandra sold it and bought a BSA "Bantam". I never liked that vehicle.

Chandra having a meal in the kitchen

Adjusting to Married Life

The first six months was our adjustment period. This is going to be the case with any marriage, but in our case there were some additional adjustments.

One area where we needed to adjust was language. My mother tongue was English, but I was fairly comfortable with Urdu and Hindi, yet I knew very little Telugu. Conversely, Chandra came from a very strong Telugu background with only a smattering of English and Hindi. Therefore, we communicated in a curious mixture of English, Telugu, Urdu, and Hindi. To a great extent, we do the same even today.

Chandra, myself, and the Bantam

I could tell that Chandra was having difficulty adjusting to the outward trappings of being married. In her community, it was a tradition that young girls wore a skirt and blouse. After they "matured" they wore a skirt, blouse, and half-*sari*. After a girl married, she then switched to a full-*sari*. This switch to a full-*sari* was not coming easy for her. Although she was comfortable wearing a full-*sari* in formal situations, she still tended to wear the half-*sari* at home. This was coupled with her retention of the habit of weaving two braids instead of the single plait as was the custom for married women. She did wear the *mangalsutra* and the *mettelu* (toe rings) of a married woman; but, this just created a confusion when mixed with the attire and manner of an unmarried girl. The whole thing was further confusing because, although she was 24 years old, she could have easily passed for 16.

On my part, most of the adjustments were related to typical household activities. These were the usual things, such as paying the utility bills, buying groceries, buying meat from the butcher, and keeping the motorcycle in running order.

I gained a totally different perspective on India after my marriage. This was due to a number of reasons. Some of which were gender oriented and some of which were communal.

From a communal standpoint, my circle of friends changed. Before marriage most of my friends were usually Muslim or Hindu, and Hyderabadi by culture. Yet after marriage, I started to move more closely with an Andhra crowd, many of whom were Christian. This gave me a different perspective on Indian world views.

Another perspective that I gained was a gender oriented one. Before marriage, it was not possible to move freely among members of the opposite sex. Therefore, I really didn't have a clear idea as to women's world views. After marriage I had access, not just to my wife's world views, but also of her girlfriends (*saheli*). There were other things that struck me as interesting, some of which may seem surprisingly simple. I had never before seen anyone wrap a *sari*. I had seen countless *saris*, but never any opportunity to see one being wrapped. I was impressed with the complexity of the process, yet how well it functioned, and how swiftly it could be done. There was one other curious point that I remember. My wife used to put coconut oil in her hair. It was extremely oily, and gave off a strong smell. Being with her was like snuggling up next to a German chocolate cake.

Daily Routine

My daily routine after marriage was not substantially different from what it had been before marriage. I still had my lessons and practice, but added to these were other duties. Some of these revolved around the upkeep of our flat.

Our day began at four o'clock in the morning. This was the time that water came in the pipes. Therefore, we had to get up and fill plastic buckets with water to last us through the day. After the buckets were rinsed and filled, we could return to sleep for a few more hours.

I was also the driver and personal assistant to my wife. Chandra was a very notable singer on TV and All India Radio, so I spent a lot of time chauffeuring her around to rehearsals, TV shootings, and performances. But I enjoyed it.

Chandra's Family

I think that I should say a few more words regarding Chandra's family. They belonged to a Telugu Christian community. In particular, her community was a Telugu Protestant community that had strong Anglican roots. However after Independence, the Anglican Church in India merged with the Methodists and several other Protestant churches to become the Church of South India.

Chandra's family converted from Hinduism into Christianity, during the time of her grandfathers. Chandra's paternal grandfather was a math teacher. I am afraid I do not have much information on his conversion.

Yet the story of Chandra's maternal grandfather's conversion was considerably more colourful. Many years ago, he and his brother got wind that their sister was involved in an illicit love entanglement, therefore the family's honour was at stake. The sister and her paramour escaped to Rangoon in an attempt to elope. But Chandra's grandfather and great uncle followed them there and killed them on the street. This was during the colonial rule, and the British took a dim view of this sort of thing. So Chandra's grandfather and great-uncle became fugitives from justice.

The departure of Chandra's grandfather and great-uncle left the family in a dire situation. Without a man to take care of the family, they fell into destitution. This was when the Christian missionaries intervened and started giving assistance. Shortly thereafter, the family converted to Christianity. At some point things settled down, and Chandra's grandfather and great uncle were able to return. They too converted. After this turbulent period was put behind them, Chandra's grandfather worked in several capacities. One of which was as a motor mechanic, but he also organised *shikars* (hunting safaris) for the British.

Telugu Christians

My marriage to Chandra brought me into close contact with the Telugu Christian community. This Christianity was somewhat of a veneer. Their culture was solidly Hindu, so beliefs in karma and reincarnation were very common. But this created deep personal conflicts as their strong cultural roots collided with the rigid and pathological world views imposed by foreign missionaries. Since they were unable to reconcile these conflicts, it caused them to concentrate on the external trappings of Christianity. On Sunday mornings I saw them going off to church, the women wore their Sunday *saris*, and the men wore their totally impractical black suits. Invariably they clutched big black Bibles and held them as though they were weapons rather than sources of spiritual peace. There was a lot of emotional energy wasted in stupid things such as whether a woman was wearing a *bottu* (*bindhi*, the red dot on a women's forehead). I felt that these were not so much to display their Christianity to others, as to convince themselves that - yes, they really were Christian.

Catholic mass in Secunderabad

Chapter 58
The Apostate

"*Undi*," said Chandra. "I think someone is outside!"

It was about 3:45 in the morning and I was sound asleep. I really didn't want to get up. Besides, I didn't hear anything.

"*Clink... clink...clink...*", came a metallic sound from outside. This time I too heard it.

"*Undi!*" She said again. "I think there's a burglar!"

Nervously we both got up and moved to the door. This door led to a small area which separated our house from the latrine. There was a seven foot wall which enclosed the area. Even though it had shards of glass embedded in cement on top, burglars could still scale the wall, steal brass vessels, and escape to sell them in the bazaar the next day. Chandra grabbed a straw broom, this was a typical response for Indian women. I came from Texas where guns were very common, so the idea of a straw broom being a suitable weapon against a burglar seemed somewhat ludicrous to me.

We both opened the door to the outside.

"*Evaru!*" exclaimed Chandra enquiring as to who was out there. All the time, she was holding the short straw broom as though it were a battle axe. But as we turned on the light, all we saw was a *bandicoot*. We upset his nocturnal foraging, and in panic, the bandicoot escaped through a small opening at the base of the wall.

We both went back to bed. It was not a bed in the Western sense, but really a cot. It had a frame of teakwood and was laced with *nawaar* (lacing) made of a long strip of heavy nylon ribbon. The bed was pulled away from the wall and had all four legs thrust into bowls of water. To do otherwise would allow ants to come crawling into our bed at night.

It was very nearly 4:00 in the morning. I wondered whether I should try to get back to sleep, since I would have to get up and fill plastic buckets with water soon. Otherwise we would have none for the rest of the day.

Normally, I would be the first to get back to sleep after being interrupted in this manner. But on this night, it was Chandra who went back to sleep first. I was busy thinking of things that I needed to pack for my trip to Tirupati. I would be leaving in just a few more hours and there were really a lot of things to take care of.

My mind began to wander. I could hear the sound of lorries coming in from Vijayawada, bound for Hyderabad. There was the sound of some bird which for some inexplicable reason had risen before the sun came up. Chandra lay there asleep with her head upon my right shoulder. She was quiet and still, the only movement was the slow heaving of her breasts as she breathed - in and out. I felt the bangles on her hands, these were always there. The only time she would remove them would be if she became a widow.

It was nearly four years since I moved to India. Suddenly it occurred to me. My life was really rather extraordinary. Everyone that I grew up with was on the opposite side of the world living totally different lives. I seldom entertained such thoughts because they just were not relevant to day-to-day life. But in the stillness of the the pre-dawn hours, I had time to reflect on this.

In order to survive here, I went through a psychological metamorphosis. I had no choice.

"But what was this process called?" I thought to myself. The closest I could come up with was "reacculturation", but it just didn't feel right. So why was there no suitable term? The first thought which came to mind was Sapir-Whorf's Hypothesis. In a nutshell, Sapir-Whorf's Hypothesis states that the only worldviews possible are those that are linguistically determined. According to this hypothesis, the lack of an acceptable term should reflect the fact that the process of reacculturation was an unfamiliar concept. But it shouldn't be unfamiliar. After all, when I moved to India, it was on the heels of half a millennium of European imperialism.

But perhaps it was this imperial mindset that was the key to this linguistic inadequacy. Only a very small percentage of native English-speakers ever went through the process of complete immersion in another culture. This seemed to be especially the case with Americans. When Americans worked for foreign oil companies, there was no effort made to integrate them while abroad. In almost every case, the approach was to create colonies that cut them off from the host country. The military, too, made very little effort to familiarise the soldier with the culture of whatever unlucky resource-rich country the US decided to "liberate." It relied almost totally on translators, often with disastrous results. Hundreds of missionaries and evangelists went abroad and acquired just sufficient cultural skills to allow them to convert the "heathen" local populations, but never enough to integrate.

It occurred to me that the lack of appropriate terms reflected a deep rooted cultural chauvinism. In the centuries of imperial rule, it was always other countries that were supposed to change to fit the requirements of the West. When a Westerner underwent a process of reacculturation in a non-Western land, it was considered to be cultural apostasy. Whenever someone "went native," they were almost always excluded from "polite society."

I was a cultural apostate! That was the answer.

"*Whoosh... chuc... chuc... whoosh... whoosh,*" came a sound from outside. It was about 4:15 in the morning, and water was coming in the taps. There was no telling how long the water would come - maybe half-an-hour, maybe an hour. Chandra and I had to get up and fill the buckets.

Additionally, I had to think about making sure that everything was in order before I left for Tirupati. So there was no time for unproductive ruminations.

Chapter 59
The Pilgrimage

A thousand feet below me, was the town of Tirupati. It was a mid-afternoon in my fourth year of living in India. I, along with a group of about 10 other people, were three-quarters of the way up a hill. We were on our way to the Venkateswara Temple in Tirumala.

Below me, Tirupati looked like a giant jigsaw puzzle. From the air, it was a random jumble of sections. These sections were trapezoidal, triangular, and rectangular, for they had boundaries that were defined by major roads that criss-crossed the town. This gigantic puzzle was punctuated by patches of green, which upon closer examination proved to be trees and clusters of vegetation.

We had all come here to attend the wedding of Rajagopal. But the wedding was to be combined with a pilgrimage to the temple at Tirumala. The presumption was that by doing so, the wedding would have an auspicious start.

We climbed the steps that led up the face of a hill. It was so steep that perhaps it wasn't correct to call it a hill, but a cliff. The gently sloping sections were verdant, with lush tropical plants exuberantly asserting their dominance over the ground. But the steep, rocky portions of the cliff saw only small plants tenuously clinging to soil lodged in the cracks. Thirty yards below me, a hawk floated effortlessly back and fourth along these steep slopes. The hawk was vigilant for signs of potential prey. My perusal of the hawk and the town below was suddenly interrupted by a misstep on my part. Perhaps it was I that should have been more vigilant. These steps were very irregular and demanded my constant attention.

We made the pilgrimage by foot. This trek was only eight kilometres (five miles), but it wound through hills. It is said that those who walked this path would be freed from the delusions of the material world. Was I becoming freed from these delusions? I didn't really know.

We came upon a white stone gate which arched several feet over our heads. It was carved with numerous, small, nameless demigods and goddesses. It was flanked on both sides by short walls to keep people from wandering out, and possibly falling over the edge of the cliff. However, as we came to the walls, we saw that they had been appropriated by a family of monkeys who were siting there grooming each other. We approached the monkeys, whereupon they grew agitated and moved away, chattering and screeching in indignation.

The sun set, but the journey continued. Periodically I heard exclamations of "*Govinda, Goooooooooovinda,*" in a characteristic singsong quality that was unique to this pilgrimage. We continued the trek at a brisk pace. A five mile walk was not a particularly long one, but this was uphill most of the way. At times, it was nearly up the shear face of a cliff, I couldn't help but feel a burning fatigue in my legs.

Our unelected, but completely uncontested leader on this trek was the bridegroom's brother, Desikan. Desikan was a thin man, about forty years old, with prematurely grey hair. He was an intelligent and highly devout brahmin who was of mixed Tamil/Telugu extraction. This ancestry was not so much a reflection of a history of mixed marriages, but the fact that the border districts do not clearly fit into either mainstream Tamil or Telugu cultures. For reasons known only to him, he decided to lead us at a pace that was so brisk that it was almost a trot. I was only 26, so it was not really a problem for me, but I feel that some of the older members of our group were having difficulty. Nevertheless, the group moved on. The firm belief in the *tapasya* (austerity) of the trek, kept people oblivious to physical strain.

It was dark, and this was a jungle. It was not too long ago that people would not make a trek like this at night for fear of tigers or other wild animals. But by the 1970s, the path from Tirupati to Tirumala had so much foot traffic that very few entertained these fears. Finally, we crossed the last summit of our journey, and there stretched below us was Tirumala, the abode of Lord Venkateswara.

The trek to Tirumala was a metaphor for my own journey. The trek was very moving, but the temple itself, with its crude commercialism was disappointing. But that was OK, for me it was the pilgrimage that was important and not the *darshan*. In a similar fashion, I realised that life was the ultimate pilgrimage, and the final destination was unimportant.

But a trek has different sections. I knew deep inside that this portion of my life - my journey - my pilgrimage, was coming to an end.

Chapter 60
Goodbye to India

"We won't need these," I said to Chandra. "I don't even know why we still have them."

Chandra and I were clearing out the contents of a large Godrej *almirah*, that she brought with her at the time of marriage. We were preparing to leave India and emigrate to the US. We had to sift through all of our possessions and decide what needed to be taken with us, what we needed to throw away, and what could be given away to friends and family.

It was 1980, and the financial opportunities were just not attractive enough for us to remain in India. So Chandra and myself made plans to move to the US. Things might have been different had it been 2000 instead of 1980, for by then the economic prospects were much better. But it wasn't, so we boarded a plane bound for Colombo and parts East, and made our way to the US. Although we returned to India many times for varying periods, it would never again be our home.

But it made me reflect upon my journey through life. Four years earlier, a person stepped of the plane in Bombay to live in a new land. That person had the same name as myself, but there the similarity ended. That person died a long time ago. Perhaps he did not die all at once, but he was dead just the same. He was slowly replaced with a new person. This new person was older, but really no wiser. This new person had a different set of world views, a different way of doing things, and a different way of relating to people. Although I didn't know it at the time, this person too would die, only to be replaced with more people.

But this was all part of the journey....

Epilogue

I am sitting on top of a multi-storied building in Secunderabad. It is a large, flat roof, which is typical of apartment buildings in any Indian city. It is completely concrete. There is a small wall along the perimeter that gives a modicum of safety for the children who play there. Wires are strung in random directions. Some wires go to antennas, some connect to satellite dishes, and some wires do not connect to anything. These are clotheslines. Although the roof is flat, there are numerous obstacles under foot. Some are water pipes. There are also small ridges about a foot high traversing the roof. These are the only indication of walls and rooms that lie below.

It is evening, and the sun is beginning to set. I am in a quiet section of West Marredpally, not too far from the cantonment area where Winston Churchill was stationed a century earlier. It is 2009, and more than three decades have passed since that first taxi ride through the streets of Secunderabad on my way to Hyderabad.

My niece Divya, an attractive young women in her early twenties, comes up with some *chai* and some glucose biscuits. "*Mama*, I brought you some *chai*," she says with her typical convent school English.

This is an excuse for me to put down my laptop computer and take in my surroundings. The hot Deccani air is starting to cool off. High above the street level it is surprisingly calm. There is a certain amount of muddy, ill-defined noise emanating from the ground; but the noises up at treetop level are much clearer. I hear a crow that is perched a few yards from where I sit. Children are on the roofs of nearby flats, some are studying, some are playing. On another roof, a women retrieves her *saris* that she laid out in the sun to dry. As she skilfully folds them, I see the crispness of starch. Elsewhere teenage girls are talking about events of the day, oblivious to my presence. There is nothing amazing or earth shattering, it is just life going on.

I am not young any more. The Hyderabad of my youth seems as far away as the India of Winston Churchill. This book is about an India that no longer exists.

I said everything that I needed to say. But I am sure many of you might be curious as to what has transpired in the thirty-some-odd years since I left. This is a sort of "Where are they now?" section.

Lasting Effects of My Reacculturation

Anyone who has gone through this process must accept the fact that for the rest of one's life, there will always be a sense of isolation. I will never be Indian, but I can never again be American. There is always a psychological and experiential gap which separates me from people I meet.

Over the years I have formed my close circle of friends around those who also share a certain sense of isolation. These tend to be people who for one reason or another, are on the edge of society. Some are on the edge by choice. These are people who have made decisions in their lives concerning things such as unpopular political ideologies,"fringe" religious affiliations, or people who are expatriates from a dozens countries. Some of my friends are on the fringe for reasons beyond their control. These are people who have had to deal with gender and sexual preference issues, or Vietnam veterans with post-traumatic stress disorders. Although we have experiential gaps that separate us, we are all united in one way. We have had to deal with our sense of self in a very conscious, and at times painful manner. Although we are all very different people, we celebrate each other's abilities to create lives for ourselves.

But what about my relations with everyone else? The world is full of people who are born, go to school, work, have families, grow old, and die, all according to culturally predetermined scripts. Over the years, I have learned to deal with such people in a cordial manner. I love and respect many of them, but I will never really be able to relate to them. No matter how hard I try, the years that I lived in India create an unbridgeable gap.

India

The India that I described is gone. It was wiped away by a tidal-wave of liberalisation and globalisation. This has produced mixed results.

On the positive side, anything can now be purchased in India. India is awash with consumer-oriented products and services. There are also many more financial, and employment opportunities.

But not everything is on the positive side. The gap between the rich and poor has increased, thus increasing social pressures. These pressures are fuelling the modern Maoists movement, which is an offshoot of the Naxalites. The modern generation of India has been gripped by consumerism and *naqali-shaan*. In the process, attention to human relations, which was always the *forte* of Indian culture, has been weakened. The media is dominated by such entities as M-TV, Zee-TV, and Star, who are putting out such crap that they even rival the American networks in their pursuit of idiocy.

Other People

Indira Gandhi's dirty tricks finally caught up with her. After stirring up trouble for years in the Punjab, her own Punjabi Sikh bodyguards gunned her down on October 31, 1984.

My Ustad Shaik Dawood Khan passed away in 1992. I am grateful for all that he taught me about the tabla.

My *pakhawaj* teacher Zakir Hussain left the Ali Akbar College of Music and is now arguably the most famous exponent of the tabla who has ever lived.

Dr. Gouribai Kirtane, with whom I lived my first two years in India, passed away after a very long and productive life. She was well into her 90s and living in Hyderabad with her son Jayant when she died.

Dr. Kirtane's youngest son Dhananjay is living in Houston, TX.

Kamal, the servant at the Kirtane household, stayed with Dr. Kirtane until Kamal was about seventy years of age. At that point, it was no longer practical to have two elderly women living together in a household like that. So Kamal went to live in a retirement home at Dr. Kirtane's expense. She remains there today.

Meena Alexander is a poet, scholar, and writer of some note. She is a Distinguished Professor at the Hunter College in New York. I particularly would like to bring to your attention her book *Nampally Road*. It is a fictionalised account of life in the Kirtane household during the 1970s. Pivotal to the novel was the Rameeza Bee Incident that crippled the area while we were there.

Kundula Bala Subrahmaniam and his mother Kundula Annapurna were convicted of the murder of Kundula Koti Nagbani and sentenced to life in prison. This is considered to be an important case, because it helped define the admissibility of dying statements in a court of law, thus putting many subsequent dowry death prosecutions on a stronger footing.

Shekhar, my guru-*bhai* was killed in a car accident in the 1990s.

Krishna Giri (a.k.a. Dumbu), son of Anasuya Devi, moved to the US and remains one of my closest friends. He has a charming wife from South Africa named Kalyani and a bright daughter named Anushka.

Anasuya Devi, sister of Vinjamuri Seetha Devi, who was instrumental in both getting my ustad and fixing my marriage, recently celebrated her ninetieth birthday.

Vinjamuri Seetha Devi, who was primarily responsible for fixing my marriage, is in her late eighties, but in declining health.

There have been many changes with my in-laws. Both my father-in-law (Samuel Sundaram) and my mother-in-law (Deva Krupavaram) have passed away. Additionally, three of my brothers-in-law have passed away. On a positive note, Jaidev, my second-to-the-youngest brother-in-law, has immigrated to the US.

My father Cecil J. Courtney, passed away just shy of his 90th birthday.

My mother Jo Anne Courtney passed away in 2001.

Kamaljit Singh Kalsi under whom I first started to learn tabla, is living in California with his wife.

Yashpal Singh Sodhi, who purchased for me my first pair of tabla, is living in retirement with his wife in Washington DC.

Texas A&M University is still there, and it is still very conservative;-)

Henry Poetker of God Has Spoken Ministries left India very suddenly during the mid 1980s. He became involved in a shady property deal. When the authorities got involved, he felt that leaving the country would be a lot better than sticking around to answer a lot of uncomfortable questions.

The *sarangi* artist Sayeed-ur-Rehman is still living in Hyderabad. He is in semi-retirement, but he has a son named Aslam Khan who is a rising artist on the *sarangi*.

Chandra and Myself

As I write this, Chandra and I are coming up on our 33rd wedding anniversary. We have two children. My son Shamsunder Courtney, was born in 1985. He lives in Austin, TX and is a security administrator for an internet hosting company. My daughter Veena Krupa Courtney was born in 1986. She just recently graduated from the University of Hawaii with a degree in Anthropology.

After returning to the US, I became interested in computers. I do a lot of HTML/XHTML work. Our website is averaging about ten million hits per month, and about seven thousand visits per day (as per the user logs). This may be seen at www.chandrakantha.com.

Chandra and myself make a lot of music. I have lost track of how many CDs we have released. In the last few years we have also been making music videos as well. Most of these can be seen on YouTube.

Since 1980, I have done a lot of writing. Most of this writing has been on Indian music.

I feel that I wasted about three years of my life in an external graduate degree program. This is in spite of the very kind mentorship of the late Dr. Marcia Herndon (1941-1997).

I became a freemason. My mother lodge is Deccan #20, Hyderabad India, but I am a joining member of Temple #4 in Houston TX.

In 2002, I could no longer sit quietly by, while the democratic and constitutional government of the US was eroded by George Bush and his gang of criminals. I became active in street level political activism. For several years I was on the steering committee of the Houston Coalition for Justice Not War. We organised protests, teach-ins, and other progressive activities. My duty was the upkeep of the website, which became the central place for information on progressive activities in the Houston area.

During this period I did not make any trips to India. I did not feel that I could travel freely. In 2001 Bush said, "You're either with us or against us in the fight against terror." That officially defined US policy. There was no room for dissension, and anyone who did not unquestioningly follow the regal dictates of the unelected President was officially considered to be a terrorist sympathizer. It was only after Bush left office, that I felt that I could again travel abroad freely.

In 2007 I developed some health problems. I'm not as young as I used to be. However, one coronary stent and three years later, I am okay.

So that is how everything stands.

Glossary

There are a very large number of unfamiliar terms used in this book. I am listing many of them here for the benefit of the readers. Many times these are terms from various Indian languages, but sometimes they are English words that have an special idiomatic usage. This is not an all inclusive dictionary, for most of the words have more meanings than are shown here:

aare - A common Hindi exclamation, which means the same thing as the English "wow!" or "oh!"

aayo papam - A Telugu exclamation which means "poor thing!"

andhra - 1) A person or thing representing the South Indian state of Andhra Pradesh. 2) The Eastern portion of Andhra Pradesh. 3) A person from the Eastern portion of Andhra Pradesh.

anna - An obsolete coinage representing 1/16th of a rupee.

anti-nautch movement - An Indian extension of the social purity movement which swept across Europe and America in the 19th century. The goal of the anti-*nautch* movement was the complete elimination of the devdasi (temple girl) and tawaif from Indian society.

araak - A potent, distilled country liquor, somewhat comparable to American "moonshine."

ashirvaad - Blessings.

ashlar - A large rectangular block of stone used in ashlar masonry, as opposed to brick masonry or rubble masonry.

azaad-e-hind - Independent India, free from foreign rule.

badmash - A scoundrel.

bakr-eid - An Islamic holiday that remembers the time when Abraham (Ibrahim) was asked by God to sacrifice his son. This holiday is marked by the sacrifice of an animal (usually a goat), and the distribution of food to the poor.

basti - A slum, usually made of thatched huts known as *jhopdi*.

bhang - 1) An extract of cannabis. 2) A sweet, milk based drink made with cannabis.

bollywood - The Bombay (Mumbai) based popular Hindi/Urdu film industry.

bombay - Present day Mumbai.

buddhu - A slang term for an idiot. An ignoramous.

burkha - A head-to-foot covering worn by traditional Muslim women.

bush shirt - A shirt, similar to a standard Western style shirt, except that it has two pockets, and is square cut at the bottom to allow it to be worn outside of the pants instead of tucked in.

chai - A very thick concoction of tea, sugar, and milk, occasionally flavoured with cardamom, ginger or other spices.

charminar - 1) A famous *masjid* (mosque) in Hyderabad. 2) The "old city" of Hyderabad which is characterised by narrow lanes, old buildings, and a predominantly Muslim population.

chaurasta - Literally "four paths." A crossroads.

chenna reddy - Indian politician who was chief minister of Andhra Pradesh during the 1970s.

chokra - A somewhat derogatory term for a boy, often used to refer to servant boys.

convent school english - A very distinctive style of English that has historically been taught in the parochial schools in India. It is essentially Victorian English with an Indian accent. In its colloquial form there is a smattering of Bombay film Hindi thrown in as well.

chudwa - Mixed khara. Namkin. A mixture of grain cereals flavoured with salt and red chillies.

dahej - Dowry.

darshan - 1) A miraculous vision of God. 2) A viewing of the deity in a Hindu temple.

deccan - 1) Literally "south." 2) The area around Hyderabad, so called because it was the southernmost part of the old Mogul empire.

decolam - Formica, a commercial laminate.

deshi - 1) A "countryman." 2) Something of local manufacture.

devnagri - A phonetic script which is used for Sanskrit, Marathi, Hindi and several other North Indian languages.

dosh - A flaw or a blemish, when referring to horoscopes, it is an inauspicious arrangement of the planets.

dukaan - A small shop, or store.

emergency - The period in the 1970s during which Indira Gandhi suspended the constitution, and set herself up as absolute ruler.

eve teasing - A form of sexual harassment. It may take the form of sexually suggestive remarks, inappropriate touching, and in extreme cases groping.

firangi - A white person, usually derogatory.

furlong - 1/8th of a mile.

gampa - A large reed or wicker basket.

gat - A fixed composition

ghairat - Self-respect.

gora - A white person, see also firangi.

gujarati - 1) A person or thing from the Western state of Gujarat. 2) The language spoken in Gujarat.

guru-bhai - Literally a "brother under the guru", a fellow student under the same teacher.

hindi - The most popular north Indian language, grammatically identical to Urdu.

hindlish - A colloquial mixture of Hindi and English, commonly found in urban areas of India, as well as among the expatriate Indian communities of the UK and USA.

hindustan - "Land of the Hindus", another name for India.

holi - A very popular spring festival where people throw colours and spray **coloured** water on passersby.

hotel - A cafe or restaurant. This peculiar Indian usage is derived from the old days when hotels were some of the few places outside of the home where one could purchase prepared food.

hyderabadi - Any person or thing from Hyderabad.

iddli - A steamed rice-cake, that is popular in South India.

interval - The intermission in a play or film.

irani hotel - A small cafe that is generally frequented and owned by Muslims.

item girl - A second tier actress who specialises in erotic song and dance numbers in the films.

item number - An indispensable part of the Indian film formula. It is a song/dance number that is completely unconnected to the story line and is included entirely for marketing purposes. The numbers have historically been erotic, but occasionally an item number may be used to present a cameo appearance of a big name star.

izzat - Reputation, prestige.

jali - Any type of grill or lattice-work.

jhopdi - A small, crude thatched hut.

joli - A traditional Indian shoulder bag.

ka'bah - A black stone in Makka (Mecca), in Arabia, toward which Muslims pray.

kaida - A form of theme-and-variation which is commonly found in tabla solos.

kallu - Country liquor.

kanduwa - A section of cloth which is folded and draped over the shoulder, worn as part of traditional Indian garb.

karnataka - A Kanada speaking state which is just south-west of Andhra Pradesh.

kerala - The Southwestern most state in India, characterised by preference for left-of-centre governments, high literacy rates, beautiful beaches, and the ability to make almost anything from coconuts;-)

khaara biscuit - Literally a hot/salty biscuit. Superficially this resembles a cookie (sweet biscuit) but it is actually more reminiscent of a cracker.

khurta - A long, loose fitting shirt.

kichadi - 1) A dish made by throwing together a mixture of dhal, rice, spices, and an almost random assortment of ingredients. 2) A hodgepodge.

konkani - 1) An ethnic Goan. 2) The language of Goa.

kotha - Literally a "mansion," but generally used to mean a mansion owned by the **tawaif**. In common usage, it is considered to be synonymous with a house of prostitution.

lakh - a) 100,000 of something. b) 100,000 rupees (a lot of money back in the 1970s.)

lok sabha - A house of the legislative branch which roughly corresponds to the House of Commons (Great Britain) or the House of Representatives (US).

lorry - Large diesel truck.

love-marriage - The opposite of an arranged marriage. This was socially frowned upon, but much more common than generally admitted.

lungi - A sarong-like garment worn by men.

madras - Present day Chennai.

madras presidency - A large portion of South India that was directly under British rule before Independence.

maharashtrian - A person from the Western state of Maharashtra.

mandir - A Hindu Temple.

mangalsutra - A thread or chain worn around the neck by south Indian women to show that they are married.

mantra - A small chant that is repeated a large number of times.

marathi - 1) The language of Maharashtra. 2) A person from the West Indian state of Maharashtra.

maryaada - Respect shown towards other people.

masjid - A mosque.

mausi - 1) Mother's sister. 2) Hindlish slang for any middle-aged to elderly women of the community.

mehendi - Temporary tattoos made by staining the skin with a preparation made from henna (Lawsonia inermis).

mehman - A guest.

modren - A common mispronunciation of the English word "modern."

mogul - A Mongol, or ethnic central Asian. In India, this generally refers to the Central Asians who ruled India from 1526 CE until the collapse of the Mogul empire with the death of Aurangzeb in 1707CE. The empire remained in name only until the deposition of Bahadur Shah Zafar in 1858.

mulghi - A very small shop opening directly onto the road.

mulki - A "countryman," somewhat similar to the English phrase "native son."

murukkulu - (a.k.a. chakli or chakri). Small, spiral shaped, snack food made from a deep fried batter of rice flour, gram flour, salt, and asafoetida. It is somewhat similar to "Fritos" in flavour and consistency.

mussarambagh - An Eastern area of Hyderabad that today is very developed, but in the 1970s was on the extreme outskirts of the city.

nadaswaram - A large double-reeded horn used in South India for auspicious occasions.

namak - Salt.

namak halal - "Faithful to one's salt." A person who is very proper in their dealings with other people, especially those who at some time have extended some kind of support.

namak haraam - "Unfaithful to one's salt." A person who behaves in an improper way to one who has extended some kind of support. An ingrate.

namaz - Prayers performed by Muslims.

nampally road - 1) A road that connects Abid Circle to Nampally Railway station. 2) The title of a book by Meena Alexander.

naqali-shaan - Ostentation.

nawaar - A strap or lacing.

nihaari - A meat dish prepared by taking pieces of beef or goat meat and slowly cooking them in a rich sauce (*shorba*). It is eaten by South Asian Muslims in the morning because it generally takes all night to cook.

nizam - The former ruler of the princely state of Hyderabad.

number-two-account - Black money.

paan - An edible concoction made of a leaf into which are placed a variety of substances. Usually these include lime (crude mix of calcium carbonate, calcium oxide, and other chemicals), the extract of trees, coconut, and other things, but it may also contain tobacco or an extract of cannabis.

pakhawaj - A very ancient barrel-shaped hand drum, with heads on both ends.

pakkah - Something that is ready, firm, fixed, or correct. In reference to houses, it is any house that is made from stone, cement, or brick.

pallu - The portion of the *sari* that hangs over the shoulder, often intricately decorated with brocade.

pardeshi - A foreigner.

paran - A tabla composition which has the strong influence of the *pakhawaj* drum.

paying guest - A relationship whereby you move into a home, and are treated like family, but you contribute financially to the household.

peshkar - Literally "to introduce," an introductory section of a tabla solo.

petticoat - A simple skirt around which the *sari* is wrapped, pleated, and tucked.

pooja - A religious ritual performed by Hindus.

poojari - A Hindu priest who officiates over rituals.

pranaam - Touching another person's feet as an extreme sign of respect.

prasad - A sacramental food, often a sweet.

punjabi - 1) The language of the Northwestern state of Punjab. 2) A person or thing from Punjab.

purdah - 1) A curtain. 2) The Islamic system of segregating women from men.

rabindra sangeet - A style of semiclassical music originated by the late **Rabindranath Tagore**, which is very popular in Bengal and Bangladesh.

ram-pyari - A sweet *paan* that is somewhat reminiscent of a *meetha paan* but not nearly as heavy.

rikshawalla - A rikshaw puller, considered in India to be synonymous with the lowest paid worker.

runanubandh - A force of karma which tends to link people's lives over multiple births.

sabji-bazaar - Vegetable market.

sada paan - A very simple *paan*.

sadhu - A wandering renunciate of the Shivite tradition.

sahib - A term of respect meaning "Sir," "Mister," or "Lord."

salaam - A salutation used by Muslims. Derived from Salaam Alikum, which means "May the peace of Allah be upon you".

sambar - A spicy vegetable soup that is popular in south India.

samosa - A deep fried snack food prepared with any of a number of fillings, usually potato, onions, or ground meat, and spices that are wrapped in dough.

samskar - 1) The actions, duties, and ceremonies of life. 2) The culture of one's position in life.

sankranthi - (also sp. sankranti) The winter harvest festival.

sarangi - A traditional bowed instrument without frets or a fingerboard.

sari - The traditional women's clothing based upon six yards of cloth which are folded and wrapped around the body.

sauda baazi - Haggling to determine a price.

second-show - A late-night showing of Indian films that generally starts after 9:00 pm and lets out around midnight.

secunderabad - The northern section of the Hyderabad Municipality, formerly a British holding.

shaan - Literally "majesty," but in the negative sense, it means "ostentation."

shalwar-khameez - The traditional dress-cum-pants, usually worn with a scarf-like piece. In the past, this was worn only by North Indians and Muslim women, but today it is the most popular women's attire in all of South Asia.

shashtipurti - A religious function performed when one completes sixty years of life.

shaukeen - One who engages in an activity for their amusement.

shendi - An alcoholic drink made from fermented palm sap.

sikh - A follower of the Sikh religion. Male Sikhs are conspicuous by their turban and beard.

sitar - A long, lute-like instrument made famous by Ravi Shankar.

streedhan - Property that traditionally belongs to a woman. This generally includes jewellery and *saris*.

suhaag ki raat - The first night after marriage.

surakai - A large, long, gourd-like squash. So named, because it is shaped like a **surai** (a water pitcher).

tabla - A pair of hand drums commonly played in India.

tamilian - 1) A person from the South Indian state of Tamil Nadu. 2) A native speaker of Tamil.

tanpura - A stringed instrument that superficially resembles a sitar both in tone and shape, but without frets or any way of playing a melody.

telangana - The northwest portion of Andhra Pradesh, which includes the city of Hyderabad.

teental - A very common north Indian rhythmic form which is composed of for measures of four beats each.

telugu - 1) The language of the people of Andhra Pradesh. 2) A person who speaks Telugu.

time-pass - A film that makes no pretence at being any great artistic achievement, rather one that is just supposed to "pass the time."

twenty20 - (a.k.a. T20) An abbreviated form of cricket that generally lasts only about 3 1/2 hours instead of the usual 5 days.

twin-cities - The metropolitan area comprising Hyderabad, Secunderabad, and a number of smaller colonies.

udipi - A small town in Karnataka which is noted for its Krishna temple, but mainly famous for its food.

urdu - A language that is grammatically identical to Hindi, but characterised by a large vocabulary derived from Persian.

zamindar - A land owner or landlord.

zee-TV - A very popular satellite based TV station.

www.ingramcontent.com/pod-product-compliance
Lightning Source LLC
Chambersburg PA
CBHW021217090426
42740CB00006B/256